Banking in France

What impact will European financial integration have on banking in member countries? What effect will deregulation and liberalization have?

Banking in France presents an up-to-date and authoritative review of the situation on the eve of European financial integration. The contributors, all leading economists and bankers, describe the evolution of the French banking sector over the last ten years, underlining the process of financial innovation, the adjustments in the regulatory framework, and the main changes in the financial structure of the French economy.

Like their foreign competitors, French banks are confronted with crucial issues to do with size, diversification or specialization, and their capital base. This book, with its thorough account of French banking today, will be a valuable source for students and analysts of the contemporary international banking scene, enabling them to judge for themselves how French banks will face up to the challenge of the future.

The Editor

Christian de Boissieu is Professor of Economics at the University of Paris-IX (Panthéon-Sorbonne). He is consultant to the World Bank and to the European Commission, economic adviser to the Paris Chamber of Commerce and Industry, and a member of the Conseil National du Crédit and the Comité de la Règlementation Bancaire. He has written widely on monetary analysis and policy.

Banking in France

Edited by
Christian de Boissieu

London and New York

First published 1990
by Routledge
11 New Fetter Lane, London EC4P 4EE

Simultaneously published in the USA and Canada
by Routledge
a division of Routledge, Chapman and Hall, Inc.
29 West 35th Street, New York, NY 10001

© 1990 Christian de Boissieu

Typeset by Pat and Anne Murphy, Highcliffe-on-Sea, Dorset
Printed in Great Britain by Billing & Sons Ltd, Worcester

British Library Cataloguing in Publication Data

Banking in France.
  1. France. Banking.
  I. Boissieu, C. de (Christian)
  332.1'0944

  ISBN 0-415-01029-2

Library of Congress Cataloging-in-Publication Data

Banking in France / edited by Christian de Boissieu.
      p.   cm.
  Includes bibliographical references (p.   ).
  ISBN 0-415-01029-2
    1. Banks and banking—France. I. Boissieu, Christian de.
  HG3028.B26   1990   82-27718
  332.1'0944—dc20   CIP

Contents

Tables

Tables

Contributors

Christian de Boissieu is Professor of Economics at the University of Paris I (Panthéon–Sorbonne).

Hugues Colmant was formerly with the French Banking Commission. He is currently with Banque Nationale de Paris.

François Henrot is Deputy General Manager, Compagnie Bancaire, Paris.

André Levy-Lang is President, Compagnie Bancaire, Paris.

Joël Métais is Professor of Economics at the University of Grenoble and at the University of Paris–Dauphine.

Robert Raymond is Head of the Research Department, Bank of France, Paris.

Philippe Szymczak is an economist with the IMF. Formerly he worked at the French Ministry of Finance.

Preface

This book contains a series of essays, written by specialists, on the evolution of the French banking sector, its comparative advantages but also its handicaps on the eve of the implementation of the ambitious financial liberalization programme settled by EC member countries.

The various essays are complementary. Taken as a whole, they intend to present a thorough and updated view of the situation of the French banking sector. The book emphasizes positive considerations, but does not rule out normative statements.

The French financial system has experienced, since the end of the 1970s, a dramatic change affecting the various compartments of the financial sector. Financial innovation and deregulation have accelerated under the pressure of the external constraint. Is the financial liberalization consistent with the traditional strong influence of French public decision-makers, and to what extent? The waves of nationalization and privatization to which the French banking sector has been exposed are just an illustration, among others, of the delicate equilibrium not only between conflicting ideologies, but also between different perspectives. The emphasis on the institutional viewpoint has led to focus on the issue of ownership (private or public) in the financial sphere, and not enough consideration on the *modus operandi* of the system (this requires a functional perspective).

Chapter 1 presents an overview of the changes that have taken place in the French financial system over the last ten years, underlining the process of financial innovation, the adjustments in the regulatory framework, and the main changes in the financial structure of the French economy.

In chapter 2 Robert Raymond highlights the dialectic between system innovations (i.e. new financial instruments) and monetary policy innovations. In France, as elsewhere, disintermediation and financial innovation have accelerated the passage from a *direct*

Preface

monetary policy (credit ceilings) to an indirect monetary policy based on interest-rate adjustments. This chapter describes the goals, the intermediate targets, and the tools of the new monetary policy.

Chapter 3, by Hugues Colmant, is devoted to a thorough analysis of the 1984 Banking Act, which introduced dramatic changes in France, and of the main regulations and prudential rules which apply to banks. The international dimension is already present here, with the perspective associated with the Cooke ratio.

In chapter 4, François Henrot and André Levy-Lang give a complementary view, underlining the development of market forces in the French system traditionally managed through administrative rules and studying the process of financial diversification. This chapter represents a contribution to the industrial economics of the French banking firm.

Philippe Szymczak, in chapter 5, is also very much influenced by the industrial economics approach. The purpose of this chapter is to give a precise picture of the relative situation of French banks as regards their profitability, the cost of intermediation, and the management of risks. Most of the conclusions drawn by the author from a deep statistical investigation condition the external competitiveness of the banking sector, and will continue to do so in the future.

Finally, Joël Métais in chapter 6 gives both an empirical and a theoretical content to the topical subject of the external competitiveness of the banking sector. There is a two-way causation between the international strategies of French banks, and their market share abroad and at home. On the one hand, French banks' international strategy depends very much on actual and also expected market shares. On the other hand, changes in market shares at home and abroad reflect in part the success or the failure of international strategies. With the challenge of European financial integration, effective as soon as 1989–90 with the application of the European directive concerning the marketing of unit trusts and mutual funds and the complete removal of capital controls, French banks will be confronted, like their foreign competitors, with crucial issues concerning their size, their diversification (or their specialization), and their capital base. In the present and future circumstances, capital is crucial not only to comply with the Cooke ratio, but also to finance external growth operations or to resist hostile take-over bids.

Christian de Boissieu
March 1989

Glossary

agent de change   stockbroker
agent de marché interbancaire (AMI)   interbank market agent,
        broker
aide personnalisée au logement (APL)   personal housing allocation
Association Française des Banques (AFB)   French Bankers'
        Association
Association Française des Etablissements de Crédit (AFEC)
        Association of French Credit Institutions
Association des Sociétés Financières (ASF)   Association of
        Finance Companies
banque d'affaires   merchant bank
banque de crédit à moyen et long terme   medium and long-term
        credit bank
banque de dépôts   commercial bank
banque inscrite   registered bank
banque de trésorerie   cash management bank
billet de trésorerie   commercial paper
bon des institutions financières spécialisées (BIFS) specialized
        financial institutions notes and boards
bon du Trésor négociable (BTN)   negotiable Treasury bill
bon du Trésor à taux fixe et à intérêts annuels (BTAN)   fixed-rate
        interest-bearing Treasury bill
bon du Trésor à taux fixe et à intérêts précomptés (BTF)
        fixed-rate Treasury bill with up-front payment of interest
caisse de crédit municipal   municipal credit institution
Caisse des Dépôts et Consignations (CDC)   Deposit and
        Consignment Office
caisse d'épargne   local savings bank
caisse d'épargne et de prévoyance   savings and provident
        institution
Caisse Nationale de Crédit Agricole (CNCA)   National
        Agricultural Credit Bank

Caisse de Refinancement Hypothécaire (CRH)   Mortgage
    Refinancing Fund
carte bancaire   bank card
Centre National des Caisses d'Epargne et de Prévoyance
    (CENCEP)   National Savings Bank Centre
certificat d'investissement   non-voting share
Chambre de Compensation des Instruments Financiers de Paris
    (CCIFP)   Paris Financial Futures Clearing House
Chambre Syndicate des Banques Populaires
    Syndicate Chamber of popular banks
Comité des Etablissements de Crédit (CEC)   Committee of Credit
    Institutions
Comité de la Réglementation Bancaire (CRB)   Committee for
    Banking Regulation
Commission Bancaire (CB)   Banking Commission
Commission de Contrôle des Banques (CCB)   Bank Supervisory
    Commission
Commission des Opérations de Bourse (CCB)   Securities and
    Exchange Commission
compte pour le développement industriel (CODEVI)   industrial
    development account
compte/plan d'épargne-logement   housing savings account/plan
Confédération du Crédit Mutuel Agricole et Rural   Confederation
    of Agricultural and Rural Mutual Credit Stock
Conseil des Bourses de Valeurs (CBV)   Securities Exchange Board
Conseil de la Concurrence (CC)   Competition Council
Conseil des Marchés à Terme (CMT)   Futures Exchange Board
Conseil National du Crédit (CNC)   National Credit Council
Crédit d'Equipement des Petites et Moyennes Entreprises
    (CEPME)   Credit for the Equipment of Small and
    Medium-size Enterprises
Crédit Local de France   French Local Credit
Direction du Trésor   Treasury Department (of the Finance Ministry)
encadrement de crédit   credit ceiling, corset
entreprise non-bancaire admise au marché monétaire (ENBAMM)
    non-bank institution admitted to the money market
établissement du crédit   credit institution
fond commun de créance   mutual claims fund
fond commun de placement (FCP)   mutual fund
habitation à loyer modéré (HLM)   council housing
Institut d'Emission des Départements et Territoires d'Outre-mer
    (IEDTOM)   Overseas Territories Issuing Agency
institution financière spécialisée (IFS)   specialized financial
    institution

livret d'épargne entreprise   business savings book
livret d'épargne populaire (LEP)   popular savings book
maison de titre   securities house
marché des options négociables de Paris (MONEP)   Paris options
        market
marché à terme international de France (MATIF)   financial
        futures market
obligation assimilable du Trésor (OAT)   fungible Treasury bonds
obligation renouvelable du Trésor (ORT)   renewable Treasury
        bonds
organisme de placement collectif en valeurs mobilières (OPCVM)
        undertaking for collective investment in transferable
        securities (UCITS)
petites et moyennes enreprises (PME)   small and medium-size
        businesses
plan d'épargne retraite (PER)   personal individual retirement
        plan
prêt à l'accession à la proprieté (PAP)   subsidized housing loans
prêt conventionné   loan under special conditions stipulated by the
        Crédit Foncier
rapport de couverture des risques   risk–asset ratio
rapport de division des risques   risk distribution ratio
réméré   repurchase agreement
second marché boursier   unlisted securities market
société de bourse   brokerage firm
société de caution mutuelle   mutual guarantee company
société de crédit différé   saving–lending institution
société de crédit immobilier   housing finance company
société de développement régional   regional development company
société de financement des télécommunications
        telecommunications finance company
société financière   finance company
société d'investissement à capital variable (SICAV)   open-ended
        unit trust
société régionale de financement (SOREFI)   regional finance
        company
société immobilière pour le commerce et l'industrie (SICOMI)
        property real-estate finance company
société de financement des économies d'énergie (SOFERGIE)
        energy conservation finance company
spécialiste en valeurs du Trésor   primary dealer
Système Interbancaire de Télécompensation (SIT)   Interbank
        Computerized Clearing Network
taux de base bancaire   banks' base lending rate

taux moyen interbancaire offert à Paris (TIOP)   average Paris
    interbank offered rate (PIBOR)
taux moyen pondéré (TMP)   average weighted rate
titre participatif   participating bond
titre subordonné à durée indéterminée   perpetual subordinated
    bond

Chapter one

Recent developments in the French financial system: an overview

Christian de Boissieu

The purpose of this chapter is to provide an overview of the dramatic changes that have taken place in the French financial system over the last ten years. An overview, since many of the subjects mentioned in this chapter are analysed in greater details in the following chapters. Four topics are discussed: (1) the process of financial innovation in France, (2) the adjustment in the regulatory framework, (3) the consequences of financial innovation and deregulation for the structure of financing of the French economy, (4) the respective elements of continuity and change in the French banking system. In conclusion the chapter deals with the relationship between 'system innovations' (i.e. innovations in financial products, markets, and technologies) and 'policy innovations' (i.e. innovations in the operating procedures of monetary policy, etc.).

The process of financial innovation

Characteristics of the financial system in the 1960s and 1970s

Until the end of the 1970s the French financial system could be (and has been) analysed by reference to the model of the 'overdraft economy'. Many studies (especially at the Bank of France) have elaborated on a distinction put forward by J. Hicks (1974) between the 'overdraft economy' and the 'auto-economy' (or, more appropriately, between the overdraft sector and the auto-sector). In an overdraft economy, deficit units do not borrow from the markets (which are non-existent or only residual), but they rely on bank credit. 'Indirect finance' (i.e. financial intermediation), to refer to the well-known terminology introduced by J. Gurley and E. Shaw (1960), predominates and 'direct finance' plays a marginal role. To use Sir John's words, 'In a pure overdraft economy, where firms kept no liquid reserves, they would be wholly dependent, for their liquidity, on the banks.'

In France, indirect finance procedures were dominant until the end of the 1970s. Capital markets were underdeveloped, compared to the United States, the United Kingdom, Canada, etc. The money market was the opposite of an 'open market', and the role of the Paris stock exchange was marginal in the saving-investment adjustment process. In 1981 financial intermediation still represented, on a flow-of-funds basis, close to 80 per cent of total financing in the French economy.

Other features, some substantially, others more superficially associated with the overdraft economy model, have been stressed in France: the commercial banks' ultimate certainty of refinancing by the Bank of France, the consequent low level of banks' excess reserves, the high rigidity in nominal interest rates (see V. Lévy-Garboua, 1982), etc.

Diversification in the 'menu' of financial instruments was limited in the 1960s and the 1970s, compared with the US or the UK. Among the few financial innovations during this period, we must refer to the development of open-ended unit trusts (SICAVs, *sociétés d'investissement à capital variable*) beginning in 1963, and to a successful diversification of savings investments with financial intermediaries (particularly contractual savings for housing finance, under the names of *plans d'épargne-logement* and *comptes d'épargne-logement*, which have been and are still very attractive to French households).

During the 1960s and the 1970s, the credit market in France was structurally 'overdetermined': the monetary authorities were controlling, in this market, both quantities, through credit ceilings (first applied discontinuously in 1958–9, 1963–5 and 1968–70, and then permanently during the period 1973–84), and interest rates. The first shock of deregulation came in 1966–7 with the reform implemented by M. Debré, then Minister of Finance, and consisted of several important steps:

1. The complete liberalization of banks' lending rates, the only remaining constraint being the legal definition of a ceiling for these rates (the ceiling is the usury rate), while deposit rates were kept under tight control by the monetary authorities.

2. The liberalization of branch banking, which created intense competition for market shares. Many large banks opened new branches – the so-called *course aux guichets* – and this phenomenon, which reached a peak in the early 1970s, had, and still has today, negative effects on banks' productivity and the cost of intermediation. Since 1986 some French commercial banks have been closing branches in 'over-branched' areas, in an attempt to reduce the cost of intermediation and to restore labour productivity.

3. The distinction between commercial and investment banking, traditional in France since the Banking Act of 1941 and the post-war legislation, was retained but somewhat relaxed.

Financial innovation

Preliminary remarks

Most recent works consider financial innovations (especially product innovations) as instruments used by private agents to circumvent discretionary measures taken by the monetary authorities. Financial innovation is, then, regarded as a challenge to monetary policy. This view, well summarized by the 'regulatory dialectic' between regulation and innovation presented by Ed. Kane (1981, 1987), is useful when describing the experience of all OECD (Organization for Economic Co-operation and Development) countries, particularly (but not only) the English-speaking countries. In France we saw some examples of financial innovation introduced to circumvent regulations. For instance, in September 1981 J. Delors, Minister of Finance, tightened the regulation on deposit rates, in such a way that many savers who, until this reform, were in a position to get rates indexed to money-market rates could no longer do so under the new regulation. They were encouraged to invest in new financial instruments offered by all financial intermediaries, namely short-term open-ended unit trusts and mutual funds. (Unit trusts and mutual funds are the two forms of what are called 'undertakings for collective investment in transferable securities', UCITSs.)

Even if the 'regulatory dialectic' is also valid in the French case, it appears that in France, as in Italy or Japan, *public* financial innovation predominates. Rather than a challenge, financial innovation is considered as a tool of economic policy.

The distinction between private and public financial innovation

Private financial innovation comes from non-governmental sectors (banks, firms, households, etc.). It arises in a decentralized way. *Ex ante* control by the monetary authorities over these new financial instruments is nil or extremely limited. The authorities intervene only *ex post*, possibly to monitor the phenomenon, to adapt the definitions of monetary aggregates and of reserve requirements, etc.

On the contrary, public financial innovation results from the initiative of the public decision-makers, who either introduce the new financial instruments themselves or impose restrictions on other parties. Public financial innovation corresponds to a centralized process, and financial institutions will not take the initiative in offering new products without having first received express authorization from the monetary authorities.

In France most of the new financial instruments have been created in the form and at the time chosen by the monetary authorities (i.e. the Bank of France, the Treasury Department). Even if the new instruments were associated with a demand, explicit or latent, by private operators, they resulted from a centralized process. This has been very clear since the starting point: in 1978 the Monory Act (named after the then Minister of Finance) promoted, through tax allowances, the development of the stock market, and this start confirms that, in France as in many other countries, financial innovation has sometimes been a tax innovation. A rather paradoxical outcome of the public innovation process was the creation, by the public decision-makers, of the commercial paper market in December 1985. Generally speaking, a commercial paper market gives private agents (lenders and borrowers) some autonomy *vis-à-vis* the banking system and the central bank, and it may reduce the efficacy of monetary policy by inducing large swings in the velocity of money. Thus it could be seen as a paradox that the monetary authorities took the initiative in this case, but the December 1985 move was also a way of transforming the shadow market for liquidity that had developed since the late 1960s ('back-to-back' operations between firms, initiated by them to circumvent credit rationing).

The French experience also confirms that the distinction between private and public financial innovation is applicable only up to a certain limit. Over a certain threshold of development, a new financial instrument introduced by the monetary authorities is totally subject to market forces. Let us take the example of certificates of deposit. CDs, authorized by the monetary authorities in February 1985, developed very quickly in 1987 (the volume of CDs was 60 billion French francs in January 1987, 200 billion frs. in December 1987), and I have the feeling that the CD market has passed the point where control by the monetary authorities is any longer effective. We cannot say that the thresholds which distinguish public and private financial innovation; and above which the distinction between them fades away, do not exist simply because they cannot easily be quantified.

The reasons for the acceleration in the pace of financial innovation

The acceleration of the financial innovation process in France after 1978 can be explained not only by factors common to all OECD countries but also by more specific factors. In the first place, apart from general technical progress, we find the arguments synthesized in W. Silber's model (1975, 1983): innovation is a way of loosening constraints when the price of adhering to them becomes high (the increase of the adherence price must be related, in particular, to the inflation rate, etc.). Traditional constraints – regulation, competition among financial institutions, increasing risks (exchange-rate risk, interest-rate risk, etc.) – have been active in generating a demand for and a supply of new financial instruments and markets. For countries like France where public financial innovation dominates, other constraints also must be taken into account:

1. The external constraint on the banking and financial system. At the end of the 1970s, France had to catch up with the leading countries in the field of financial innovation (the United States, the UK, Canada, etc.), in order to maintain the competitiveness of the banking system and the role of Paris as a financial centre. The comparison with West Germany, where there was very little financial innovation until 1986, could be useful: the content of what is called the 'external constraint' is different in the two countries, since France, traditionally a weak-currency country exposed to structural external deficits, had to follow the leading countries in the field, whilst the problem of Germany, a hard-currency country with structural external surpluses, was to limit capital inflows.

To be sure, the Single European Act adopted in 1985 and the prospect of the internal market in 1993 will at the same time reinforce the external constraint on the French financial system and induce greater harmonization among individual member states. For instance, the West German authorities will need to soften their position concerning financial innovation if they want Frankfurt to remain a leading financial centre.

2. The government budgetary constraint. An important aspect concerns co-ordination between monetary policy and fiscal policy. The constraint associated with monetary targeting by the central bank has led the French Treasury Department to issue new instruments (*obligations renouvelables du Trésor*, ORTs; *obligations assimilables du Trésor*, OATs; etc.) in order to finance, through non-monetary means, public-sector deficits.

3. Constraints of financing bearing on certain categories of firms: nationalized firms, small to medium-size enterprises (SMEs). The 'Delors Act' of January 1983 created several financial instruments (*titres participatifs, certificats d'investissement*, etc.) tailored to nationalized enterprises and SMEs, since they serve to increase the capital of the firm without changing the structure of property

rights (these instruments completely separate pecuniary from voting rights).

The content of the financial innovation process

The use of new payment technologies in the banking sector The French banking sector has recently gone through a rapid process of computerization. While banking represents 4 per cent of the gross national product, it accounts for 20 per cent of total computer expenses. Electronic money has been extended very rapidly since the early 1980s, as table 1.1. suggests. In international comparisons, France is close to the UK, and far ahead of West Germany. The diagnosis is confirmed by looking at the density of the point-of-sale system. In France the number of POS outlets rose to 70,000 at the end of 1987 (which corresponds to 780 inhabitants per terminal) from 10,000 at the end of 1983 (5,470 inhabitants per terminal). This technological dimension has to be kept in mind when looking at the prospects of open competition associated with the implementation of the Single European Act.

Table 1.1 Automatic cash dispensers and automatic teller machines, 1978−88 (year ends)

Country		1978	1983	1987	1988 forecasts
France	(1)	1,000	5,100	10,000	12,000
	(2)	54,800	10,940	5,470	4,600
USA	(1)	9,750	48,118	76,231	*n.a.*
	(2)	22,513	4,896	3,222	*n.a.*
West Germany	(1)	*n.a.*	1,600	7,500	*n.a.*
	(2)	*n.a.*	38,500	8,147	*n.a.*
UK	(1)	2,189	5,653	11,500	*n.a.*
	(2)	24,852	9,659	4,930	*n.a.*

Notes: (1) Number of machines. (2) Number of inhabitants per machine.

Source: Bank for International Settlements.

A list of financial innovations Table 1.2 gives a chronological list of new financial instruments and markets introduced since 1978, a year which is often considered the starting point of the financial innovation process in France.

Table 1.2 The main financial innovations in France, 1978–88

1978	*July.* Monory Act, which included tax incentives for the development of the stock market
1979	*July.* Creation of mutual funds (*fonds communs de placement*, FCPs)
1981	*September.* Short-term UCITSs (undertakings for collective investment in transferable securities: SICAVs and FCPs)
1982	*June.* The LEP (*livret d'épargne populaire*), a financial instrument offered by all depository institutions to low-income groups, with a ceiling on savings and indexation of the capital to the rate of inflation
1983	*January.* The Delors Act, which created new financial instruments for the capitalization of nationalized or private firms (and financial institutions): *titres participatifs, certificats d'investissement*, etc.
	February. Unlisted securities market (*second marché bousier*)
	October. CODEVI (*compte pour le développement industriel*), a financial instrument open to all depository institutions and to all agents. The resources collected through the CODEVIs are channelled into the financing of industry
1985	*March.* Negotiable certificates of deposit, denominated in French francs or in foreign currencies, mainly US dollars, sterling, ECUs, etc.
	December. Commercial paper market (*billet de trésorerie*)*
1986	*January.* Negotiable Treasury bills (*bons du Trésor négociables*, BTNs), and notes issued by specialist financial institutions (*bons des institutions financières spécialisées*)*
	February. Financial futures market (before September 1988, *marché à terme d'instruments financiers*; thereafter *marché à terme international de France*, MATIF). Began with a long-term contract (a 'notional' bond with ten-year maturity), supplemented in June by a short-term contract
1987	*September.* Options market, with three underlying securities (Lafarge Coppée, Paribas, Peugeot) to start with (*marché des options négociables de Paris*, MONEP). At present (September 1988) there are eleven underlying securities
1988	*January.* The PER (*plan d'épargne retraite*), corresponding to an individual retirement account, created by an Act of June 1987, is proposed, as from this date, to households by credit institutions, insurance companies, pension funds, etc. The PER resorts to several tax incentives
	September. Future contract on a stock index (with forty underlying securities), introduced on the MATIF. (An option contract on the same index will be offered by the end of 1988)

* This financial instrument is analysed in chapter 2.

The adjustment of the regulatory framework

Main characteristics of the new Banking Act (1984)

From the end of the Second World War to the early 1980s, banking activity in France was governed by a set of regulations adopted in 1941 and largely confirmed in 1945. These regulations, unlike the German 'universal banking' system, favoured a high degree of specialization and compartmentalization. They established a clear-cut classification of credit institutions and bank activities, according

7

to several criteria: the main distinction between commercial and investment banking was supplemented by taking into account the average maturity of the credits, the field of intervention (agriculture, export financing, etc.), the degree of control exercised by the monetary authorities, etc. With the increased openness of the economy, the development of 'direct finance', and a progressive tendency towards universal banking, it was clear in the early 1980s that the 1941–5 legislation had to be updated. During the discussion and approval of the nationalization programme in 1982 the government announced the preparation of a new Banking Act, which was adopted by Parliament in January 1984.

An enlarged definition of banking

The 1984 Banking Act introduces more uniformity in the banking sector by referring to the notion of a 'credit institution' (*établissement de crédit*), already introduced under the European directive adopted in December 1977. Under French law, a credit institution is now defined as an institution that engages in at least one of the following activities: (1) collecting deposits from the public, (2) extending loans, (3) issuing means of payment (e.g. credit cards, travellers' cheques, bankers' drafts).

Without exception, all credit institutions are subject to the same rules (e.g. the same liquidity ratio, solvency ratio, etc.) and the same supervisory institutions. The broad definition of credit institutions implies that there is no incentive for the development of 'non-bank' banks in France. Prior to a 1987 change in the definition of a bank, 'non-bank' banks could be established in the United States under a loophole in the Bank Holding Company Act and their number has grown dramatically since the mid-'80s. In France, a firm which only extends credits *or* only collects deposits is subject to the same regulations as a full-service banking concern.

Within the class of credit institutions, there are several categories, the main distinction being between financial institutions which can collect demand and short-term deposits (ordinary banks, members of the French Bankers' Association – Association Française des Banques, or AFB – mutual and co-operative banks, savings banks, etc.) and others. However, some important agents are excluded from the coverage of the Banking Act: the Treasury, the Bank of France, the Caisse des Dépôts et Consignations (which centralizes the deposits with the *caisses d'épargne* and invests them in social housing, municipalities, etc.) and the Postal financial services. As in West Germany, Italy, and some other countries, French Postal financial services are a part of the Postal administration. They are allowed to offer a wide variety of financial instruments to collect resources, but are not permitted to grant credits.

While preserving the distinction between financial institutions and non-financial organizations, the new Banking Act allows credit institutions to find a better equilibrium between the opposing forces of specialization and diversification. Credit institutions are allowed to engage in activities collateral to their main functions, but ceilings are imposed to limit the extent of diversification. For example, under a rule adopted by the Committee for Banking Regulation (see below) in November 1986, the net income derived from ancillary activities (insurance business, etc.) must not be greater than 10 per cent of the global net income of a credit institution.

Adjustment in the organization of banking supervision

The widened definition of banking implies more uniform procedures for supervision. Before 1984 banks were supervised by two committees, the National Credit Council (Conseil National du Crédit) and the Bank Supervisory Commission (Commission de Contrôle des Banques), and most of the other financial intermediaries were under the direct or indirect supervision of the Ministry of Finance (particularly of its most influential department, the Direction du Trésor, or Treasury Department).

Under the new Banking Act, most credit institutions (with the exception of some financial institutions with a special status, such as Crédit National, Crédit Foncier, etc.) are supervised by three bodies working closely with the Bank of France:

1. The Committee of Credit Institutions (Comité des Établissements de Crédit), chaired by the Governor of the Bank of France and responsible for *individual* decisions (authorizations to conduct banking activity, individual derogations, etc.).

2. The Committee for Banking Regulation (Comité de la Réglementation Bancaire), chaired by the Minister of Finance (the governor of the central bank being the vice-chairman), in charge of regulatory decisions (e.g. the creation of new financial instruments, rules concerning the liquidity ratio, the solvency ratio, etc.).

3. The Banking Commission (Commission Bancaire), which replaced the Commission de Contrôle des Banques. Chaired by the Governor of the Bank of France, this commission has extensive powers to monitor the compliance of credit institutions with the regulations and to impose sanctions in cases of violation.

In the present regulatory framework, the National Credit Council has only a *consultative* role that involves both the activity of credit institutions and the implementation and the effectiveness of monetary policy.

The deregulation/reregulation dialectic

The deregulation of interest rates, commissions, and fees

As noted earlier, lending rates were deregulated in 1967. As far as deposit rates are concerned, the deregulation process has been more gradual and controversial. Since May 1986 interest rates on time deposits with a maturity over three months have been freely determined, and they follow money-market rates closely.

Interest payments on demand deposits have been prohibited since 1967. In the present discussion between the banks and their customers, a zero interest rate on demand deposits is seen as the counterpart of free banking services (cheque books, no penalty for small-denomination cheques, etc.). In France, as elsewhere, this regulation has been circumvented by financial innovation. UCITSs, the MATIF, and all kinds of cash management techniques generate market interest rates on financial instruments that are a close substitute for demand deposits. In the coming months and years, several factors will speed up a complete deregulation of deposit rates. Two of them should be emphasized:

1. The external constraint associated with the completion of the great internal market in Europe, since in most European countries demand deposits bear positive interest rates. Even if the yield is not the main motivation for the holding of sight deposits, interest-rate differentials on demand deposits in the different member countries cannot be neglected in a situation of perfect capital mobility.

2. The search for more 'transparency' in the cost and price structure of the banking sector, which means the introduction of fees and commissions for many services that are now offered without charge, with one or several compensating adjustments for banks' customers (positive interest rates on demand deposits, but also a likely change in the 'float', which, in its present form, is costly to non-financial agents, especially to households).

The regulatory framework is one aspect, to be complemented by the study of concrete procedures of financing. Traditionally the financing of the French economy has been effected largely through subsidized interest rates. The proportion of subsidized credits – which involve agriculture, housing, exports, and some investment expenditures – in the total amount of credits was 42 per cent in 1975, 44·6 per cent in 1984. The stock-flow dimension means great inertia in this matter, despite the implementation of financial deregulation and liberalization. Although the growth rate of subsidized credit has been negative since 1986 (see table 1.3), the proportion was still about 42 per cent as at the end of 1987.

Table 1.3 Medium and long-term credits to firms and households with concessionary interest rates: rate of growth, 1982−7 (%)

Type of credit	1982	1983	1984	1985	1986	1987
Subsidized credits	+ 19·8	+ 15·6	+ 8·2	+ 0·4	− 13·2	− 3·9
Total credit to firms and households	+ 15·0	+ 12·7	+ 10·8	+ 10·3	+ 7·5	+ 9·0

Source: Conseil National du Crédit.

Aggregate data conceal a significant change in the structure of subsidized credits. Not only has the subsidy of the privilege (i.e. the gap between market interest rates and interest rates on housing credits, export credits, etc.) been reduced during the recent years, but also the proportion of credits with subsidized interest rates *de facto* (i.e. through a procedure of revision) or *de jure* indexed to market interest rates has risen dramatically. No doubt, behind the apparent stability in the proportion of subsidized credits, the share of the French financial system indexed on market rates has increased and is now close to what can be observed in many European economies.

As for banks' commissions and fees, they have been completely deregulated since 1986, and are now subject to full competitive pressures.

The deregulation of volume

The removal of credit ceilings at the end of 1984 (but actually at the end of 1986) is a major component of the deregulation process. This change is analysed in detail in chapter 2.

Branch banking

Branch banking in France is a good illustration of a cycle of deregulation and reregulation. Between 1945 and 1967 any new branch had to be authorized by an individual decision of the National Credit Council. The full liberalization of branch banking in 1967 was effective until 1982, and the period 1982−6 was characterized by reregulation of branch banking and some rationing of the demand presented by financial intermediaries. Since 1986 French credit institutions have not needed an authorization from the monetary authorities to open new branches. Only a few financial intermediaries, keeping some form of privilege (e.g. the savings banks' 'A' pass-book deposit or the mutual credit 'Blue book', both exempt from tax, the privilege of Crédit Agricole in the allocation of loans at subsidized interest rates) need this authorization. To be sure, the residual regulation of branch banking is less of a constraint for the banks under present circumstances, since the credit institutions are closing some branches, rather than opening new ones, in order to reduce their overheads.

The rapid growth in the number of branches during the 1970s is illustrated by table 1.4. This table also documents the recent slowdown and even decline (in 1986) in the branch banking process that has occurred because of growing consciousness of the costs of 'over-branching'.

Table 1.4 Number of permanent branches, 1966–87 (year ends)

Type of bank	1966*	1970	1975	1980	1985	1986	1987
AFB banks	4,483	6,426	9,508	9,664	9,908	9,917	9,939
Mutual and co-operative banks	n.a.	6,361	8,580	10,365	11,095	11,125	11,175
Savings banks (caisses d'épargne)	n.a.	2,250	2,989	3,630	4,626	4,374	4,378
Other	n.a.	n.a.	n.a.	n.a.	47	47	58
Total		15,037	21,077	23,659	25,676	25,463	25,550

* Before 1967 there is no official record concerning the number of branches of Crédit Agricole and of *caisses d'épargne*.

Source: Banking Commission.

Table 1.5 Number of inhabitants per branch (permanent or occasional), 1983

Belgium	968	Canada	1,934
Switzerland	1,300	UK	2,283
France	1,524	USA	2,310
West Germany	1,541	Japan	2,780

Source: Bank for International Settlements.

Table 1.4 could be usefully complemented by the OECD data concerning the average number of branches per institution, which give joint information about branching and banking concentration. The figure for France – close to sixty branches per institution in 1986 – is much higher than the comparable figure for West Germany (nine) or Switzerland (nine), but much lower than that for Japan or the UK. By international standards, taking into account not only permanent but 'occasional' branches (i.e. branches that are open only during certain seasons or on certain days), France is second to none in the group of the seven most industrialized countries. The ratio given in table 1.5 is quite stable in France. At the end of 1987 it was equal to 1,535 inhabitants per branch.

The 'big bang' in Paris

The deregulation of commissions and fees has been, in Paris as in London, an important aspect of the 'big bang'. In addition, a major change results from the adoption of the Act of January 1988, which adapts the status and the functions of stockbrokers to the new environment. Before the reform there were rigid 'Chinese walls' between banks and stockbrokers, and the latter had a monopoly of negotiation and intervention on the stock market. With the January 1988 Act, gradually implemented, the stockbrokers became specialist brokerage firms (*sociétés de bourse*), and they were induced to increase their capital in order to cope with the challenges of 1992. The recapitalization of the *sociétés de bourse*, in most cases, implies close co-operation between banks and stockbrokers and the acquisition by the former of a stake in the latter. As at July 1988 thirty-one out of sixty-one *sociétés de bourse* had opened their capital, mainly to credit institutions but also to other organizations (for example, the purchase by the holding Compagnie du Midi, which controls insurance companies but also some non-financial firms, of a controlling interest in Meeschaert-Rousselle). The proportion is much higher if we consider only Paris stockbrokers: twenty-nine agreements out of forty-five *sociétés de bourse*. These agreements have been made with domestic financial institutions (e.g. Crédit National has invested in Dupont-Denant), and with foreign ones (e.g. Warburg controls Bacot-Allain, James Capel controls Dufour-Koller-Lacarrière). 'Chinese walls' have been displaced rather than completely removed. Indeed, the *sociétés de bourse*, which are now open both to other financial intermediaries and to non-financial agents under the January 1988 Act, retain their monopoly on the trading of securities.

The adjustment in the tools of prudential control

In France, as in other countries, financial innovation and financial fragility (associated with the international debt crisis, but also due to the large indebtedness of French firms during the 1970s) have led to new definitions of the various types of prudential ratio (liquidity ratio, solvency ratio, etc.). The reregulation involves extending the area of prudential control (a logical consequence of the new concept of banking embodied in the Act of 1984), and adapting the concrete definition of the ratios (taking into account off-balance-sheet operations and other items). Greater attention has been paid · to deposit insurance: even though the issue is less topical in France than in English-speaking countries, because of the low rate of banking mortality in France and the direct guarantee given by the state to deposits collected by the *caisses d'épargne*, by the Caisse des Dépôts et Consignations, or by the nationalized banks, the Banking Act gave official status to the agreement initiated by the French Bankers' Association, which involves reciprocal support between bankers in case of major difficulty (see article 52 of the Banking Act and its actual application in the case of Al Saudi Bank in autumn 1988).

The prudential ratios imposed by the monetary authorities are analysed in chapter 3. In the present transitional situation there are numerous constraints, since sufficient harmonization among domestic rules, international guidelines (e.g. the risk-related capital adequacy requirement proposed by the Cooke Committee for countries of the BIS – Bank for International Settlements – zone), and European norms associated with the completion of the internal market has not yet occurred. Just to take the example of the Cooke guideline – a risk-based capital ratio of 8 per cent, effective in 1993 – French banks reveal great diversity in their capital ratios but, generally speaking, the adjustment to the Cooke target will not be too difficult, since part of the provisions against claims on less developed countries (LDCs), rather high in France by international standards (the provision for LDCs' debt is close to 50 per cent in the case of major commercial banks), is included in the numerator of the ratio. Some banks will find it more difficult to comply with the 4 per cent sub-ratio (which concerns genuine capital, i.e. capital and reserves) than to respect the global 8 per cent ratio.

The structure of financing of the French economy

Financial innovation and deregulation were the main forces behind the dramatic change in the structure of financing. The rapid development of 'direct finance', disintermediation, and securitization has to be assessed in a macro-economic framework.

The macro-economic framework

From a national accounting viewpoint, developments between 1983 and 1986 are characterized by a progressive reduction in the financing deficit of non-financial firms, and relative stability (in nominal values) in the household surplus. The progressive improvement in firms' net position resulted from several factors, the most important being the policy of wage de-indexation that was implemented in 1982. The figures for 1987 show a slight deterioration in the net position of firms and a reduction in the households' surplus.

Table 1.6 Deficits (−) and surpluses (+), 1983−6 (fr. billion)

Type of credit	1983	1984	1985	1986
Households	+ 157	+ 154	+ 152	+ 169
Non-financial firms	− 108	− 98	− 84	− 76

Source: National accounts.

When the above-mentioned nominal values are converted into ratios, they exhibit two significant changes: (1) a marked decrease in the households' savings rate, (2) a continuous improvement since 1982 in the self-financing ratio of firms.

The drop in the households' savings rate (table 1.7a) took place despite a dramatic increase in real interest rates, which after having been often negative in the 1970s became highly positive in the 1980s. Most econometric works explain the decline in the households' savings rate by the wages de-indexation policy and its impact on the time profile of real incomes.

Table 1.7 Households' savings, 1980−7

Year	(a) Households' savings rate (%)	(b) Financial and non-financial savings rate (%)	
		Non-financial	Financial
1980	17·6	12·5	5·1
1981	18·0	11·3	6·7
1982	17·3	11·0	6·3
1983	15·9	10·4	5·5
1984	14·5	9·6	4·9
1985	13·8	9·3	4·5
1986	13·3	9·2	4·1
1987	12·0	9·2	2·8

Two important factors must be kept in mind in interpreting the aggregate data. First, the drop in financial savings has been more pronounced than the decrease in non-financial savings (housing etc.), especially since 1985. This phenomenon, which has consequences for the relations between households, banks, and activity on capital markets, means that, in France, financial savings of households have been the main variable to bear the burden of the adjustment not only to de-indexation but also to financial instability. Growing uncertainty before and after the October 1987 crash explains the dramatic drop in the financial savings rate in 1987. Second, the drop in the households' savings rate has occurred concomitantly with the institutionalization of savings through the development of SICAVs and other types of mutual funds.

As for corporate savings, the rapid rise in the self-financing ratio since 1982 (see table 1.8) has been a consequence of de-indexation (and the related increase in firms' margins) and, in the early 1980s, of the low rate of investment. Since 1985 it has coincided with a significant increase in the investment rate (defined as the ratio of investment to added value).

Table 1.8 Self-financing and investment ratio of non-financial corporations (excluding large nationalized corporations), 1979−87 (%)

Year	Self-financing ratio	Investment rate
1979	83·2	14·8
1980	66·3	15·8
1981	60·3	15·4
1982	64·2	15·3
1983	71·2	14·5
1984	76·0	14·2
1985	76·5	14·7
1986	93·4	15·1
1987	91·0	15·9

With enlarged liquidity, French firms first reduced their net debt to the banking sector. Thereafter they have invested in physical plant, and some of them, as elsewhere, were attracted to financial assets because of high real interest rates and expectations of a further drop in nominal rates. Without doubt, numerous non-financial firms have invested a significant portion of their wealth in short-term SICAVs (in December 1986 firms held 38 per cent of the outstanding amount of short-term UCITSs), in time deposits with deregulated interest rates, in certificates of deposit, futures, and options, etc. But a study prepared at Crédit National by Michel Fried and Olivier Gaudry (1988) points to the limited substitutability between physical and financial investment: among French firms, those having high rates of investment in financial assets have had, at the same time, the highest rate of capital accumulation.

An assessment of disintermediation

We present two convergent measures. The first is global, since it corresponds to the aggregate rate of intermediation, whilst the second concerns only the structure of corporate financing.

There are several competing measures for the intermediation ratio. Here I refer to the series of the National Credit Council, which takes the viewpoint of borrowers (how deficit units satisfy their needs) and considers the UCITSs as pure channels of disintermediation. (Clearly, this is a controversial issue, since most UCITSs are managed, directly or indirectly, by credit institutions and since, like any financial intermediary, they operate maturity transformation on a large scale.)

Table 1.9 presents the rate of intermediation in terms of flows. The flows are very sensitive to short-run movements (e.g. the drop in intermediation in 1987, before and after the financial crash). But the stock approach raises many difficult issues, including complex problems of valuation.

Table 1.9 The intermediation ratio (in terms of flows), 1981–7

1981	1982	1983	1984	1985	1986	1987
0·78	0·77	0·71	0·64	0·63	0·42	0·48

Source: Conseil National du Crédit, Annual Report, 1987.

Turning to the structure of corporate financing, we see a parallel development of 'direct finance'. It appears, from a flow-of-funds perspective, that 'direct financing' (i.e. financing through domestic or international capital markets) jumped to 80 per cent in 1986 from 36 per cent in 1981. For 1987 we see the same slow-down – 'direct financing' is close to 64 per cent – which began well ahead of the crash.

The securitization process

Securitization began in France in the early 1980s, with the development of capital markets, the progressive substitution of negotiable securities for credits in banks' balance sheets, etc. In practice, disintermediation and securitization are so closely related that it is difficult to give a separate estimate of the latter phenomenon. However, a global securitization ratio, which considers from a flow approach the proportion of securities in total financing, has been calculated by Régine Montfront (1988). The ratio, which was stable at around 15 per cent during the sub-period 1970–9, jumped to

60 per cent in 1986 and then dropped significantly in 1987 to only 42 per cent.

Securitization began later in France than in the United States or the United Kingdom, but it has developed very rapidly under the influence of a 'catching-up' effect. This phenomenon is illustrated by the portion of commissions and fees in aggregate bank net income (table 1.10). Between 1984 and 1988 the share of commissions increased markedly. For large commercial banks it was close to 25 per cent in 1987, and some were close to figures seen in English-speaking countries (for instance, Crédit Commercial de France had a ratio of 37 per cent in 1987).

Table 1.10 Ratio of commissions in bank net income, 1980–4 (%)

Japan	15·1
France	15·4
USA	24·4
West Germany	27·4

Another proxy variable for disintermediation and securitization is given by the growth of off-balance-sheet operations (back-up lines of credit, stand-by commitments and letters of credit, swaps, etc.). Off-balance-sheet operations correspond to 26·2 per cent of the total of balance-sheet operations as of December 1987, as compared with 22·8 per cent at the end of 1980 (for banks belonging to the French Bankers' Association). Given the relative inertia of stocks, these figures illustrate the rapid change in the French financial system.

Securitization will accelerate with the gradual implementation of the December 1988 law creating specialized *fonds communs de créances*. Through such institutional changes, the monetary authorities want to extend competitive pressures in the banking sector and to induce downward adjustments in the intermediation cost. Nevertheless, owing to macro-economic constraints, short-term lending has been excluded from the securitization process, which will affect only credit over a two-year initial maturity.

Elements of continuity and change in the banking sector

Market structures

The observer is struck by the low variability in the number of banks which are members of the French Bankers' Association (since 1950 the number has fluctuated around 400). Another persistent feature is that the banking sector remains highly concentrated: as of December 1987 the three largest depository institutions nationalized· in 1945 (Crédit Lyonnais, Société Générale, Banque Nationale de Paris[1]) accounted for 49 per cent of total bank credit and 55 per cent of demand and time deposits (including certificates of deposit) with commercial banks. If we add to these figures Crédit Agricole (the largest depository institution by size of balance sheet), Crédit Industriel et Commercial, Banque Indosuez, Banque Paribas, and Banques Populaires, we arrive at close to 90 per cent of banking activity in France. The concentration ratio did not change significantly during the period 1960–87. It has to be complemented by some qualitative information concerning interbank co-operation. Besides the participation of large depository institutions in European associations (like Europartners, ABECOR, etc.), domestic co-operation has developed in the recent past, sometimes as a substitute for mergers or acquisitions.

But the high concentration ratio in the banking sector is not an idiosyncrasy of the French system. Equivalent ratios are observed in many European countries. This means that, until the opening up of the French banking sector to external competition, it was necessary to resort to oligopoly theory in order to model the functioning of this sector. Oligopolistic competition but also collusion are the basic ingredients when we analyse the market for financial services and the determination of banks' base lending rate (*taux de base bancaire*) in France until the early 1980s. Two consequences must be underlined:

1. The high concentration ratio explains, at least partially, the low rate of banking mortality. Some failures did occur but they involved only small local and regional banks. Owing to the constraints of the 'systemic risk', the Bank of France could not allow a nationwide bank to fail. For instance, the 'lender of last resort' was very active when Crédit Lyonnais faced a liquidity squeeze in 1974.

2. The risk of diseconomies of scale became increasingly well understood by large depository institutions, which have been closing some branches and reducing the number of employees since the mid-1980s. Renewed and more intense competition associated with the 1992 programme of financial liberalization in Europe will oblige many commercial banks to take into account not only economies of scope but also economies and diseconomies of scale, and to determine the optimal size and the optimal volume of activity more carefully.

But the overall stability in the concentration ratio has coincided with significant changes in market shares. The banks that are members of the French Bankers' Association lost ground in the mobilization of liquid savings (their market share fell to 35 per cent in 1987 from 43 per cent in 1950), to the benefit of mutual and co-operative banks (particularly Crédit Agricole) and, to a lesser extent, of savings banks (*caisses d'épargne*). From the viewpoint of credit allocation, the decline in AFB banks' market share is similar (from 35 per cent in 1978 to 30 per cent in 1987), but it has mainly benefited specialized financial institutions (Crédit National, Crédit d'Equipement des Petites et Moyennes Entreprises – Credit for the Equipment of Small and Medium-size Enterprises).

Some features of banks' balance sheets

The permanence of sizeable interbank operations

For all credit institutions, interbank operations represent a high proportion of the total balance sheet: 32 per cent in December 1987 (the figure is quite stable over time). The share of interbank operations is much higher for fund management banks (*banques de trésorerie*) and for discount houses; it is much lower for local and regional banks. Even when considering large depository institutions such as Crédit Lyonnais or Banque Nationale de Paris (BNP), size-able interbank operations appear not only on the asset side but also on the liability side of the balance sheet. For example, as of December 1987, resources from other financial intermediaries amounted to 27 per cent of total liabilities of BNP. Interbank operations involve traditional financial instruments and also financial innovations (e.g. the market for negotiable certificates of deposit). The high degree of credit reciprocal dependence among credit institutions has to be taken into account for the management of 'systemic risks' in France.

The extent of maturity transformation

Maturity transformation is often associated with interbank operations, but in France it was also required by the different needs of non-financial agents: households had a strong preference for liquid savings, whereas firms wanted to raise long-term funds. This canonical configuration still holds in France as elsewhere. But market and policy answers to this challenge have evolved, under the influence of financial innovation and policy-makers' analysis.

In the 1960s, French policy-makers encouraged maturity trans-formation by banks in order to facilitate the financing of rapid real growth. Retrospectively the official position could be justified by several arguments: at the time, the financial system was close to the paradigm of the 'overdraft economy', and the reduced volatility of domestic interest rates (a counterpart of the implementation of credit ceilings) meant that the interest-rate risk generated by maturity mismatching was low. The monetary authorities changed their mind in the '70s, perhaps because of the extension of interest rate risk (mainly due to the international environment, the credit ceilings being maintained), but also because some economists were arguing that maturity transformation could speed up inflation. On this controversial issue no rigorous proof has ever been supplied. Nevertheless, monetary policy resorted, and is still resorting, to incentives that encourage credit institutions to extend their equity and quasi-equity (*titres participatifs, certificats d'investissement,* etc.) base, and therefore the average maturity of the liability side of their balance sheet. The coefficient of term transformation, computed by calculating the average maturity of the asset side and of the liability side (a ratio above 1 means the existence of maturity lengthening through transformation) fell to 1·6 at the end of 1987 from 2·2 in December 1980. This figure covers only bank operations in French francs, but a parallel evolution is observed for operations denominated in foreign currencies.

The heterogeneity of the banking sector

The concept of heterogeneity has been widely used since the 1960s to characterize some features of the banking sector. It has various meanings. At first, it was (and still is in certain circumstances) referred to when pointing out the coexistence of permanent lenders (i.e. banks with large branch networks) and structural borrowers (i.e. credit institutions without a branch network) on the money market. For a long time this coexistence was put forward as an argument to justify credit ceilings and to show the difficulties of the transition to flexible interest rates, which would create large and perhaps unsustainable transfers between lenders and borrowers.

Nowadays the analysis of heterogeneity has several dimensions. An interesting study by the Banking Commission (1988) chooses 100 criteria to approach the notion of heterogeneity (among these criteria we find many ratios concerning the structure of the balance sheet, the conditions of production, profitability, etc.) and develops a typology with fairly homogeneous sub-categories: (1) the three largest depository institutions (other than Crédit Agricole): BNP, Crédit Lyonnais, and Société Générale; (2) other large and diversified banks with branch networks; (3) small and medium-sized diversified banks; (4) small local and regional banks; (5) fund management banks (*banques de trésorerie*); (6) banks dealing mainly with non-residents and in foreign currencies.

It is very difficult to present international comparisons on banking heterogeneity. Perhaps, owing to the conjunction of several factors – historical legacy, government intervention, the traditional specialization of some bank networks (e.g. Crédit Agricole, Banques Populaires, etc.) – the banking sector is more heterogeneous than in many other OECD countries. But, with extended competition, the picture is changing rapidly. Despecialization and diversification have, to a certain extent, raised homogeneity ratios at the domestic level, and they will continue to do so in the future. Like the issues of monetary policy and banking regulation, the issue of banking heterogeneity must henceforth be dealt with at the European level or, even better, at the world level.

The issue of ownership in the banking sector

In France, since the Second World War, much of the economic and political debate concerning the banking sector has focused on the issue of ownership and the role of the public sector in the global and intersectoral allocation of credit. The two waves of the nationalization process, the first in 1945, the second in 1982–3, were followed by the privatization programme implemented at the end of 1986 by the Prime Minister, Jacques Chirac, and Edouard Balladur, Minister of Finance. Privatization of banks stopped at the end of 1987 with the October financial crash and the change in political majority in June 1988. Two conclusions could be drawn from table 1.11. (1) Privatization has been quite successful, according to the ratio of demand to supply. For several reasons (e.g. partial saturation of the market, general economic conditions) the rate of attraction, as measured by this ratio, has diminished in the second half of 1987. (2) The prices of privatized banks' stocks recovered their initial values only several months after the October 1987 crash, and as of September 1988 some are still below their initial values.

In 1982 the socialist government justified the nationalization of banks by its desire to influence the objective function of the banking firm in a direction more favourable to the financing of small and medium-size enterprises and by the need to articulate industrial policy and monetary policy more clearly. The results have been rather disappointing. In 1986 the conservative government justified privatization by the pressures of competition and the need for French credit institutions to increase their capital. It is too early to assess how far these goals have been fulfilled. The question of ownership is relevant when analysing the distribution of resources and profit among activities and among agents. Ownership does not always indicate accurately the location of power. This is one lesson

Table 1.11 Privatization of financial institutions

Name	Date	Demand/Supply	Initial price	Price on 1 March 1988	Price on 30 September 1988
Paribas	January 1987	40	405	303	443
Société Générale Alsacienne de Banque (SOGENAL)	March 1987	46	125	115	119·8
Banque du Bâtiment et des Travaux (BIP)	April 1987	65	130	130	129·1
Banque Industrielle et Mobilière Privée (BIMP)	April 1987	29	140	196	184·5
Crédit Commercial de France (CCF)	May 1987	10·7	107	114	135
Société Générale	June 1987	5·4	407	323	451
Compagnie Financière de Suez	October 1987	4·7	317	267	305

to be drawn from the French experience. Before the implementation of the 1982 nationalization programme, the actual control of the banking sector by the monetary authorities was already stringent through 'moral suasion' exercised by the Bank of France, the Ministry of Finance (particularly the Direction du Trésor), and other public bodies. The change in ownership resulting from privatization does not necessarily mean less influence for the monetary authorities. Everything depends on the practical use of 'moral suasion'. As remarked earlier, the French financial system has been, for a long time, exposed to 'overdetermination', since policy-makers were, at the same time, influencing the determination of interest rates and, through credit ceilings, both the volume of credit and its intersectoral allocation. Perhaps overdetermination has been reinforced by nationalization, but *institutional* features give only one side of the picture. They need to be complemented by a *functional* perspective, as discussed in the following chapters.

Concluding remarks

The French financial system has gone through a dramatic change during the last ten years. The rest of this book is dedicated to a thorough analysis of the main dimensions of this change, with emphasis on the present situation of the banking sector in the context of generalized domestic and international competition.

This chapter has stressed what I call *system innovations* (new financial instruments and markets, etc.), even if, in the case of France, these innovations took place under the leadership and the stringent control of the monetary authorities. But there is a necessary dialectic between system innovations and *policy innovations*, i.e. adjustments in the goals and operating rules of monetary policy that are required by structural modifications in the financial system. The next chapter documents the system/policy dialectic in more detail.

Note

1 Banque Nationale de Paris, created as such in 1966–7, was the outcome of the merger of Banque Nationale pour le Commerce et l'Industrie (BNCI) and Comptoir National d'Escompte de Paris (CNEP).

References

Banking Commission (Commission bancaire) (1988) *Rapport annuel pour 1987.*

de Boissieu, C. (1987) 'Lessons from the French experience as compared with some other OECD countries', in M. De Cecco (ed.) *Changing Money. Financial Innovation in Developed Countries*, Oxford: Blackwell.

Fried, M. and Gaudry, O. (1988) 'La politique de placements financiers des entreprises industrielles', *Revue d'Economie Financière*, September.

Gurley, J. and Shaw, E. (1960) *Money in a Theory of Finance*, Washington, DC: Brookings Institution.

Hicks, J. (1974) *The Crisis in Keynesian Economics*, Oxford: Blackwell.

Kane, E. (1981) 'Accelerating inflation, technological innovation, and the decreasing effectiveness of banking regulation', *Journal of Finance*, May.

Kane, E. (1987) 'Competitive financial reregulation: an international perspective', in R. Portes and A. Swoboda (eds) *Threats to International Stability*, Cambridge: Cambridge University Press.

Levy-Garboua, V. (1982) 'Note sur les taux d'intérêt dans une économie d'endettement', in C. de Boissieu and J.L. Guglielmi (eds) *Formation et rôle des taux d'intérêt*, Paris: Economica.

Montfront, R. (1988) 'L'évolution du système financier français à travers le TERF', Bank of France, unpublished.

Silber, W. (1975) 'Towards a theory of financial innovation', in W. Silber (ed.) *Financial Innovation*, Lexington, Mass., DC: Heath.

―――― (1983) 'The process of financial innovation', *American Economic Review*, May.

Chapter two

Money market and monetary policy

Robert Raymond

In France, until the end of the 1970s, credit policy served as monetary policy. Negotiable government securities and private-sector bond markets remained modest. Since World War II, corporate and housing financing has depended to a very large extent on bank credit. Under these circumstances, any sizeable increase in nominal interest rates might have directly affected the financial balance of commercial and industrial firms and crippled the housing sector at a time when needs were considerable. In order to avoid disrupting the real economy and triggering blunt criticism from the public, the monetary authorities preferred on several occasions (and for the last time as from December 1972) to resort to credit ceilings (*encadrement du crédit*).

As stated in the previous chapter, this picture has undergone far-reaching changes since the beginning of the 1980s. The greater openness of the economy as well as the oil shocks increased the external constraint – which led to raised short-term interest rates – sufficiently to protect the exchange rate. Budget deficits induced by the slowdown in growth were for the most part soundly financed; issues of long-term government securities brought interest rates, in the capital market, to the equilibrium level between supply of and demand for funds. As a result, interest rates regained a significant role as indicators of inflationary expectations and as adjustment tools.

The payment of interest on liquidities could not escape this general trend. It was, and partly remains, subject to the regulation of deposit interest rates. Nevertheless, it can now be easily eluded. Indeed, banks have created different types of mutual investment funds.[1] They take in at any time capital deposited with them by individuals or by firms that have a temporary cash surplus. They invest these resources either in liquid assets and in bills or in variable-rate bonds and in bonds close to maturity and offer, therefore, a yield linked to money or capital market conditions according to their asset structure. Shareholders may sell their shares at any time. Other formulas have also developed, such as repurchase agreements against long-term securities between banks, mutual investment funds, and other capital holders.

Under these circumstances it was easier to allow banks to issue directly marketable certificates of deposit. Along the same lines, the Treasury decided to issue negotiable Treasury bills through auctions open to any subscriber and not only to banks, as previously. A concomitant step consisted in allowing industrial and commercial firms to issue commercial paper. These reforms were implemented, under the lead of the authorities, in 1985 and at the beginning of 1986.

These innovations also influenced banks' asset management. Banks started to increase their long-term bill portfolios. Large firms, with the size and financial capacity to issue paper direct to the public, demanded that their banks grant them terms closely matching money-market rates and not the prime rate, which consequently lost part of its previous reference role. The link between the cost of credit and market interest rates was strengthened, on the one hand because commercial paper induced competition and, on the other, because a growing proportion of bank resources avoided regulatory limits and was subject to market terms.

Monetary policy had to acknowledge this transformation. The ability to substitute disintermediated financing for bank credit sooner or later rendered the credit ceiling system inefficient. Interest rates became the natural transmission mechanism to the whole economy of impulses given by the central bank to short-term capital markets. This chapter is devoted to the description of these markets and of monetary policy.

The money market

The money market is the short-term funds market; it takes several forms.

Credit institutions are regulated by the 1984 Banking Act. They are registered with the Committee of Credit Institutions (Comité des Etablissements de Crédit) and have current accounts with the Bank of France. Their activities lead them to mutual lending and borrowing of central-bank money in the interbank market; by definition, non-bank entities, which cannot hold central-bank money, are excluded from the interbank market.

The new money-market securities, introduced as from 1985, are issued respectively by the government, by banks, and by firms, and are traded on the three markets concerned (negotiable Treasury bills, certificates of deposit, commercial paper). Futures operations supplement short-term investment and borrowing opportunities offered to professionals and to the general public.

The interbank market

The purpose of the interbank market

Credit institutions' current accounts with the central bank must in no case show a debit balance. They are debited daily with the numerous payments which every credit institution has to make for the benefit of other banks (cheque clearing settlements, credit transfers, purchases of foreign exchange and of securities, etc.) and with withdrawals of banknotes. They are credited with the reverse operations (payments received, deliveries of banknotes at the Bank of France). Every day these operations show either a deficit, which must be compensated for by buying central-bank money from other banks, or a surplus which should be invested. As elsewhere, from a technical point of view, money-market operations aim at allocating temporary cash surpluses among those who have financing needs.

Money-market operations are also connected with the obligation to maintain a credit balance which enables credit institutions subject to reserve requirements to set them up. Reserves are calculated on monthly periods. Credit institutions must ensure that the average daily credit balance of their current account with the Bank of France on successive monthly periods (from the 16th of month m to the 15th of month $m + 1$) should be equal to the amount of compulsory reserves to set up (see 'Monetary policy instruments', below). At the beginning of the computation period, banks can allow movements in their central-bank money holdings. They may get ahead of requirements, if they think interest rates will go up, and keep a higher-than-average daily balance, or lag behind, if they expect a decline in interest rates, and keep a lower-than-average balance. Of course, reserves in excess of the required amount have normally to be cancelled out by the end of the period; since they do not bear interest, they may partly be carried forward to the following period. Conversely delays must be compensated for, otherwise, at the end of the period, it would infringe the regulations.

Thus every bank has to adjust its cash according to its central-bank money flows in and out of its account with the Bank of France, according to the average amount of reserves it has to set up and according to the deviation from this amount which it wants to accept or according to the previous excesses or shortfalls which it will have to cancel out anyway.

Main types of interbank operations

The operating procedures of the interbank market have been specified by a regulation of the Committee for Banking Regulation (Comité de la Réglementation Bancaire) of 17 December 1985.

Operators are credit institutions subject to the Banking Act of January 1984, as well as the Treasury, the Bank of France, the Postal financial services, the two Overseas Territories Issuing Agencies (Instituts d'Émission des Départements et Territoires d'Outre-mer) and lastly the Deposit and Consignment Office (Caisse des Dépôts et Consignations). This last body, which manages the main part of resources collected by the two savings bank networks (one belongs to the Postal financial services) is a structural lender on the interbank market.

This market has no specific location; the various operators get in contact with each other or with intermediaries by modern transmission methods. Transactions are made all day long. This 'continuous quotation' method, introduced in October 1986, put an end to the previous fixing procedure, which consisted in fixing every morning a call-money rate which applied to all orders placed 'at the best price' for that day. Henceforth rates fluctuate all day long according to the development of demand and supply.

Intermediaries are either so-called cash management banks (*banques de trésorerie*), specializing in this role, which lend and borrow on their own behalf, or interbank market agents (*agents des marchés interbancaires*, AMIs). These brokers, who number about thirty, bring together potential contracting parties but must not act as counterparts. Direct transactions are also realized between banks.

Transactions take the form either of transfers of funds without actual delivery of securities (so-called unsecured lending and borrowing), or of operations against securities settled in central-bank money between interbank market operators. Repurchase agreements are a case in point. They are of two kinds: securities-backed credit facilities (*pensions*), or sales with option to repurchase (*rémérés*). Of course, there are also outright purchases and sales.

In the case of repurchase agreements, the borrower is generally not obliged to hand over the securities used as collateral; segregating them from his own assets ('hold in custody' arrangements) is enough. Treasury bills, however, which are in book-entry form and held in current account with the Bank of France, are transferred for the duration of the repurchase agreement from the central-bank money borrower's current account with the Bank of France to the lender's.

29

Two kinds of securities are likely to be traded or to be used as collateral for repurchase agreements. Some are specifically earmarked for the interbank market: private-sector bills representing credits (in France promissory notes as well as bills of exchange are still widely used), bills representing credits eligible for the mortgage market, and lastly negotiable bank acceptances. In addition, market operators can trade in securities and in the new money-market instruments which will be examined below. These securities are also accessible to non-bank entities.

Financial innovation has introduced all sorts of new operations which share common features in every market: interest-rate swaps, interest-rate futures, options, etc.

The maturity of operations is unrestricted but in practice short-term, especially day-to-day operations, represent an overwhelming proportion.

The Bank of France determines an average weighted rate (*taux moyen pondéré*, TMP) for day-to-day transactions settled on that very day and circulates it the following day. The French Bankers' Association publishes, for the forward market, the average Paris Interbank Offered Rates, PIBOR (in French TIOP, *taux moyens interbancaires offerts à Paris*), which are determined at the end of the morning upon information drawn from a representative panel of operators.

The markets for short-term bills

Common features

Introduced into the French financial sphere in 1985−6, short-term negotiable instruments, often called money-market securities, expanded rapidly. Previously the money market was identified with the interbank market, in which, besides banks, only a limited number of large entities, called ENBAMMs (*entreprises non-bancaires admises au marché monétaire*, 'non-bank entities admitted to the money market'), were allowed. These included insurance companies, stockbrokers, UCITSs and pension funds. Creating active markets for short-term bills opened the money market (in the economic sense) to all non-financial agents. Under these circumstances the specific category of ENBAMMs died out. The former ENBAMMs are no longer admitted to the interbank market, since they can acquire liquid marketable assets elsewhere.

Short-term bills were gradually phased in in order to avoid too sharp transfers, which might have had a distorting effect on monetary aggregates. Rules applying to the maturity and the amount which at the outset were quite stringent, were later relaxed. The minimum maturity has been set at ten days since 1 March 1987, which ensures a certain standardization of assets thus traded. Nevertheless, in practice, each category of securities shows specific features. Maturities may reach the limit beyond which securities belong to the category of bonds (i.e. seven years for private-sector issues and five years for government securities). For their part, bonds are dealt with under other regulations, are listed on the stock exchange, and come under the supervision of the Securities and Exchange Commission (Commission des Opérations de Bourse).

The minimum denomination required for short-term bills remains high. Set for a long time at 5 million frs., it has been lowered to 1 million frs. since July 1988. Because of the amounts involved, these instruments are only exceptionally held directly by households. They are, rather, bought by UCITSs and held by non-banks through these bodies. Of course, banks themselves may include these securities in their portfolios. The corresponding markets are therefore open both to non-banks and to financial institutions. Accordingly it can be seen that the share of inter-mediated and disintermediated financing provided to the economy varies in a flexible way according to market forces and banks' strategy. This is one of the reasons why credit ceilings would now scarcely be effective (see below).

When the income from these securities is received by physical persons (directly or through a UCITS) it is subject to a withholding tax at 32 per cent plus a tax for the social security system, at present 2 per cent. When the income is received by a company it is included in items taken into account to determine the taxable profit. Non-profit-making bodies are liable to a 10 per cent tax.

The main securities and their markets

Table 2.1 includes the amount of these securities held by resident non-financial agents and table 2.2 shows the total outstanding amount of these securities.

French franc-denominated certificates of deposit   These were created by a regulation of the Committee for Banking Regulation on 1 March 1985. The minimum subscription has been 1 million frs. since July 1988. Maturities range from ten days to seven years. Issues with an initial maturity exceeding one year may bear interest at a reviewable rate. Banks issuing certificates of deposit have to publish a financial leaflet as from 1 October 1988, and a rating as from 1 July 1989 for issues of certificates at more than two years. Banks issuing certificates of deposit at less than two years have to

Table 2.1 French monetary aggregates: amount outstanding at end of June 1988 (billion frs.)

M1		
Banknotes and coin		223·7
Sight deposits (credit institutions, Treasury, Postal giro system)		1,194·5
Total	1,418·2	
M2 – M1	1,244·7	
Taxable passbook accounts		221·7
Mutual credit bank 'blue' books		86·9
Industrial development accounts (CODE VI)		78·4
Popular savings books		64·5
Housing savings accounts		105·7
Savings bank A passbook deposits		687·5
Total M2	2,662·9	
M3 – M2	995·8	
Sight deposits, other deposits, and money market securities, denominated in foreign currencies (credit institutions and the Treasury)		41·2
Time deposits		376·8
Notes, bills, and savings certificates		374·3
Money-market securities issued by credit institutions		203·5
(*of which*: certificates of deposit)		(191·0)
Total M3	3,658·7	
L – M3	548·8	
Treasury bills		108·3
Commercial paper		55·5
Housing savings schemes		376·4
Contracts with savings and loans institutions		6·4
Business savings books (*livrets d'épargne entreprise*)		2·2
Total L	4,207·5	

Table 2.2 Money-market securities: amount outstanding at end of June 1988 (billion frs.)

Certificates of deposit*	252·2
Bills issued by finance companies	17·6
Bills issued by specialist financial institutions (IFSs)	35·5
Treasury bills	433·3
Commercial paper	59·5
Total	798·1

* Outstanding amount of French franc foreign currency-denominated issues with residents.

make it known whether they have obtained a rating from a specialist agency and, if so, disclose the result. For certificates of deposit at more than two years, issuers must disclose the rating obtained.

They may be issued by depository institutions, namely banks (including mutual banks) and the Deposit and Consignment Office. They are subject to reserve requirements on the same conditions as time deposits, i.e. when their initial maturity is two years or less. Certificates of deposit at more than two years do not represent more than 25 per cent on the whole.

These securities have different amounts. Therefore their secondary market, which is under the Bank of France's supervision, takes the form of OTC (over-the-counter) transactions. In practice their yield is comparable with the rates prevailing on the interbank market for the same maturities.

Commercial paper (billets de trésorerie)   Allowing industrial and commercial firms (including *groupements d'intérêt économique* – consortia – and agricultural co-operatives) to issue paper direct to the public required a law (title V of the Act of 14 December 1985). The Committee for Banking Regulation was entrusted with the task of determining its main features. It must be to bearer and be of fixed maturity, which may range (since 1 March 1987) from ten days to seven years.

From the outset, issues of commercial paper have been subject to specific precautions designed to protect savings. Indeed, unlike banks, issuing firms are neither obliged to comply with prudential ratios, nor do they come under the supervision of the monetary authorities.

A first safeguard consisted in requiring that the issuer of commercial paper of more than 5 million frs. should obtain a back-up line of credit from a bank; this credit line is not a guarantee that the bank will grant to the holder of the paper in the event of the failure of the issuer; nevertheless it provides a guarantee to the extent that the bank pledges to grant the issuer a loan if the market does not enable the latter to renew its paper. Since 1 March 1987 this back-up line must be equal to 75 per cent of the amount of the issue (instead of 95 per cent originally). A guarantee may nevertheless be granted by another firm issuing (or potentially issuing) commercial paper and owning at least 20 per cent of the capital of the issuer. This option is used within a group.

When, in July 1988, the Committee for Banking Regulation lowered the minimum value of an issue to 1 million frs. it opened the primary market to small-sized issuers. As a matter of fact, this measure was aimed at enabling efficient PMEs (small to medium-size firms) to raise short-term funds at a market rate and to strengthen their bargaining power with banks. However, widening the population of issuers increased the risk of default. Therefore it was allowed that issues of commercial paper between 1 million frs. and 3 million frs. should be combined with a real warranty in favour of the holder; at the same time, the back-up line of credit became optional. The rules concerning information and rating (mentioned above) for certificates of deposit have been applied to commercial paper.

In practice, commercial paper is sold direct to subscribers on the primary market, and there are only a few transactions on the secondary market. It must be domiciled in a bank, and transactions are declared to the Bank of France, for statistical purposes. In 1987 159 companies sold a total of 481·3 billion frs. of commercial paper, and the outstanding amount rose from 24 billion frs. to 40·8 billion frs. The most customary maturities range from twenty to forty days.

Negotiable Treasury bills Before December 1985 the government issued two types of Treasury bills. The first type, in paper-based form, was earmarked for non-banks, and bore interest at rates fixed according to a scale seldom changed and complying with the regulation of interest rates paid on time deposits. The second type, in book-entry form, held in current accounts with the Bank of France, was earmarked for banks and was offered at a market rate through an auction procedure every ten days.

The reform implemented in December 1985 aimed at allowing the Treasury to offer non-banks the equivalent of certificates of deposit, i.e. Treasury bills bearing interest at a market rate, like those that were offered to banks. Therefore negotiable Treasury bills (*bons du Trésor négociables*, BTNs) were created. At present they exist in two forms, first the discount Treasury bills with up-front payment of interest (*bons du Trésor à taux fixe et intérêts précomptés*, BTFs) issued on a discounted basis, and, second, the fixed-rate interest-bearing Treasury bills (*bons du Trésor à taux fixe et à intérêts annuels*, BTANs). In addition, the Treasury issued variable-rate Treasury bills at the beginning of 1986 (*bons du Trésor à taux variable*, BTVs) which were reserved to banks and financial institutions.

The typical minimum subscription of negotiable Treasury bills (BTNs) was lowered from 5 million frs. to 1 million frs. in July 1988. In theory their maturities range from ten days to five years. In practice they are between four and fifty-four weeks for discount

Treasury bills (BTFs) (clustering around thirteen weeks) and between two and five years for fixed-rate interest-bearing Treasury bills (BTANs).

These bills are issued through auctions and exist only in registered form. They gradually substituted for bills held in current accounts earmarked for banks and for paper-based bills offered to the public. Recently, these latter had been severely hit by the competition with other savings instruments owing to financial innovation, and in particular with SICAV shares.

Several prerequisites for the development of a secondary market have been fulfilled:

1. Regular issues and a substantial outstanding amount (more than 400 billion frs. at 30 June 1988).

2. The attractiveness to banks and UCITSs of these securities, which offer a market rate and entail no risk at all.

3. The creation, in June 1986, of a ninety-day Treasury bill contract on the financial futures market (MATIF).

4. The creation of a group of Treasury securities specialists, in December 1986.

5. The ability to effect securities loans through the Bank of France as from September 1988.

Nevertheless the secondary market turnover is not as high as had been expected. Indeed, Treasury bills are assets appreciated by banks, since they must comply with a liquidity ratio, and by so-called 'monetary' SICAVs (similar to money-market funds) that aim at offering their shareholders a money-market yield.

Other bills Various institutions that do not belong to any of the three above-mentioned categories of issuers that are banks, industrial and commercial companies and the government, may nevertheless raise funds on the money market for their cash requirements. They were thus authorized to issue their own bills, under similar conditions. This is the case of:

1. Specialist financial institutions, like the Crédit Foncier de France, the Comptoir des Entrepreneurs, the Crédit National.

2. Finance companies specializing in granting certain types of credit (housing credit, consumer credit) but which may not collect deposits, strictly speaking.

3. Securities houses, specializing in securities operations on behalf of their customers.

These securities have roughly the same characteristics as certificates of deposit.

Extension of money-market conditions to non-negotiable instruments

1. Part of banks' assets and liabilities, other than money-market securities, bear *de facto* interest at money-market rates. This is the case, on the liability side, of time deposits that are not subject to interest-rate ceilings and therefore bear interest at a market rate (as a matter of fact, interest-rate ceilings do not apply above a certain amount and beyond a certain term). This adjustment merely reflects the competition between banks. Indeed, a bank attracting a deposit previously held by another bank receives central-bank money for the duration of the deposit and is thus willing to pay interest on it at a market rate.

It is also the case, on the asset side, of certain credits. Indeed, a company of such a size and performance as to be able to issue commercial paper directly on the market can put pressure on its banker(s), as can readily be appreciated, by threatening to issue commercial paper; as a result, it obtains spot credits, usually at short term and up to a given amount, roughly at the money market rate corresponding to the same maturity.

For these categories of resources (as well as by issuing certificates of deposit) and of credits, the bank, in adjusting to market conditions, renounces almost all profit on its intermediation. It has therefore to charge a higher price for operations of other kinds and higher fees for services to customers.

2. For the moment, genuine money-market funds do not exist in France. Actually, the regulation obliges short-term UCITSs (of which monetary SICAVs) to hold listed securities for at least 40 per cent of their assets. However, this measure should be removed soon. It has not prevented some SICAVs from arranging their assets in such a way as to provide a yield close to the terms applicable on the money market. They specialize in holding either variable-rate bonds, or bonds near maturity, or bonds with an option to repurchase (*rémérés*). These instruments bring in the equivalent of a short-term rate.

3. It has become common practice to conclude repurchase agreements against long-term securities. These operations, being at short term (a few days), are effected at money-market interest rates. They constitue *de facto* a special compartment of the money market in the economic sense. They are frequent between SICAVs and banks: SICAVs may thus lend banks liquidity collected from subscribers and receive as counterpart in their portfolios long-term securities which are returned on the maturity date of the contract.

Complementary and substitutability of money-market compartments

Although they are distinct by the category of their issuer and their technical characteristics, the various money-market instruments form a consistent group. They offer a continuous range of maturities. For each of them, interest rates are very homogeneous, i.e. very close, whatever the instrument considered. Any differential that would not be warranted by objective factors, i.e. obvious to any operator, like the issuer's creditworthiness, the market liquidity, and the operation costs, would immediately trigger arbitrages. For example, banks or financial institutions managing sizeable resources (SICAVs, insurance companies, etc.) would do better to buy undervalued (i.e. offering a high yield) securities and sell the others, which would restore uniform yields.

Such arbitrage mainly concerns the secondary market. Substitutions can occur on the primary market as well, but more slowly. However, shifts between different instruments happen, rather, for other motives. There are, for instance, changes in the respective share of intermediated short-term finance (bank credits) and disintermediated (commercial paper). It is quite clear that subscribers to commercial paper may be led, under certain circumstances, to consider that the creditworthiness risk associated with these securities had become too high; then they would prefer certificates of deposit. The result would be partial reintermediation of the finance previously raised directly on the market.

Substitution may also occur between Treasury bills and certificates of deposit. Outstanding amounts of both instruments depend on the financing policy of issuers, and their distribution between banks' and non-banks' portfolios fluctuates. As a matter of fact, the amounts and the maturities of these instruments are standardized. What differs is, for subscribers, the issuer's category (the government or a bank) and, for issuers, the specific cost of bank liabilities subject to reserve requirements.

These various phenomena are not specific to France and they develop as in any active and integrated market.

Future prospects

The development that has just been described, characterized by the gradual, although rapid, introduction of securities and operations at market rates, appears to be a trend which has not yet reached its limit. It raises three questions. (1) In a market in which demand for and supply of finance can freely meet, how much room is there for

bank intermediation? (2) With products offering the entire
spectrum of maturities, from the very short to the very long-term,
are interest-rate ceilings still justified? (3) Will not international
integration, and particularly European integration of financial
markets, push towards the adoption of similar techniques? The
third question is not specific to France. But the first two deserve
some explanation.

1. In France, as elsewhere, the direct relation between saver and
borrower is limited by the wish of the former to escape the creditworthiness risk attaching to a company he does not know. Therefore the number of commercial paper issuers is limited. It may
grow if commercial paper is accompanied by bank guarantees. In
that case, banks would not really be squeezed out; they would
continue to be involved and earn fees; the situation would
approach that in which the bank grants a spot credit.

The connection between the credit market and the securities
market may increase if the securitization of credits expands in the
future. Adjustments to the legislation in this sense are contem-
plated. Banks could then trade, in a market, securities representing
credit originally recorded among their assets.

2. The regulation of interest paid on deposits comprises three
main thrusts: (a) It forbids the payment of interest on checkable
sight deposits. (b) It sets (at present at 4·5 per cent) the interest rate
on passbook savings accounts: withdrawals of cash or credit transfers may be made without notice but cheques cannot be drawn on
such accounts. (c) It limits interest paid on time deposits according
to the terms shown in table 2.3.

Table 2.3 Interest-rate ceilings, as from May 1986

Type of deposit	Amount (frs.)		
	Up to 500,000		*Above 500,000*
Short-term deposits and notes:			
From one to three months	4·5		$(MM \times 2)/3$
Three months and beyond	Free		Free
Bank passbook accounts		4·5	
Housing savings:			
Accounts		2·75	
Schemes		6	
Savings bank passbooks:			
A		4·5	
Blue		4·5	

MM Monthly average of day-to-day interbank rate for transactions on the money market during
the previous month.

Whereas market operations expand, maintaining such regulation may appear completely outdated. At the same time it can be asserted that any saver or deposit holder has the opportunity to find investments, in the form of money-market securities or, more commonly, of mutual funds which meet his needs. The complete abolition of the regulation would be very much in line with present developments but it is not a priority. Besides, each of the three thrusts listed above has specific features.

Historically the fact that interest is not paid on sight deposits is a trade-off for free cheques. Cheques are a very commonly used means of settlement in France. Three and a half billion cheques were cleared in 1987. Printing and clearing constitute a heavy expense for the banks. It would therefore be relevant that the payment of interest on chequebook sight deposits should be associated with the payment of fees for services.

Table 2.4 The structure of deposits, June 1988

		Amount (billion frs.)	Proportion in M3 (%)
Subject to interest-rate ceilings		2,735·1	74·8
Zero rate		1,418·2	(38·8)
Banknotes and coin	223·7		
Sight deposits	1,194·5		
Other rates		1,316·9	(36·0)
M2 − M1*	1,244·7		
Time deposits (7%)	15·9		
Notes	56·3		
At market rates		923·6	25·2
Foreign currencies	41·2		
Repurchase agreements	149·1		
Time deposits	211·8		
Notes	318·0		
Money-market securities	203·5		
M3		3,658·7	100

* These figures include savings bank passbooks.

Individual passbook accounts also fit in with the habits of the public. Savings bank A passbook accounts (national savings banks and ordinary savings banks) and Mutual Credit blue books, the ceiling on which is at present 80,000 frs., bear interest at 4·5 per cent, tax-exempt. They have withstood quite well the competition from market products. The collected resources are compulsorily earmarked for certain uses, and in particular are used for financing council house building. Funds collected by both savings bank networks are centralized by the Deposit and Consignment Office. The decline of these accounts would imply changing the financing conditions of certain low-rent council houses (which is conceivable) and rebuilding collecting institutions into universal banks (which would take time).

There are a few other tax-exempt savings accounts, CODEVIs, whose funds are in part earmarked for lending to industrial companies, popular savings books (*livrets d'épargne populaire*). In addition, banks open passbook accounts, the interest on which is liable to tax. However this product represents only a modest share of their resources.

Actually the regulation of time accounts, which compete directly with short-term securities, could be removed or at least conform to the characteristics of these securities.

Table 2.4 shows the part of M3 (June 1988) which is subject to the regulation of deposit interest rates, the removal of which could only increase the costs of the banks.

Monetary policy

The situation which still prevailed in France in the 1970s was characterized by:

1. A narrow securities market, both for short-term instruments (short-term interest rates were tightly monitored) and for long-term securities (the bond market expanded, impelled by the banks, which saw a means of escaping credit ceilings, and by the government, since the budget posted a deficit after the second oil shock).

2. The dominance of bank credit in the financing of economic agents.

3. Tightly regulated, monitored, or subsidized interest rates.

4. Strict controls of capital outflows.

The preceding pages emphasized certain aspects of the recent restructuring of the financial system, the main features of which are:

1. Rapid securitization, combined with a significant degree of disintermediation.

2. The availability of a continuous range of maturities for borrowing, investments, and financial transactions.

3. The importance of market rates.

4. Increasing involvement in foreign financial markets, owing to the gradual dismantling of exchange controls, which will be furthered by the creation of a totally unified European financial market.

Monetary policy had, of course, to adapt to this development. Since December 1972[2] it had been based on quantitative restrictions on credit granted by banks, net of bank bond issues and of other bank permanent resources. This net lending was closely related to the money stock. Credit ceilings thus made it possible to monitor the money stock in accordance with the following identities (on the assumption that the external position of the banking sector remains unchanged):

Bank credits − Bank permanent
   resources   = Credits subject to quantitative
                               controls
                        = Bank monetary resources

But these measures were destroyed by innovation and greater involvement in international markets:

1. The continuous range of maturities blurred the distinction between money and other financial assets.

2. Banks lost the monopoly of issuing liquid assets, negotiable Treasury bills and commercial paper being substitutable for certificates of deposit and time deposits.

3. Banks also lost their quasi-monopoly in the new financing of the economy, which can henceforth be partly provided by markets without bank intermediation, or by external borrowing hedged against the exchange-rate risk.

An increase in disintermediated financing and in capital inflows hedged against the exchange rate risk would cancel out credit ceilings.

The credit ceiling system, which had been in force since December 1972, was abolished as from 31 December 1984 and replaced by a transitional system. The latter, which was not very different, came to an end on 31 December 1986.

A pattern adapted to the financial sphere

The same phenomena which tended to make quantitative credit controls ineffective restored the regulating function of interest rates freely determined, in broadened and integrated financial markets, by supply and demand and, through them, by operators' expectations. With banks (to a certain extent only, because of the regulation of interest paid on deposits), with certain UCITSs and with money-market securities, savers find assets bearing interest at a free-market rate. Borrowers can raise loans at market terms, either directly from the market or, when their creditworthiness is high, from banks. Credit is more closely linked than previously to market terms; indeed, specific procedures of credit selectivity through interest-rate subsidizing, or preferential refinancing terms, have been gradually phased out. Once a credit policy, monetary policy has become an interest-rate policy.

In fact until 1985 the monetary authorities could resort simultaneously to two instruments: money-market interest rates (which, through the payment of non-regulated interest on non-resident accounts, influenced the speculative behaviour of non-residents) and credit ceilings (which, in the face of the demand for funds corresponding to the prevailing interest rates, could induce rationing). Today, they have only one instrument at their disposal, short-term interest-rate fine-tuning, supplemented if need be by changes in reserve requirements. However, monetary policy could not be said, in a country such as France, to have one final target only. It aims at achieving, simultaneously:

1. A moderate rate of inflation, and in any case one close to that of the country's main economic partners.

2. A stable exchange rate *vis-à-vis* the currencies participating in the exchange-rate mechanism within the European Monetary System (EMS).

3. Current payments in balance, or at least not showing an unsustainable surplus or deficit.

Wanting to monitor so many macro-economic variables through a single preferred instrument may appear to be asking for too much. However, these variables are interdependent. It is clear that the stability of the exchange rate of the French franc *vis-à-vis* other European currencies cannot be maintained in the medium term without a suitable convergence of prices and current payments. However, difficulties must not be overlooked. They spring from the unequal responsiveness of these variables to interest rates. Thus the relationship between interest rates and the exchange rate is immediate through capital movements; they create a close link between domestic interest rates and other countries' interest rates, since stable exchange rates are maintained. But the relationship between domestic interest rates on the one hand, and prices or foreign trade on the other, is much looser: the effects of a change in interest rates emerge only with a long time lag. Thus changes in interest-rate policy designed to influence one of the three variables may have on the others swifter or more belated, and therefore ill-timed, impacts. These are only potential difficulties and they hardly arose, thanks to the rather satisfactory balance of the economy from 1986 to 1988.

Setting out monetary policy

1. The definition of money and credit aggregates was reformed as from January 1986 so as to take into account financial innovation and the 1984 Banking Act, which noticeably increased the number of institutions coming under its provision. The savings banks and all finance companies are treated as banks. On the other hand, UCITSs, which do not come under the Banking Act, are included in the category of non-banks. Residents' assets only are taken into account.

M1 includes banknotes, coin, sight deposits with banks, and similar entities like the Post Office giro system. Such assets are included only when they are held by resident non-banks, UCITSs being assigned to the category of non-banks. Foreign currency-denominated deposits are excluded.

M2 includes, in addition to M1, interest-bearing sight deposits: savings banks A (and other) passbook deposits, other passbook accounts of any kind, housing savings accounts.

M3 comprises, besides M2, foreign currency-denominated deposits, time deposits and non-negotiable time bills, certificates of deposit and bills of a similar kind. Repurchase operations carried out by banks with non-banks (especially UCITSs), being perfect substitutes for time deposits, are also included in M3.

L (liquidity) includes, in addition, two categories of assets held by non-banks: first, contractual saving schemes offered by banks to their customers (mainly housing saving schemes), which cannot easily be converted into means of payment; second, negotiable short-term bills issued by non-banks, i.e. Treasury bills and commercial paper (of course, only the part which is held by non-banks, including UCITSs).

Table 2.4 shows the amount of these aggregates at the end of June 1988.

2. Since 1976 it has been common practice in France to have an intermediate target for the calendar year in terms of money stock. In the present system, M3 appeared to be too subject to transfer from or towards other categories of assets, especially the bills included in L-M3. This would justify resorting to a narrower aggregate that should be a good transaction assets proxy. M1 proving unstable in the short run, the monetary authorities chose M2, a single target base for 1988, whereas it had been targeted together with M3 in 1987.

The aggregate used before the January 1986 reform was even narrower, since it corresponded to the part of the current M2 managed by commercial banks *stricto sensu* and excluded the

Table 2.5 Monetary growth targets and outcomes since 1977 (% change over the year)

Year	M	Target	Outcome
1977	M2	12·5	13·9
1978	M2	12·0	12·2
1979	M2	11·0	14·4
1980	M2	11·0	9·8
1981	M2	10·0	11·4
1982	M2	12·5−13·5	11·5
1983	M2 (1)	9·0	10·2
1984	M2R(1)	5·5−6·5	7·6
1985	M2R(1)	4−6	6·9
1986	M3 (2)	3−5	4·5
1987	M2 (2)	4−6	4·1
	M3 (2)	3−5	9·1
1988	M2 (2)	4−6	4·0

Notes: Changes between two quarterly averages centred on (1) December, (2) November.

savings bank networks. Table 2.5 summarizes targets and outcomes since the beginning of the practice of targeting in France.

The choice of the target refers to growth and inflation estimates made with models of central government agencies and the Bank of France. It takes into account the expected effect of a tightening (or expansionary) action. The calculation is supported by the projection of a table of flow of funds.

Targeting proved particularly useful for the years of the fight against inflation. It made it possible to calculate accurately the authorized percentage for credit growth at a time when monetary creation needed to be curbed. As in every country, interpreting monetary aggregate development has been complicated by financial innovation. Indeed, it is always difficult to single out pure portfolio arbitrages from spontaneous velocity changes.

The monetary authorities also watch closely the broader aggregates M3 and L, which include crucial information for assessing the results of monetary policy, as well as a credit aggregate, total credit to domestic non-financial sectors, which gathers households', companies', and public-sector finance obtained from the banking system or from the domestic financial market, as well as medium and long-term external borrowing.

Monetary policy instruments

1. Banks must set up compulsory reserves with the Bank of France at a rate of 5 per cent on sight deposits and of 2·5 per cent on

passbook accounts and time accounts. Savings bank networks are not subject, at least for the moment, to this requirement as regards tax-exempt A passbook accounts.

Compulsory reserves do not bear interest. They are calculated on the basis of the average of daily balances of each bank's current account with the Bank of France from the 16th of month m to the 15th of month $m + 1$. This average is compared with the amounts of resources subject to minimum reserve requirements at the end of the month m situated in the middle of the period under review (contemporaneous reserves).

The concept of excess reserves materializes in case of possible surpluses at the end of the period. Seventy-five to 90 per cent (according to the amount) of these excess reserves may be transferred to the following period. During a period, institutions may be ahead of requirements (higher-than-average daily balances) or lag behind, according to their expectations of foreseeable developments in interest rates over the rest of the period. Any shortfall in setting-up reserves induces a penalty but it is most unusual to show a shortfall.

The need for central-bank money thus determined is about 60 billion frs. at present. Banks lose central-bank money because of customers' withdrawals of banknotes, or payments to the Treasury, or because of possible sales of foreign currencies by the Bank of France on the exchange market. They receive central-bank money when the situation is reversed. Their liquidity is also affected by the float.

2. Relations between the Bank of France and the Treasury give rise to fewer difficulties than in other countries, since the budget deficit is not directly financed to any great extent by the central bank.

The government has the benefit of an overdraft facility with the Bank of France, governed by an agreement signed between the Minister of Finance and the Governor of the Bank of France. This agreement is approved by Parliament and is seldom changed. The one currently in force dates from 17 September 1973 and was approved by an Act of 21 December 1973. Originally, the maximum amount of advances to the government was set at 20·5 billion frs., of which 10·5 billion frs. did not bear interest, and the rest bore interest at the money-market rate. This maximum amount has been changed half-yearly since then, by an amount equal to exchange gains or losses on the value of official foreign-exchange assets; these gains or losses are transferred to the Treasury's account. It will be noted that gains or losses on the value of the gold stock are recorded, in the liabilities of the Bank of France, in a frozen account called the 'gold official asset revaluation reserve'. This reserve appeared for the first time when the gold stock was valued at market price instead of the conventional price.

In addition, the Treasury has an interest-bearing creditor account with the Bank of France, which is its sole banker. The balance of this account undergoes fluctuations which reflect timing differences between the revenue being collected and the payment of expenditure, as well as government refinancing techniques through the issue of securities.

3. France participates in the narrow-margins exchange-rate mechanism, within the European Monetary System. Actually the authorities endeavour to provide for the macro-economic consistency of their decisions with a view to keeping the French franc exchange rate within the fluctuation margin. Nevertheless, on a day-to-day basis, and with a view either to restricting the exchange-rate volatility, or to delaying a realignment due to lack of convergence, the Bank of France is led to carry out intervention that reduces or increases foreign currency-denominated official reserves. These operations alter one counterpart of the monetary base and affect the stock of central-bank money that banks have at their disposal. Left to themselves, banks should change the inter-bank interest rates that they apply also to their foreign correspondents so as to induce short-term capital movements warranting reverse intervention by the Bank of France. Thus the excess or deficit of central-bank money due to former intervention would be cancelled out. But this would lead to extreme volatility in the inter-bank rate. Since the Bank of France discretionarily sets the money-market rates, it is led more or less to sterilize its foreign currency-denominated intervention, which does not prevent it from raising or lowering the money-market rates to alleviate tensions arisen on the exchange market if they are deemed lasting.

4. Interbank interest rates are in a way channelled between the Bank of France's two key rates, at which it supplies banks with the bulk of the central-bank money they need, in view of the interaction of the above-mentioned factors (flows of banknotes in and out, government cash movements, foreign currency-denominated intervention, float).

The major part of the central-bank money needed by banks is supplied to them through a procedure of calls for tender in which the Bank of France sets both the quantity and the price. If it has given too much (or too little), deliberately or because of misjudgement, interbank interest rates, and especially day-to-day interest rates, tend to decline (or to rise). The Bank of France is always free to withstand this movement by means of conventional operations conducted at market rates either directly or through a bank specializing in money-market operations. In practice, calls for tender are realized with the help of a limited number of banks acting as intermediaries between the borrowers and the Bank of France (*opérateurs principaux du marché*).

Calls for tender entail the delivery, by the borrowing institution, of a promisory note. This institution must be able to show that its assets include a corresponding amount in Treasury bills or in loans to companies which have been granted a good rating by the Bank of France. The maturities of these notes are generally at twenty or thirty days. Normally calls for tender take place every ten days. The collection of notes thus coincides more or less with a call for tender, which occurs at the time when the collection increases the need for central-bank money.

When interbank interest rates rise enough, they reach the second key rate, that of five to ten-day repurchase agreements (as from 1 August 1988; previously seven-day repurchase agreements) that are available without any limit and are made against Treasury bills and high-quality loans. The overnight interbank rate may exceed the official repurchase agreement rate in so far as banks prefer to borrow at a higher price for a few days, rather than for five days at the repurchase agreement rate.

The rate of repurchase agreements is usually higher than that of calls for tender by 50 or 75 basis points. The Bank of France sets this spread with complete freedom.

5. The Bank of France is legally empowered to intervene by purchases and sales of securities so as to create or destroy central-bank money.

Occasionally it engages in purchases and sales on the secondary market for Treasury bills. These open-market operations proper as yet play a marginal role, but they are bound to develop.

Although it is empowered to do so, the Bank of France has not intervened, up to now, in the long-term securities market but has preferred to let the yield curve spontaneously reflect operators' expectations.

Appendix 2.1[3]   The mortgage market

The period 1966–85

The mortgage market was created in 1966 with two aims: on the one hand, to expand the financing of private-sector housing; on the other, to organize financial channels so as to make it possible to use savings directed more towards the short-term for the long-term finance required for housing.

In order to fulfil these general requirements, the scheme implemented was associated with operating regulations concerning the transactions and the operators as well as the mobilization techniques.

Transactions and operators

Only credit institutions with a certain level of funds of their own, and approved by Crédit Foncier de France (state-owned mortgage bank), which oversees this market, may apply for refinancing on this market. In the event of their own funds being inadequate the guarantee of bigger institutions, authorized for this purpose, is required.

Loans eligible for this market must comply with norms relating to the purpose (financing of domestic housing), the term (between ten and twenty years), the guarantees tied to the claims (debt obligatorily secured by a mortgage or property pledged as collateral), and the borrowers' minimum personal capital contribution (20 per cent as a rule, at the beginning).

Mobilization techniques

These are not the claims themselves that are traded on this market but promissory notes representing their capital amount, issued by the institution wishing to apply for refinancing; in addition, notes to bearer represent the amount of interest payable annually.

The issuer binds himself, in regard to the holder of these notes, to hold permanently a volume of eligible loans of at least the same amount as that of capital notes issued, so as to give investors full guarantees of liquidity and security.

The holders of notes can apply, at any time, for the 'handing over' of mortgage claims. Thus, in the event of default (should a capital note or an interest note not be paid), the holder may obtain the conveyance, at his benefit, of the ownership of the loans.

The 1985 reform

The reasons for the reform

Nearly twenty years after it was created, the mortgage market appeared as a system aimed too exclusively at reallocating money and quasi-money among a quite limited number of principal operators. As a result of this kind of supply, the property sector was too dependent on the short term and on monetary policy.

This spilled over into the rates prevailing on this market, and notes were issued with an average maturity of about six years, whereas the maturity of eligible loans was much more than twelve years. This induced lending institutions to include a large spread for 'transformation risk', which did not help the desired reduction in intermediation costs. These various reasons led the authorities to embark on the extensive reform of 1985, on the basis of a report by G. Bonin, the governor of Crédit Foncier.

The main thrusts

The mortgage market reform was enforced by an Act of 11 July 1985. It made it possible to provide authorized institutions with a new source of finance based mainly on long-term non-monetary savings.

The overhaul of the techniques   The reform did not create a new category of property loans but diversified the methods of mobilizing them.

Authorized institutions may still resort to the mortgage market in its 1966 form, but they may also offer to an approved body the mobilization notes that they have issued, if underlying claims comply with stricter rules: (1) first-mortgage security, (2) financed part not exceeding 66 per cent or, alternatively, 125 per cent coverage by underlying claims of the notes issued (125 claims to borrow 100).

In return for the notes purchased, this entity issues long-term bonds (with a minimum maturity of twelve years, at present), whose main features must be similar to those of the notes initially subscribed.

The creation, as from 1985, of the Caisse de Refinancement Hypothécaire (CRH, Mortgage Refinancing Fund), the only entity approved at present, made possible the starting of the new scheme. The shareholders of this fund, created in the form of a financial company, are the credit institutions that lend (commercial banks) or borrow (specialist entities) on this market.

In order to promote the introduction of the CRH in the market, its issues have been, up to now, guaranteed by the government.

The new definition of the mortgage market   From now on, two channels of supply of the mortgage market coexist corresponding to specific needs and techniques: (1) on the one hand, an old mortgage market, brought closer to the money market, because of its operators (institutional investors have been excluded), the instruments used, and the resources, involving mainly depository institutions; (2) on the other, a second compartment forming part of the bond market, therefore of long-term savings, and trading securities representing mortgage loans which comply with stricter requirements as to guarantees.

Moreover, the techniques which have just been described could be amended with the securitization scheme.

Acknowledgement

I would like to express my thanks to Ms Bogard who translated the text into English.

Notes

1 Generally known as UCITSs, undertakings for collective investment in transferable securities, or, in French, OPCVMs, *organismes de placement collectif en valeurs mobilières*. Their main forms are SICAVs (*sociétés d'investissement à capital variable*, open-ended unit trusts) and FCPs (*fonds communs de placement*, mutual funds).
2 There had been previous experiences: see chapter 1.
3 The appendix was prepared by Denis Villarubla, Deputy General Secretary, Crédit Foncier de France.

Chapter three

The evolution of institutional structures and regulations

Hugues Colmant

The dramatic changes that have occurred in the 1980s (removal of credit ceilings, creation of new financial instruments and new financial markets, reform of the Paris stock market) had been preceded by another structural revolution. In consequence of the new Banking Act promulgated in January 1984, the banking system has changed from an old-fashioned, rigid, and compartmentalized system to a uniform and harmonized one. This change has allowed the strengthening of competition on a fair basis among the various actors of the banking community and has already contributed to increase the efficiency of the banking system.

The situation before the new Banking Act

Under the former legislation dating back to 1941 and 1945, different rules applied to institutions that were members of either the French Bankers' Association (AFB) or the Association of Financial Companies (ASF) and to other institutions (mutual and co-operative banks, savings institutions, specialist financial institutions, etc.), which were all subject to specific rules. This meant that only about 40 per cent of total banking activity was subject to the control of the former Bank Supervisory Commission (Commission de Contrôle des Banques) and of the National Credit Council (Conseil National du Crédit). Other institutions were regulated according to special laws and were, in most cases, controlled by the Treasury Department. Moreover, among banks there was a legal distinction between commercial banks (*banques de dépôts*), merchant banks (*banques d'affaires*), and medium and long-term credit banks (*banques de crédit à moyen et long terme*). This system was based on the idea that it is basically unsound and risky to finance long-term credit or equity investment by means of short-term deposits (less than two years).

This framework proved to be ill adapted in the long run to

51

changes in banking activity. By the 1980s there was a sharp contrast between the traditional banking system, which was properly supervised and subject to a whole range of prudential rules, and the mutual and savings sectors, which, being less regulated, were increasing their market share. In practice the major mutual banks (Crédit Agricole, Crédit Mutuel, Banques Populaires) had developed more and more activities beyond their initial legal field of activity and become fierce competitors of the commercial banks on an unequal footing.

The need for a move towards harmonization was felt before 1984, and some measures were taken before that date, particularly in 1971 (beginning of tax regime harmonization) and in 1979 (the solvency rules applying to registered banks, *banques inscrites*, were extended to mutual and co-operative banks). However, these measures were rather incomplete in so far as the constraints in terms of rules, of reporting, and of on-site inspection were very different from one category to another. Besides, the boundaries between commercial banks and merchant banks had already been largely blurred in 1966 as a first move towards a less compartmentalized banking system.

The 1984 revolution

The new Banking Act was promulgated in January 1984. This measure for the first time groups together nearly all financial institutions in the same legal framework and under the control of the same supervisory bodies. It also includes a very wide definition of banking business which gives the authorities the possibility of bringing all financial actors under the same rules. Moreover this law reinforces the power of the prudential authorities in order to safeguard the safety and the soundness of the financial system.

The only institutions which remain outside the scope of the new Banking Act are the Treasury, the Bank of France, the financial services of the Post Office, the Overseas Territories Issuing Agency (Institut d'Emission des Départements d'Outre-Mer), the Institut d'Emission des Territoires d'Outre-Mer and the Deposit and Consignment Office (Caisse des Dépôts et Consignations). These institutions and services may carry out the banking operations specified in the laws and regulations governing them.

These exceptions are largely explained by the fact that they are either part of the administration or under the direct control of Parliament. None the less, in order to prevent any distortion in competition, the Committee for Banking Regulation (Comité de la Réglementation Bancaire) may, *mutatis mutandis*, and according to conditions fixed by a decree, extend its rules to the financial services of the Post Office, the Caisse des Dépôts et Consignations, and the Treasury accountants providing a deposit facility for private individuals. Such action has already been undertaken, in August 1984.

For the opening of branch offices and the regulation of deposit rates, these bodies also have to provide the Banking Commission with accounting information on banking activities which are of the same nature as those provided by banking institutions. It should be mentioned that the French Bankers' Association has recently[1] expressed strong opposition to any development of the financial services offered by the Post Office or to any idea of banks using the branch network of the Post Office in any way. Moreover the French Bankers' Association is demanding the abolition of the Postal monopoly if a new private structure is to be created in order to render acceptable the development of financial services offered by the Post Office.

Institutions covered by the Act

Thanks to the adoption of a very broad definition of banking business, all credit institutions fall under the scope of the Act, apart from those mentioned above. This common rule affects more than 2,000 bodies called credit institutions (*établissements de crédit*),[2] compared with the former registered sector, which included no more than 800 institutions. This result was achieved through a very broad definition of credit institutions.

Section 1 of the 1984 Banking Act specifies that 'credit institutions are legal persons carrying out banking operations as their regular business. Banking operations comprise the receipt of funds from the public, credit operations and making available to customers or managing means of payment'. It has to be stressed that according to this definition any institution which grants credit, whatever the way such activity is financed (deposits from the public, borrowing on financial markets), is to be considered a credit institution. This definition appears to be far more extensive than is found in most countries, where the criterion used for defining a credit institution is the receipt of funds from the public, as for instance in Great Britain.

Moreover the Act gives a broad definition of a credit operation, which, according to section 3, shall be understood to mean any act by which a person, against consideration of value, places or promises to place funds at the disposal of another person or assumes a commitment in favour of the latter in the form of an

53

endorsement, guarantee, or the like. Leasing and, in general, any rental operation with a purchase option shall be treated as a credit operation. This provision gives French credit institutions a monopoly of the management of means of payment. Others companies can only make available to their customers cards which allow them to buy goods sold by those companies but no other goods or cash. Fifty companies such as American Express, etc., are subject to the banking laws and the prudential rules that are applied to credit institutions.

According to the Act, all specialist financial institutions, which in many countries are not subject to banking legislation, are governed by the same rules and supervised by the same supervisory bodies. The problem of unfair competition between banks and 'non-bank banks' or between commercial banks and merchant banks has ceased to exist, owing to this universal regime. This situation is sound on a domestic basis but could present some disadvantages for specialist financial institutions when competing on international markets with some of their foreign competitors. In that respect the French authorities and the French banking community are in favour of an international move towards a harmonized broad definition of credit institutions.

Compared with the former compartmentalized financial system, the new Banking Act has represented a dramatic change in the institutional environment.

Distinctions abolished

First, mutual and co-operative banks (17 per cent of the total balance sheet of all credit institutions at the end of 1987), savings banks (8 per cent), and specialist financial institutions (8 per cent) are now subject to the same rules as traditional commercial banks (55 per cent) and finance companies (11 per cent). This change has been accompanied in parallel by a move towards despecialization. For example, the volume of subsidized-interest loans has dramatically diminished and at the same time Crédit Agricole and the savings banks have more and more freedom to grant loans outside their original activities. Barriers to competition between different financial institutions have been cut back, even if some sources of dispute still exist within the banking community.

Second, the Banking Act abolished the former distinction between commercial banks, merchant banks, and medium- and long-term credit banks. Such a distinction, created by legislation in the early 1940s and a view to eliminating the risks believed to attach to universal banks, had already been blurred in 1966 and 1967. However, various institutions have continued in their specialist areas of activity, and it is likely that the flexibility allowed by the new Act will not lead to fundamental changes in that respect.

This change is another consequence of the aim of the legislation to encourage a move towards universal banks, competing with each other on an equal basis, as in Germany or in Switzerland. However, the French legislature has, within this common and unique regime, respected the diversity of financial institutions. Taking the 'population' of credit institutions as a whole, there exist strong differences between large universal banks (such as Banque Nationale de Paris) and small specialist finance companies. In addition, co-operative and mutual banks and savings banks have particularities in their legal status and in their organization which have been taken into account.

Distinctions retained

For these various reasons the law draws a distinction between six broad categories of credit institutions which have a monopoly of banking operations as regular business and of the use of any trade name or any denomination which would lead to the belief that they are to be considered a credit institution.

Institutions entitled to receive funds from the public at sight or at less than two years Four categories of credit institutions are authorized to accept deposits from the public at sight or at less than two years:

1. *Banks* which may carry out all banking operations. This category nearly corresponds to the former registered banks (*banques inscrites*): at the beginning of 1988, 394 institutions which account for 55 per cent of the total activity, as measured by the amount of the balance sheet, of all credit institutions, and to which 9,939 domestic branches belong.

Mutual or co-operative banks, savings and provident institutions (*caisses d'épargne et de prévoyance*), and municipal credit banks may carry out all banking operations, subject to restrictions arising from the laws and regulations governing them.

2. *Mutual or co-operative banks* at the beginning of 1988 comprised 190 institutions accounting for 17 per cent of the total activity of credit institutions and had 11,175 domestic branches. They are mutual associations, owned by their members, originally created to grant credit to their members, who once had in common some characteristics related to their status or their business. Crédit Agricole, the most important institution by size, was originally intended to grant credit to farmers and by extension to the rural population. This original mission has left Crédit Agricole with a

very large domestic network (around 5,600 branches) to fulfil its local role.

From now on Crédit Agricole still has a monopoly of the distribution of subsidized loans to finance the purchase of agricultural equipment. But this basic activity has steadily diminished in importance in relation to the overall loan portfolio. At the same time, house-purchase finance has become a growing part of its activities. In fact, Crédit Agricole is gradually extending its area of operation and is now entitled to grant credit to virtually any customers except big companies which are located in urban areas. These new powers have allowed Crédit Agricole to increase dramatically its presence in house-purchase finance and more recently in the financing of small-to-medium companies and private customers.

In addition, Crédit Agricole has developed an international network of subsidiaries and branches and has taken an equity participation in various sectors of the economy. So the range of its activities, since the loss of its privileged tax status, is now so large that it can be seen more as a universal bank with specific features than as a specialist institution.

Another big institution is Crédit Mutuel, which also has an extensive network of domestic branches (around 3,300) and which was created in the nineteenth century to meet private local needs. The main characteristic of Crédit Mutuel is its monopoly of making available to its customers a special savings deposit bearing tax-exempt interest (*livret bleu*) which still represents more than 55 per cent of its total deposits. Thanks to this attractive instrument, Crédit Mutuel rapidly expanded its activities to collecting other deposits and granting credit to individuals. Its speciality is much criticized by the French Bankers' Association, which is calling for any bank to be allowed to offer its customers such a deposit.

The third main institution belonging to the category of mutual or co-operative banks is the Banques Populaires, which have a domestic network of around 1,600 branches. Created by a law promulgated in 1917, their main activity consists in financing small and medium-sized companies, commercial customers, and craftsmen. Their former role of granting privileged loans to craftsmen is now diminishing as all banking networks tend gradually to be put on an equal footing.

3. *Savings and provident institutions (caisses d'épargne et de prévoyance)* are non-profit-making institutions, unincorporated and without shareholders. At the beginning of 1988 the 394 savings banks had a large domestic network of around 4,400 branches and accounted for 8 per cent of the total activity of credit institutions.

Traditionally savings banks collect funds on tax-free savings accounts which are centralized by the Caisse des Dépôts et Consignations and earmarked for housing and local authority finance.

From the beginning of the 1980s savings banks have been allowed to diversify their activities. They now offer checkable deposits, mutual funds, and all types of savings accounts. Moreover the local savings banks have now allowed themselves to use a large part of the funds collected and may grant credit to individuals and even to small and medium-sized companies.

Banks in this category have undertaken a merger process which explains why the number of local savings banks has diminished year after year (364 at the beginning of 1988 as against 468 in 1984). The trend is due particularly to the necessity of raising capital adequacy in relation to the prudential rules which have to be respected by every local *caisse d'épargne*.

4. *Municipal credit institutions (caisses de crédit municipal)* comprise twenty-one municipal institutions, all affiliated to the central union of municipal credit depository institutions, intended to combat usury by granting loans against the pledge of physical objects (pawnbroking, of which they have a monopoly), against securities, and against pensions by a charge on the salaries of civil servants or the like. Their importance is now low in terms of the local activity of credit institutions (0·17 per cent at the beginning of 1988) because of the security system and of the competition of savings banks. The bulk of their activity is now represented by loans granted to civil servants.

Institutions which may not receive funds from the public at sight or at less than two years Two categories of credit institutions – finance companies (*sociétés financières*) and specialized financial institutions (*institutions financières spécialisées*) – are not allowed, unless authorized to do so as a secondary activity in accordance with the conditions laid down by the Committee for Banking Regulation, to receive funds from the public at sight or at less than two years.

5. At the beginning of 1988 the 1,067 *finance companies* (hire-purchase companies, mortgage credit banks, leasing companies, etc.) accounted for 11 per cent of the total activity of credit institutions. These institutions may carry out only such banking operations as are covered by the laws and regulations applying to them (group A) or by a decision authorizing them to operate (group B).

In group A (nearly 600 finance companies) were to be found at the beginning of 1988 around 300 mutual guarantee companies (*sociétés de caution mutuelle*), two-thirds of which depend upon the Banques Populaires, and around 160 low-cost housing finance companies (*sociétés de crédit immobilier*), founded by an Act of 1908, which are non-profit-making institutions whose directors are not remunerated and which are subject to a limit on the dividend they may pay (6 per cent of nominal capital). Their activities consist primarily in financing the building and maintenance of council houses (HLM) through the provision of subsidized mortgages. (Around eighty property finance companies, SICOMIs, specialize in property leasing operations with commercial and industrial customers.) The SICOMIs have recently enjoyed rapid growth in their activities, partly because this form of loan is now relatively cheap for customers, for whom the rents paid are tax-deductible.[3]

Group A also included at the beginning of 1988 four saving–lending institutions (*sociétés de crédit différé*), five telecommunication finance companies (*sociétés de financement des télécommunications*), twenty companies for financing energy conservation (SOFERGIE), and around thirty other various institutions. Group B (nearly 480 finance companies) includes a wide range of institutions individually authorized for a special activity (leasing, factoring, hire-purchase, credit sales, real-estate finance, etc.).

It should be mentioned that most finance companies are subsidiaries of larger groups and that only a few are independent. Not only credit institutions but also industrial companies have set up or acquired subsidiaries, sometimes for tax considerations, in the form of a finance company for performing specialized operations.

6. At the beginning of 1988 the thirty-one *specialist financial institutions* accounted for around 8·5 per cent of the total activity of credit institutions. This category is very heterogeneous, each institution having been created by the authorities for a special purpose. The law specifies that 'specialist financial institutions are credit institutions carrying out a permanent public-interest task assigned to them by the state. They may not carry out banking operations other than those relating to this task, except as a secondary activity.' Their market share in some activities is particularly large: around 20 per cent for housing finance (Crédit Foncier de France, Comptoir des Entrepreneurs), for investment credit to domestic companies (Crédit National, Crédit d'Equipement des Petites et Moyennes Entreprises and Sociétés de Développement Régional) and for loans to local and central authorities (Crédit Local de France).

A feature common to nearly all these institutions – but not, for example, to the CCIFP, which is in charge of the MATIF (the financial futures market) – is that their activity consists mainly in granting long-term credits, which often benefit from government assistance in the form of privileged terms or of a guarantee. Owing to the new policy of the authorities favouring a reduction in subsidized loans, most of these institutions are now granting more and more loans on normal market terms. More than 40 per cent of the total loans granted by this category must now adapt its structures and its competence to a highly competitive environment.

7. *Article 99 institutions.* Apart from these six broad categories of credit institutions, article 99 of the Banking Act provides that 'Institutions whose principal business is to manage portfolios of securities on their customers' behalf, to this end receiving funds together with management authority, or to assist in the placing of such securities, shall be subject to the present Act'. This article implies that the *maisons de titres* (securities houses) specializing in portfolio management and trading securities are subject to the Act and are now called article 99 institutions. However, these institutions (112 at the beginning of 1988) are not allowed to engage in banking activities on a regular basis (receiving deposits from the public, granting loans, or managing means of payment).

Until recently, securities houses were concerned only with portfolio management or with underwriting operations on national and international markets, and in most cases were affiliated either to banks or to insurance companies and pension funds. Recently foreign investors have created article 99 institutions in order to develop an activity of securities and commercial paper trading in Paris (at the beginning of 1988, twenty-two article 99 institutions were controlled by foreign investors, compared with only four in 1985) and some others have been registered for the sole purpose of securing access to the MATIF (fourteen belong to this last category of article 99 institutions).

From 1986 to 1988 the number of article 99 institutions has risen from sixty-seven to 112. This trend has been favoured by the fact that the prudential rules applied to these institutions are less stringent than those applying to other credit institutions, in particular for capital requirements.

One supervisor for all credit institutions

The 1984 Banking Act has brought all credit institutions under one common regulatory framework. Compared with the former situation, a clear distinction is now drawn between institutions which have advisory powers or regulatory powers and banking supervision. Above all, the new law has reinforced the powers of the Banking Commission, which is entrusted with banking supervision.

Advisory institutions

The Conseil National du Crédit (National Credit Council), which had been created by the law of December 1945, has been restored by the 1984 Banking Act but it now has only an advisory role as opposed to the previous situation. The Minister of Finance is the chairman of the Council and the Governor of the Bank of France is vice-chairman, while fifty-one other members represent the government, Parliament, credit institutions, professional and consumers' organizations, and trade unions and professionals chosen for their competence in banking and financial matters.

Article 24 of the Banking Act states that the Council shall be consulted on the stance of monetary and credit policy and shall study the working of the banking and financial system, particularly as regards customer relations. It may issue opinions in these areas and set up working parties or study groups for conducting any research it deems necessary. It may be asked by the Minister responsible for economic affairs and finance to give an opinion on Bills and draft decrees falling within its competence. Apart from its traditional meeting devoted to monetary and credit policies, the recent activities of the Council have been characterized by a growing number of study groups on various issues such as the impact of financial innovation in banking (securitization, etc.).

The Act has established a new entity which is called the Comité Consultatif (Advisory Committee) and which has to study matters concerning credit institutions' relations with their customers and to suggest appropriate measures in this sphere, in particular by putting forward opinions or general recommendations. The committee is composed predominantly, and in equal numbers, of representatives of credit institutions and representatives of their customers and is chaired by a prominent person chosen for his competence in banking and financial matters. This advisory committee reports annually to the National Credit Council and this annual report is published. In 1986, for instance, it conducted three studies concerning the pricing of banking services, the responsibility of banks in case of non-renewal of credit lines, and the problems connected with usurious loans.

Regulatory powers

The Banking Act has concentrated all regulatory powers concerning credit institutions in the Comité de la Réglementation Bancaire, the Committee for Banking Regulation. This new committee has only six members, so as to be able to take decisions rapidly and efficiently. It comprises the Minister responsible for economic affairs and finance, as chairman, the Governor of the Bank of France as deputy chairman and four other members appointed by a decree of the Minister of Finance for a period of three years. These four other members are a representative of the Association of French Credit Institutions (Association Française des Établissements de Crédit), a representative of the trade unions representing the staff of the credit institutions, and two prominent members chosen for their competence.

This description shows that the Ministry of Finance clearly has the leadership in regulatory matters. It is also specified in the Act that it is within the framework of guidelines laid down by the government that the Committee for Banking Regulation sets the general regulations applicable to credit institutions. During the parliamentary debates that took place in 1983 right-wing parties tried to give more powers to the Governor of the Bank of France, whom they would have preferred to be the chairman of the Committee for Banking Regulation. All they obtained was that when the Minister of Finance and Economic Affairs does not chair the committee in person it is the Governor of the Bank of France who does so, with a casting vote in the event of a tie, in place of the substitute for the Ministry of Finance and Economic Affairs.

According to article 33 of the Act, the Committee for Banking Regulation is competent to define:

1. The amount of credit institutions' capital and the conditions in which equity participation in these institutions may be taken or increased. This means that the committee defines the conditions under which any person may acquire, hold, or lose voting powers in a credit institution.

2. The requirements for establishing branch networks. The committee is free to authorize the opening of branch offices by credit institutions or not.

3. The conditions in which these institutions may take an equity participation in other companies.

4. The conditions of transactions that may be carried out by credit institutions, particularly in their relations with customers, and the conditions of competition. At present the committee exercises its power to fix interest rates only for rates of interest paid on deposits and savings accounts and no longer for interest received on loans. Banks are not allowed to pay interest on current accounts and they must comply with ceilings on interest paid on term deposits and on savings deposits, for monetary purposes. As for competition, the ordinance of December 1986 relating to price controls and competition put credit institutions under the authority of the new Conseil de la Concurrence (Competition Council).

5. The organization of joint services.

6. The management standards to be observed by credit institutions with a view in particular to safeguarding their liquidity and solvency and the equilibrium of their financial structure. The responsibility for ensuring compliance with the regulations rests with the Banking Commission.

7. The accounting plan, the rules for the consolidation of accounts, and the disclosure of accounting documents and information intended both for the authorities concerned and for the public. This means that the 1984 Act transferred responsibility for defining accounting rules and the type of information to be published from the Banking Commission (formerly the Commission de Contrôle des Banques) to the Committee for Banking Regulation.

8. Without prejudice to the competence of the Bank of France, the instruments and rules of credit policy. Basic principles are then defined by the Committee for Banking Regulation, but the directives to banks are issued by the Bank of France.

Considering this list, the regulatory powers of the Committee for Banking Regulation are very large indeed. Only some limited aspects are excluded from its responsibility.

It is worth mentioning that the rules of the Committee for Banking Regulation may differ according to the legal status of the credit institutions, the extent of their branch network, or the characteristics of their business. This provision allows it to maintain a certain diversity of treatment according to the nature of the institutions, which none the less must all abide by all the common rules formulated in the Banking Act. So far the Committee for Banking Regulation has scarcely used its ability to differentiate rules from institution to institution. All major prudential rules (solvency, liquidity, financial structure) have to be observed under the same conditions by all credit institutions whatever category of credit institution they belong to. However, the committee has sometimes resorted to its power of elaborating various rules according to the institution. Apart from the amount of the minimum capital, which can differ according to the category or the size of the balance sheet (see below), the main example is related to the authorization of new branch offices.

It is worth remembering that the rules concerning the setting up of branch networks have changed constantly. No authorization was required from 1967 to 1982. Then from July 1982 to 1987 prior authorization was needed. From 1987 the principle of freedom is applied to banks, the Banques Populaires, finance companies, and article 99 institutions, and, more recently, to municipal credit institutions. On the other hand, prior authorization before opening a new branch is still necessary for all credit institutions which may offer specific tax-free savings deposits or may grant subsidized loans: Crédit Agricole, Crédit Mutuel, Caisse Centrale de Crédit Coopératif, savings and provident institutions.

So the authorities have abandoned their policy of administrative control over the opening of new branches in order to allow some flexibility in the management of those institutions. Considering the pressing need for strict control of overheads and the fact that French commercial banks are now tending to cut back the number of their domestic branches, there is no danger that freedom will result in excessive development of their domestic networks. However, given the remaining advantages of some categories as regards competition and the very rapid expansion in the networks of the mutual or co-operative banks during the recent past, freedom has not been extended to all credit institutions.

The Committee for Banking Regulation has been very busy, because there were a lot of rules to be enforced in relation to the Banking Act and also because the need for new rules has emerged. For example, more than seventy regulations have been adopted by the committee since its inception.

The Comité des Établissements de Crédit (CEC, Committee of Credit Institutions) authorizes individual institutions to operate as credit institutions or as article 99 institutions. The Committee of Credit Institutions is responsible for taking the decisions and granting the individual authorizations or exemptions provided for in the laws and regulations applying to credit institutions, with the exception of those within the competence of the Banking Commission. It is the CEC which gives individual authorization to credit institutions concerning the granting or withdrawal of licences, significant changes in shareholdings when they affect control or the acquisition or loss by a group of shareholders of a blocking minority, modifications to legal form, business name, location of head office, scope of activities, and branch networks. The CEC must be kept informed of any changes related to credit institutions' management, shareholding, or statutes.

The CEC consists of the Governor of the Bank of France, as chairman, the Director of the Treasury, and four members or their substitutes, appointed by a decree of the Minister of Finance for a period of three years. These four other members comprise a representative of the Association of French Credit Institutions, a representative of the trade unions representing the staff of the credit institutions, and two prominent persons chosen for their competence. Also present, with a right to vote, shall be a representative of the professional body or central organization to which the credit institution or enterprise whose situation is being studied by the committee belongs or is eligible to belong. Thus it can be seen that within the Committee of Credit Institutions there is a rough equilibrium between the powers of the Bank of France and those of the government.

Before giving the authorization to start business, the committee verifies whether:

1. Credit institutions have paid-up capital, or a paid capital endowment in the case of a foreign branch, at least equal to the amount fixed by the Committee for Banking Regulation.

2. At least two persons are responsible for the effective direction of the credit institution's business policy.

3. The enterprise's legal form is appropriate to the activity of a credit institution.

The CEC takes into account the business programme of the enterprise, its proposed technical and financial resources, and – as do authorities of many countries – whether the persons investing capital and, where applicable, their guarantors are deemed fit and proper. In particular the CEC emphasizes in this connection the problems encountered in the past by credit institutions in which shareholdings were too fragmented, and expresses a preference for partners who feel responsible for the management of the institution on a long-term basis. When the investors do not have sufficient recognized experience in the management of institutions similar to the one they want to create or in which they want to acquire a controlling stake, the patronage (*parrainage*) of a reputable bank is traditionally asked for by the committee. In the latter case, the sponsor institution must hold a significant share of the capital and play an active role in management and in supervision. The committee may also refuse authorization if the managers of the enterprise are not deemed fit and proper, i.e. if they lack the necessary integrity and adequate experience for their duties.

It can also be added that the authorities have adopted a very liberal and open attitude towards foreign newcomers opening a branch or a subsidiary in Paris. For example, some 156 foreign banks were operating in France at the beginning of 1988, of which sixty-six had branches and ninety subsidiaries.

It is worth noting that appeals against decisions affecting individual institutions taken by the committee come directly before the administrative courts.

Banking supervision powers

Banking supervision powers are the responsibility of the Commission Bancaire (CB, Banking Commission) which has replaced the former Commission de Contrôle des Banques. The Banking Commission enjoys wider powers and fuller scope for action. Of course it has lost to the Committee for Banking Regulation the regulatory tasks such as the definition of accounting rules. It does, however, retain responsibility for defining the reporting intervals and the types of documents which have to be submitted by credit institutions.

The Banking Commission comprises the Governor of the Bank of France or his representative, as chairman, the Director of the Treasury or his representative, and four members, or their substitutes, appointed by a decree of the Minister of Finance for a period of six years, namely two high-ranking magistrates and two members chosen for their competence in banking and financial matters. In the case of a tie the chairman has the casting vote. This structure differs a little from that of the former Banking Supervisory Commission, since it no longer includes representatives of the banking industry and of the staff of credit institutions. It makes the Banking Commission a top-level institution characterized by its highly technical nature and competence.

First, its authority now extends to all credit institutions that come within the scope of the Banking Act, which means that more than 3,000 institutions are under its control, instead of only around 800 as before. Second, the Commission is required by law not only to check that credit institutions abide by the regulations, but also to supervise the quality of their financial situation and of their management and to ensure their compliance with the professional banking code of ethics. The Commission shall examine the way credit institutions operate and monitor the soundness of their financial condition. It shall also ensure that the rules of sound banking practice (*règles de bonne conduite*) are observed.

This means that the Banking Commission is not strictly bound by the rules enacted by the Committee for Banking Regulation, which constitute the minima which credit institutions have to respect, but can go beyond those rules in order to take account of the particular nature of the risks faced by institutions. Whenever a credit institution's situation justifies such action, the Banking Commission may issue an injunction calling upon it, *inter alia*, to take all necessary measures within a given period to restore or strengthen its financial equilibrium or rectify its management methods.

If a credit institution has contravened a law or a regulation relating to its business, or has not complied with an injunction or a warning, which can be issued in case of a breach of the rules of sound banking, the Banking Commission may impose disciplinary sanctions. The list of sanctions has been defined in the new Banking Act. Before 1984 such sanctions were a warning, a reprimand, a prohibition on the execution of certain operations, and any other limitations on the carrying on of business, temporary suspension of managers with or without the appointment of a provisional administrator, and, as a last resort, withdrawal of the institution's authorization. Two further measures are now at the disposal of the Commission, namely the automatic dismissal of managers and the imposition of fines. The presence of all members or of their substitutes is necessary when disciplinary decisions are taken.

In exercising its powers the Banking Commission arranges for supervisory data analysis, and on-the-spot individual inspections were conducted and special horizontal enquiries made in a dozen housing finance banks, and for assessing the impact of the October 1987 stock market crash in more than 120 institutions.

The efficacy of the on-the-spot inspections has been increased thanks to three new arrangements introduced under the Banking Act. First, the findings of the inspection visits shall be forwarded not only to managers but also to the board of directors and to the external auditors. Second, inspection visits can be extended to a credit institution's subsidiaries, to the legal persons directly or indirectly controlling it, and to their subsidiaries. Third, they may be extended, in the framework of international agreements, to the branches or subsidiaries abroad of credit institutions incorporated under French law.

Concerning supervisory data analysis, all credit institutions are required to submit quarterly financial statements to the Banking Commission, and in the case of larger institutions monthly reporting is required. Moreover the Banking Commission may ask to be sent the external auditors' reports and, in general, all accounting documents (and, where necessary, for them to be certified), as well as all relevant information and data. In practice the Commission and external auditors (*commissaires aux comptes*) tend to collaborate more and more extensively.

The Bank of France, which is entrusted, on behalf of the Banking Commission, with organizing data analysis and carrying out inspection visits through its officials, has considerably increased the number of staff (more than 200) at the disposal of the Banking Commission. All these staff belong to the Secretariat Général de la Commission Bancaire, headed by a general manager of the Bank of France, and work exclusively for the Banking Commission.

In practice, owing to the stability of the banking system and certainly also to the efficiency of the supervisory system, the role of the Banking Commission has consisted mainly in taking preventive measures rather than punitive ones.

It must be added that the Bank of France has been given the scope for playing a major role in case of difficulties. Article 52 of the Banking Act provides that:

> where such action appears justified by a credit institution's situation, the Governor of the Bank of France shall call upon the shareholders or members of the institution to provide the latter with the support it needs. The Governor of the Bank of France may also arrange for the assistance of the credit institutions as a group with a view to taking the measures needed to protect the interests of depositors and third parties, ensure the smooth functioning of the banking system, and safeguard the reputation of the financial centre.

This power is in essence a moral suasion power in so far as no legal sanction is attached to any refusal by any person to obey the wishes of the Governor. It is also to be noted that article 52 gives the Governor of the Bank of France alone the possibility of getting the assistance of credit institutions when he deems it necessary. The occasion of this decision and the form it would eventually take are entirely in the hands of the Governor.

In its concern to respect the diversity of the various credit institutions, the Banking Act has allotted an important role to the central bodies of the mutual or co-operative banks and of the savings and provident institutions. Several central bodies are mentioned in the Act: Caisse Nationale de Crédit Agricole, Chambre Syndicale des Banques Populaires, Confédération du Crédit Mutuel Agricole et Rural, and Centre National des Caisses d'Épargne et de Prévoyance (CENCEP).

These central bodies are responsible for ensuring cohesion within their network and the smooth functioning of their member institutions. To this end they must take all necessary measures, in particular to safeguard the liquidity and solvency of each of the institutions and of the network as a whole. They must ensure that the laws and regulations applying to those institutions are implemented, and exercise administrative, technical, and financial supervision over their organization and management. Within the scope of these powers, they may take disciplinary action as provided for in the laws and regulations applying to them.

Without prejudice to the powers conferred on the Banking

Commission to conduct supervision by data analyses and inspection visits over their member institutions, the central bodies must, each in its respective area, assist in implementing the laws and regulations governing the credit institutions. As part of these responsibilities, they must bring any infringements of such provisions to the notice of the Banking Commission.

Prudential rules

A common set of prudential rules

According to article 51 of the Banking Act:

> credit institutions are required, subject to conditions laid down by the Committee for Banking Regulation, to observe management standards designed to safeguard their liquidity and solvency in relation to depositors and, more generally, third parties, and the equilibrium of their financial structure. They must in particular observe risk asset and risk distribution ratios.

On the basis of this article the Committee for Banking Regulation has worked out management standards; the main ones are described below in detail. It should be added that these rules are to be respected under the same circumstances by all branches and subsidiaries of foreign concerns which are licensed in France.

Minimum capital According to article 16 of the Banking Act, credit institutions must have a paid-up capital or a paid capital endowment (for foreign branches) at least equal to an amount fixed by the Committee for Banking Regulation. Moreover all credit institutions must be in a position to prove at any time that their assets effectively exceed their liabilities of third parties by an amount at least equal to the minimum capital. Branches of credit institutions with their registered office abroad are required to give proof of a capital endowment employed in France at least equal to the minimum capital required of credit institutions incorporated under the French law.

In 1988 the amount of minimum capital required was:

1. For *banks* and mutual or co-operative banks, 15 million frs., or 30 million frs. when the total of their balance sheets exceeds 1·2 billion frs.

2. For *savings and provident institutions* and for *caisses de crédit municipal*, 5·15 million frs. or 30 million frs., depending on

whether the total of their balance sheet is lower than 600 million frs. or between 600 million frs. and 1·2 billion frs.

3. For *finance companies*, 7·5 million frs., but only 2·5 million frs. for the *sociétés de caution mutuelle* (mutual guarantee companies) when the total of guarantees is below 1·2 billion frs. and also for finance companies specialising in issuing travellers' cheques.

4. For *article 99 institutions*, 7·5 million frs. when they assist in the placing of securities or 2·5 million frs. when they concentrate their activities solely on portfolio management.

These amounts are already in conformity with the future European rules as outlined in the proposal for a Second European Directive from the Commission of the European Communities. They are to be considered the minimum initial commitment in capital which any newcomer, whatever its nationality, has to make to enter the French market. Far more demanding is the solvency rule, namely the risk–asset ratio.

The risk–asset ratio The *rapport de couverture des risques* (risk–asset ratio) is determined by calculating the ratio of capital base to risk items. All credit institutions are required to observe a minimum target of 5 per cent on a consolidated basis. When their ratio is lower than this 5 per cent, the capital base must increase at a rate of at least 6 per cent of the increase in the risks.

The numerator of the ratio is mainly composed of paid-up share capital, disclosed reserves, general provisions with the character of reserves, and other similar elements. This last item comprises hybrid debt capital instruments (notably the *titres participatifs* and *titres subordonnés à durée indéterminée*, that is to say, perpetual subordinated debts) and subordinated term debt of at least five years to maturity. To take into account subordinated debts in the capital base, credit institutions must obtain prior approval of the Banking Commission, which carefully checks that these instruments are satisfactory from the prudential viewpoint. Intangible assets and all investments in other credit institutions are to be deducted in order to prevent multiple use of the same capital resources by different institutions. The denominator is the total of the weighted risks relating to on-balance-sheet and off-balance-sheet transactions.

This approach has always been preferred to a gearing ratio approach, which uses the total of the balance sheet as a denominator, because it takes into account the relative risk involved in transactions and it allows off-balance-sheet business to be taken into account. In addition it should be noted that the degree of relative risk of transactions is considered purely from the credit risk aspect, that is to say, the risk of signature, and is not connected to other kinds of risk such as investment risk, interest-rate risk, or exchange-rate risk.

The main weights used in 1988 are 100 per cent for claims on the private sector (including claims on companies owned by the public sector) and 20 per cent for claims on credit institutions. This more favourable regime for interbank claims is due to the fact that there is a sizeable interbank market among the high-quality credit institutions, which makes this activity statistically far less risky than standard commercial loans. Some other weights lower than 100 per cent are used – namely 75 per cent for loans fully secured by mortgages on residential property (the most secured transactions are only weighted at $33\frac{1}{3}$ per cent) or for claims on domestic public-sector bodies and leasing transactions.

One of the main characteristics of the French solvency ratio is that it takes off-balance-sheet transactions into account from the start. Thus direct credit substitutes (e.g. general guarantees of indebtedness) are treated exactly in the same way as direct loans (a 100 per cent coefficient). This treatment has prevented French credit institutions from resorting to artificial practices, as, for instance, in the United States, where in order to escape capital requirements, traditionally linked to the total of the balance sheet, some banks have tended to 'empty out' their balance sheets on a large scale by giving guarantees instead of financing loans directly. Other off-balance-sheet items (such as stand-by facilities, lines of credit, documentary credits, guarantees, etc.) are generally weighted at 25 per cent, or at 10 per cent if the beneficiary is a credit institution.

It should be stressed that the note issuance facilities (NIF) and the revolving underwriting facilities (RUF) have been captured since their creation in the solvency calculations.

The risk distribution ratio   The *rapport de division des risques* (risk distribution ratio) limits to 40 per cent of the capital base the total risks (calculated according to the weights as defined for the solvency ratio) concentrated on a single beneficiary. These limits are also to be respected on a consolidated basis. Moreover the total of large loans (exceeding 15 per cent of the capital base) must not exceed eight times the capital base. It should be added that branches of foreign firms licensed in France are not subject to the risk–asset ratio or to the risk distribution ratio when in their home countries similar rules, at least as severe, exist.

The liquidity ratio   The liquidity ratio obliges credit institutions to cover their liabilities at less than one month by at least an equivalent amount of liquid assets or amounts receivable at less than one month. This new liquidity ratio replaced in 1988 the former rules, which dated back to 1948.

The measure of the liquidity of credit institutions is now far more comprehensive than was obtained with the former ratio, from three points of view:

1. All credit institutions and article 99 institutions are now subject to the new rules and not just banks only, as before 1988.

2. The ratio is calculated for all currencies together and no longer for each national currency.

3. Foreign branches of credit institutions, and even subsidiaries if credit institutions are willing, are now taken into account.

The present ratio has four main characteristics which make it suitable for the new world of banking.

1. It is basically a short-term liquidity ratio, as the time span retained is only one month (the former rules were based on a three-month period). As a warning signal of future difficulties, credit institutions have none the less to send reports on assets an liabilities by term to maturity (on a quarterly basis), showing the remaining maturities of assets and liabilities up to one year.

2. It tends to give a quite realistic picture of the liquidity of a credit institution by taking into account the observed stability of liabilities (such as deposit accounts) which are only taken into account for one fifth of their amount in the denominator of the ratio and by giving a higher weight to interbank liabilities. Recent experience has effectively shown that, in cases of difficulty, bankers are far quicker to cut their lines of credit than small depositors are to withdraw their deposits.

3. It tries to take into account the subjective character of the liquidity situation of a credit institution. What is fundamental for a bank which borrows on the market is the judgement made by market participants on the quality of its signature (its creditworthiness). One of the main factors which influence that judgement is the level of the capital base. For this reason, the capital base is retained as a favourable factor in the calculation of the liquidity ratio.

4. Finally, the new ratio aims at inducing credit institutions to have sufficient liquid assets in an autonomous manner notwithstanding the volume of loans eligible for discount by the central bank.

The ratio of permanent resources (mismatch ratio) was also recently introduced. Credit institutions and article 99 institutions must finance 60 per cent of the amount of their fixed and long-term assets (i.e. those with a residual maturity beyond five years) by means of long-term liabilities. This ratio affects only transactions carried out by domestic branches and denominated in French francs. The restrictions show that this ratio serves not only prudential concerns but also monetary considerations. When the monetary authorities removed the credit ceilings, which led credit institutions to issue large volumes of domestic debentures in order to obtain the right to grant new credits, this ratio was thought of as a means of keeping a desired volume of issued debentures by French credit institutions.

Equity participation and non-banking operations   Strict limits are also to be observed concerning any equity participation that credit institutions may hold in non-banking companies. Under the previous legislation, only commercial banks were stricly limited in their ability to take an equity participation in non-banking companies. Now all credit institutions are subject to the same rules, which means greater flexibility for the former commercial banks but stricter rules for the former merchant banks.

The Committee for Banking Regulation has tried to maintain a balance between necessary freedom of enterprise and prudential requirements. Hence, no limit exists on participation in other credit institutions or article 99 institutions. It is also specified that investments in non-banking companies are freely permitted when they do not represent more than 10 per cent of the capital of such companies. For other types of participation three limits have to be respected:

1. No single participation must exceed 5 per cent of the capital base, as calculated for the solvency ratio, of the credit institution.

2. The total of participation in non-banking companies must not represent more than 50 per cent of the capital base.

3. The total of controlling stakes in the companies concerned must not exceed 15 per cent of the capital base.

These rules are somewhat more stringent than what is specified in the proposed Second Banking Directive.

The freedom of credit institutions to carry on activities other than banking and related operations is strictly limited. According to article 7 of the Banking Act, such operations must in any case remain of limited importance in relation to the institution's normal business as a whole and must not hinder, restrict, or distort competition in the market concerned. The Committee for Banking Regulation has recently indicated that the total earnings derived from these activities must not exceed 10 per cent of the net interest income.

It is, however, to be stressed that, according to the Banking

Act, credit institutions are allowed to carry out a wide range of activities other than receiving funds from the public, granting credit, and managing means of payment. They are indeed free to carry out operations such as:

1. Foreign exchange transactions and transactions in gold, precious metals, and coins.
2. The placing, subscription, purchase, management, and custody of securities and any financial product.
3. Advice and assistance in the management of assets.
4. Advice and assistance in financial management, financial engineering, and, generally all services designed to facilitate the setting up and development of enterprises, subject to the legislative provisions relating to the illegal exercise of certain professions.
5. Operations involving the simple rental of movable or immovable property, in the case of institutions authorized to effect leasing operations.

These proposals have allowed the banks to play a major role in securities activities such as portfolio management or underwriting and trading operations. Banks also control more than two-thirds of the UCITSs. In 1988 fees from these activities represented for all French banks around 8 per cent of the net total of interest income and various fees.

It is important to stress that the banks are not allowed to undertake insurance business, an activity which is the monopoly of institutions placed under the control of the Minister of Finance. However, they are allowed to offer savings accounts which are related to life insurance, and in recent years, they have actively done so. They are also allowed to offer their customers loans with an insurance clause in case of unemployment or of any accident. On the whole, they are coming to distribute insurance products, more and more.

Moreover, cross-ownership between banks and insurance companies has multiplied in recent years. In 1988 French banks held around twenty-five participations of over 5 per cent in insurance companies, while insurance companies also had around twenty-five participations of over 5 per cent in banking institutions. This cross-holding could increase, considering the present number of planned operations of this nature.

Major recent developments in prudential rules

Since the early 1980s, the banking industry has been confronted, in all countries, with a deterioration in the quality of assets, in relation to financial difficulties encountered by domestic and international borrowers. Some major defaults have been observed in big

73

financial centres and this has led the supervisory authorities in France to strengthen prudential rules. The other major trend which can be observed is related to the increase in the use of new financial instruments (swaps, options, futures) which offer means of hedging market risks (e.g. interest-rate risk or exchange-rate risk) but can also be used in a speculative way.

In response to these developments a continuous reinforcement of the prudential rules has been recently undertaken. In 1986 the ratio of permanent resources was established, in 1987 the rules concerning both the risk coverage ratio (solvency ratio) and the risk distribution ratio (limits for one single borrower) were strengthened, and in 1988 the liquidity ratio was updated and close monitoring of the use of new financial instruments was set up.

The reinforcement of the solvency of French banks The supervisory authorities have adopted a strict policy of increasing by all possible means the ability of the banks to face any major deterioration in the quality of their assets. The solvency ratio, which was introduced in 1979, is now a rigorous constraint. First, weights given to interbank claims which were initially only equal to 5 per cent were raised to 20 per cent in 1987. Second, since 1985 any credit institution whose solvency ratio is still under 5 per cent must, in that case, increase its capital base by at least 6 per cent of the increase in the risk exposure. At the beginning of 1988 only 4 per cent of the banking population still had a solvency ratio below 5 per cent instead of 28 per cent in 1985.

At the same time, the Banking Commission has put very strong pressure on banks concerning provision against sovereign risk. Since 1982 very detailed information has been required from credit institutions on their bad loans (domestic and international) and corresponding provision. On the basis of this information, the Banking Commission obliges all banks operating in France, even foreign banks, to make general provision for sovereign risks. More precisely, all credit institutions working in France are firmly invited to raise their level of provision for sovereign risks up to the weighted average rate observed for a very large representative sample of more than forty major French institutions.

The tax authorities have adopted a favourable regime in that field: from March 1987 all provision made for uncovered exposure on beneficiaries (public or private) which have the nationality of more than seventy countries are tax-deductible. A huge financial effort has been undertaken by the banks: the total annual net amount of provision against sovereign risk has exceeded 10 billion frs. since 1984. In consequence, at the beginning of 1988, the average rate of provision against sovereign risk was around 40 per cent, instead of 31 per cent a year before and only 23 per cent two years before. For the major commercial banks this rate amounts to 50 per cent. In that respect the situation of the major French banks is again stronger than that of many of their foreign competitors, in particular the big American, British, and Japanese banks.

It is also worth mentioning, as a matter of interest, that, traditionally, domestic bad debts are very highly provided against in France. Thus, at the beginning of 1988, the rate of provision against domestic risks reached 57 per cent (53 per cent one year earlier). Thanks to these two factors – capitalization which is much higher than three years ago and large amounts of general provision against sovereign risk – the major French banks will probably be able to meet without any great difficulty the new international solvency ratio in 1992.[4]

This situation is encouraging when it is considered that the minimum ratio will be 8 rather than 5 per cent. In addition, a more comprehensive definition of the risks (in particular, the risk of counterpart failure is taken into account for new financial instruments) will probably induce a rise by 20 or 25 per cent in the denominator of the solvency ratio for French banks. For example, the Banque Nationale de Paris, the biggest of the commercial banks, has publicly announced that its present 'Cooke ratio', calculated according to the rules which will be used in 1992, is already above the minimum rate of 8 per cent.

According to certain unofficial estimates, the average 'Cooke ratio' would be around 7 per cent at the beginning of 1988 for a representative sample of international French banks. Of course, this relatively favourable situation is due partly to the fact that the Basle Committee on Banking Regulation and Supervisory Practices has fairly recognized the value of general provision in assessing the solvency of any bank. For this reason, the inclusion in the capital base of sovereign risk provision, which can be considered in large part as good as general provision, is admitted up to 2 per cent of the total risks. However, most international French banks will have to raise their capital base substantially before 1992 by retaining large amounts of their profits and also by raising funds on the market.

Fortunately, enough major French banks have issued only small amounts of subordinated term debt, which is a type of resource relatively easy to get on the financial markets. This situation allows major banks considerable room for manoeuvre, because term subordinated debt can be included in the capital base of the Cooke ratio up to 50 per cent of the amount of the core capital (capital plus reserves).

The extended monitoring of the new financial instruments   Several basic principles have been adopted in this field by the supervisory authorities.

They do not intend to prohibit or limit the use of financial instruments such as swaps, futures, or options, because that would prevent French banks from heding some sizeable risks and so put them in an unfavourable position *vis-à-vis* their foreign competitors. What is at stake is only the need for a sensible use of these instruments. For example, any idea of closing the MATIF has been clearly rejected by the authorities.

The White Paper on the new financial instruments and the risks for banks published in March 1987 by the Banking Commission and the Bank of France describes clearly the approach adopted by the authorities. They consider that the judicious use of market instruments presupposes the fulfilment of three conditions:

1. Market risks (e.g. interest-rate risk or exchange-rate risk) must be identified, which implies that a global position must be ascertained for each risk on the basis of all current, future, and contingent claims and liabilities (on and off-balance-sheet). A separate measure of the position taken by means of options, for instance, is clearly of little value because this position may have been taken for hedging purposes. So, for measuring sensitivity to interest-rate movements, the White Paper proposes as a first step to include all transactions, converted into loans or borrowing equivalents, in a schedule of maturities.

2. The results of operations on these instruments must be ascertained with rigour and prudence, the aim being to achieve continuous revaluation of profits and losses.

3. Internal structures must be adjusted by introducing a permanent control system continuously fed with information.

Recent rules for new financial instruments   At the end of 1987 a survey by the Banking Commission of the French banking sector showed that internal procedures were quite satisfactory for the measurement of exchange-rate risk but, as for interest-rate risk, nearly half the credit institutions were not yet satisfied with their present tools. As a result, the Committee for Banking Regulation recently adopted a new regulation concerning the measurement and the control of risks in regard to new financial instruments. According to this new regulation, all credit institutions which regularly use new financial instruments must:

1. Have a permanent system for measuring the volume and profitability of their transactions. They must also be able at any time to assess their open positions.

2. Manage their risks by defining and respecting limits for their net open positions.

3. Control the way their internal procedures are functioning.

Each year French credit institutions must now send the Banking Commission a description of their internal procedures related to the measurement and control of the risks concerning new financial transactions. They have also, on a quarterly basis, to send a report on their results and on the open net positions they have taken. This last information has to be broken down according to various criteria (undertaken on a regulated market or over the counter, denominated in French francs or in foreign currencies, hedging or speculative transactions, etc). A close examination of the efficiency of internal procedures will also be undertaken by means of on-site inspections. Moreover the Banking Commission has announced that, when it deems that risks taken exceed what is reasonable in view of the present level of the capital base, credit institutions will have to take corrective measures.

It is worth remembering that the Committee for Banking Regulation also introduced prudent accounting rules for new financial instruments. In a simplified presentation, speculative transactions are now treated in a more conservative way than hedging operations and transactions made on regulated markets, where the presence of clearing houses eliminates the risk of default by the counterpart.

Foreseeable future development of prudential rules

First of all, the supervisory authorities adhere to the basic principles which have been established by the Cooke Committee and will strictly apply common rules which will be defined at the EEC level. Considering that the future EEC solvency ratio will be very close to the one adopted by the Cooke Committee, it can be assumed that, at least by 1993, all French credit institutions will be subject to a new solvency ratio. Concerning limits on large loans, French regulations have already been strengthened (in 1987) in accordance with EC recommendations. So no major change is foreseen for the moment.

The same kind of situation prevails concerning the French deposit protection scheme. The present system is already in conformity with EEC recommendations. Every category of French credit institution has its own scheme which guarantees small depositors reimbursement in case of default. As for banks, the present contractual agreement concerns all deposits denominated in French francs up to 400,000 frs. As for liquidity, we have seen that the new rules established in 1988 are somewhat in advance of what can be found in most countries, and it seems likely that future work on the subject at the EC level could keep some main characteristics of the present French system.

The main developments will probably relate to market risks. For exchange-rate risk, the French authorities are now concerned that the near complete removal of foreign exchange controls, which have long prevented French banks from taking global open positions against francs, will require the establishment of some form of supervision of exchange rate risks, as in Great Britain or in Germany. As for interest-rate risk, the authorities will examine closely the information they will collect thanks to the new rules. The possibility cannot be excluded that more stringent rules, probably in conformity with future international recommendations at the BIS level or at the EC level, will be imposed on French banks.

In conclusion, it is interesting to look at the way French credit institutions have reacted to the October 1987 stock market crash. It seems that the main lessons to be drawn, from a prudential viewpoint, were the following ones.

First of all, French banks' profitability has not been too much affected, on the whole, by the strong movements observed in the markets. This situation is largely due to the traditionally cautious attitude of the major banks, whose open foreign exchange positions are, for instance, pretty low, and also to the large scope for hedging offered by the new financial instruments.

Second, certain unpleasant surprises encountered by some institutions in the use of the new financial instruments have led the banking community to pay more attention to the risk of counterparts, to the efficiency of their back offices, and to the quality of their hedging policy. All this is linked with the necessity of increasing the reliability of their internal procedures.

Third, the merits of increased co-operation between the different supervisory bodies (the Banking Commission, the Securities and Exchange Commission (Commission des Opérations de Bourse), the Stock Exchange Board (Conseil des Bourses de Valeurs), the Futures Exchange Board (Conseil des Marchés à terme), the Paris Financial Futures Clearing House (Chambre de Compensation des Instruments Financiers de Paris, CCIFP) have appeared. The new law concerning the Paris stock exchange has facilitated this development because it liberalizes the exchange of information between the different bodies. According to the common wishes of the Ministry of Finance and of the Governor of the Bank of France, a special joint committee was created in 1988 with the specific task of defining the ways of increasing co-operation between all supervisors.

Notes

1 See the 1987 annual report of the Association Française des Banques.
2 At the beginning of 1988 2,067 credit institutions plus 103 securities houses (article 99 institutions) were subject to the Banking Act (see annual reports of the Banking Commission).
3 See the annual report of the Banking Commission for 1987, where a special study is devoted to the SICOMIs (created in 1967).
4 See 'International convergence of capital measurement and capital standards', *Committee on Banking Regulations and Supervisory Practices*, July 1988.

Chapter four

Markets and products in the banking sector

François Henrot and André Levy-Lang

The French banking sector can be approached from an institutional viewpoint, as the various banking institutions are categorized in the Banking Act of 1984: all credit institutions must, according to this law, belong to one of the recognized groups, namely: the Association Française des Banques for institutions that take deposits with maturities under two years, Crédit Agricole, Crédit Mutuel, and Crédit Populaire for mutual savings institutions, the *caisses d'épargne*, the *institutions financières spécialisées*, the Association Française des Sociétés Financières for specialist finance houses – all of these institutional groups being in turn part of the Association Française des Etablissements de Crédit (AFEC).

But this classification of credit institutions, while very logical and complete, tells little about the markets actually served and the products offered by banks. In practice the various credit institutions have either broadened the range of their business beyond their offical and legal specialization, or are in the process of so doing, or, on the contrary, have elected to specialize, although their banking charter allows them to offer all products. For instance, the *caisses d'épargne* now offer investment products, unit trusts, and business loans, while some banks specialize in leasing or in consumer loans. The same variety can be observed in almost all the categories of credit institutions existing within the AFEC. We shall therefore look beyond regulatory classifications and into the markets and products – as they exist today and as they may evolve in the coming years.

In the first section we remain within the regulatory classification of credit institutions to describe their activities, but analyse, for each category of institution, the markets it covers: individual households, small businesses, large corporations, local authorities. This analysis will lead to a finer description of the structure of the banking industry, in some cases distinguishing between specific institutions. It will show that the classification of credit institutions set up by the Banking Act of 1984 leaves ample room for diversity within each category and that credit institutions can choose to specialize or to diversify without great difficulty within the legal framework.

In the second section we analyse the products offered to the public by the banking system, and indicate the market shares of the various types of credit institutions. These products range from payment systems (which include demand deposits, cash dispensers, cards) to merchant banking and venture capital – and, between these extremes, the various types of savings and investment products on one hand, and of loans and debt products on the other. For each product, the regulatory status and its evolution must be analysed as well as the degree of disintermediation, the competition from new entrants, and the possible changes in pricing and tax treatment.

These successive approaches leave an impression of great diversity – with a highly developed banking system that covers all the sectors and essentially all the financial needs of the economy – and, at the same time, the prospect of very substantial changes in the next few years: changes in the products in response to regulatory changes which will be necessary in preparation for the unification of financial markets in Europe; changes in the structure of the industry as new entrants appear in market segments where, until recently, competition was relatively restricted.

The structure of the banking system

The Banking Act of 1984 gives a very broad definition of the credit institutions which fall within its domain. This definition is based on a broad definition of 'banking operations' which include: receiving deposits from the public, lending, and offering or managing payment systems. This definition is broader in France than in most other countries. For instance, equipment leasing (on a full pay-out basis) or the distribution of credit cards is very often treated as a commercial rather than a banking operation in other countries. In France a retailer who wishes to offer a private-label credit card to his customers must do so through an *établissement de crédit* which falls under the Banking Act. In practice the Banque de France, which grants all *établissement de crédit* licences (through the Comité des Etablissements de Crédit) has not restricted entry, and the Banking Act has so far achieved its purpose, which was to enforce common rules on all banking operations without restricting competition.

Before describing the markets served by each category of credit institution, it may be useful to have a broad view of their relative

importance. This can be seen by comparing their shares in the total
savings and deposits on one hand, in total loans on the other (tables
4.1–2). Another rough indication of relative size is given by the
number of branches and the staff – although these clearly have
different meanings for banks which take demand deposits and for
other credit institutions (table 4.3).

Table 4.1 Deposits and savings by category of credit institution, 1987

Category	Million frs.	%
AFB banks	1,278·4	35·1
Co-operative and mutual banks:	1,012·5	27·8
of which: Banques Populaires	*281·5*	*16·2*
Crédit Agricole	*653·0*	*64·5*
Crédit Mutuel	*175·0*	*17·3*
Caisses d'épargne	1,191·0	32·7
Other (Post Office, Treasury)	160·3	4·4
Total	3,642·2	100

Note: Includes all demand and term deposits as well as savings in monetary form, the total being
the aggregate L.

Table 4.2 Loans to French residents by category of credit institution,
1987

Category	Million frs.	%
AFB banks	1,183·5	29·8
Co-operative and mutual banks	779·1	19·6
Caisses d'épargne and CDC	801·5	20·2
Sociétés financières	408·1	10·3
IFSs*	767·9	19·3
Other	36·9	0·8
Total	3,977·0	100

* *Institutions financières spécialiseés* (Crédit National, Crédit Foncier, Crédit d'Equipement des
Petites et Moyennes Entreprises, etc.).

The three categories of banks that take short-term deposits have
in common a large number of branches and large staffs, as opposed
to the *sociétés financières* and the IFSs, which specialize in lending
and other financial services. The differences between AFB banks,
mutual banks, and *caisses d'épargne* have been reduced over the
past few years, both in the regulations that apply to them and in
practice.

Table 4.3 Relative size of French banks, by number of branches and staff, 1987

Category	Permanent branches	Staff
AFB banks	9,939	2,226,985
Co-operative and mutual banks	11,175	121,058
Caisses d'épargne	4,378	26,970
Sociétés financières	n.s.	21,516
IFSs	n.s.	9,938
Total	25,492	2,406,467

The AFB banks

There are about 400 institutions in this category, of which 155 are foreign-owned. Only part of this total number can be classified as truly universal banks. Many are in fact specialized, or limit their activity to a region of France, or to a small number of markets. The truly universal banks are the three largest ones: BNP, Crédit Lyonnais, and Société Générale, which offer essentially all banking services to all customers, in France and abroad. They have a large network of retail branches, investment banking and corporate finance departments, a network of foreign branches or subsidiaries, and have, since the stock exchange reform of 1986, acquired brokerage houses and operate on the Paris stock market. The other large banks are, by choice, slightly less universal – Banque Indosuez and Banque Paribas are much less active in retail banking, and have limited branch networks to serve medium and large corporate clients, and the more affluent households. Their international and capital-market activities are therefore more important, in relation to their size. They are, however, part of the larger Suez and Paribas groups, which have, in addition to these banks, other activities, including such retail financial services as the Compagnie Bancaire group in the case of Paribas.

The other large banks in the AFB category are the CIC group, the CCF and Crédit du Nord (a Paribas subsidiary). These banks are more oriented towards retail banking and less international than the largest five, although they all have substantial capital-market activities and international business.

Altogether, the eight largest banks (BNP, Crédit Lyonnais, Société Générale, Banque Paribas, Indosuez, CIC Group, CCF, Crédit du Nord) account for more than three-quarters of the business of the 400 AFB banks.

The other AFB banks are all, in one way or another, less than universal. They may be regional retail banks, such as Banque de

Bretagne or Société Marseillaise de Crédit, which lack the international networks of the larger banks and specialize in the small and medium-size businesses and in banking for households.

Or they may specialize, by choice, in consumer loans (this is the case for Cetelem, Sovac, and Sofinco) or real-estate loans (Banque La Hénin) or equipment finance and leasing (UFB-Locabail). These specialist banks cater to specific market segments, to which they offer a limited range of products, and do not collect demand deposits from the public. They fund their loans through the money markets and, in this respect, are closer to the *sociétés financières* than to the banks. They have chosen to have a banking licence in order to be free to broaden the range of products they offer, which may include demand deposits for certain customers.

Other specialist banks have been created in recent years to take advantage of the expansion of the money and currency markets. These so-called *banques de trésorerie* specialize in fund management for institutions, and trade on their own account on the money, securities, and currency markets.

They have prospered during the boom years of the securities market, from 1982 to 1986, when volumes and prices both went up, and have since had to adjust, more or less successfully, to a fluctuating market with stable volumes. Again, these institutions have a banking licence in order to receive deposits from their institutional clients but make very limited use of it and are highly specialized.

As for the foreign owned banks which are also members of the AFB, they usually specialize in corporate finance for their customers, with activities in capital markets for a few of them and, in a few cases, a retail network of branches. For instance, J.P. Morgan is a primary dealer (*spécialiste en Valeurs du Trésor*) in French government bonds and has acquired a stockbroker on the Paris market. Barclays Bank has a retail network. The Japanese banks are active in capital-market operations in relation with their London branches. The development of foreign banks was indirectly restricted between 1973 and 1986 by the *encadrement du crédit*, which was a corset imposed on lending volumes. Since the removal of this corset, foreign banks have been able to expand without constraints, while a significant number of new banks established subsidiaries in Paris (twenty-eight subsidiaries or branches of foreign banks were established between 1985 and 1987). Overall, foreign banks account for 10−13 per cent of the business (deposits and loans) of the AFB banks. This is comparable with the share of foreign banks in the United States; it is less than in Great Britain or Belgium, but significantly more than in Germany or in Italy.

The co-operative and mutual banks

Until 1984 the co-operative and mutual banks were not subject to the same rules as the AFB banks. For historical reasons they were under the direct authority of the Treasury and had special privileges and assorted constraints as a result of their specialized purpose. This has changed with the passage of the Banking Act, but the co-operative and mutual banks still retain some distinctive features, partly by law and partly by choice.

The largest mutual bank is Crédit Agricole. It still is the farmers' bank but has long been much more. Its main strength is the large network of branches that the decentralized *caisses régionales* have built. The ninety-four *caisses régionales* are mutual banks, owned by their customers, and they in turn own (since 1987) the Caisse Nationale de Crédit Agricole (CNCA). The Caisse Nationale runs international and capital-market operations and, through its subsidiaries, can lend to the few market segments not directly open to the *caisses régionales*, mainly the corporate sector in larger cities.

Crédit Agricole has thus become the leading lender to consumers, the leading mortgage and real-estate lender, and a dominant force in the retail savings business, with a very strong position in unit trust and life insurance distribution. Its international and capital market operations, still relatively less developed, can benefit from the strong retail distribution capacity of the branch network.

The limits to Crédit Agricole's growth may appear in the next few years: they are financial and structural. Financial limits, as Crédit Agricole is now subject to the same tax treatment and the same prudential rules as banks, and will have to generate a significantly higher return on assets than in the past (although its mutual status is an advantage when it comes to raising equity). Structural limits, as its earnings base is very much in the form of retail deposits, and, like all retail banks, it will have to face the mounting costs of savings together with the fixed cost of the branch network. It is still likely to remain a very powerful force in French banking in spite of these constraints.

A similar development route has been followed by Crédit Mutuel, with two key differences: it has no strong central agency to link its mostly urban local and regional *caisses*, and, as it started expanding much later than Crédit Agricole, its expansion was held back by *encadrement du crédit*. It is strong in the east of France (Alsace Lorraine) and in Brittany; in both areas it is the dominant retail organization. It still benefits from a regulatory advantage, as it is allowed to offer a tax-free savings passbook, the *livret bleu* (actually the bank pays a partial tax on interest, which is tax-free to the saver). It has an obligation to lend part of the funds thus collected to local authorities.

Crédit Mutuel stands to benefit most from the deregulation of interest paid on savings and demand deposits. It still has a low market share in many areas of France and would probably try to increase it if allowed to open branches without restriction and pay interest on deposits. To bring Crédit Mutuel back into the fold of non-regulated banks is certainly a difficult endeavour for the Treasury if overcrowding of the retail banking market is to be avoided.

The third co-operative bank is the Crédit Populaire. It comprises thirty-six regional co-operative banks and a central bank which handles capital markets and international activities. The Banques Populaires are largely a retail organization, with a strong customer basis among small businesses and craftsmen. They used to distribute subsidized loans to these customers, but this is no longer a very significant part of their business. Although the Banques Populaires are no longer different from the AFB banks in terms of regulatory status or activities, they retain from their origin a strong retail orientation towards small business and households.

The three mutual bank networks, Crédit Agricole, Crédit Mutuel, and Banques Populaires, have therefore common features: a decentralized organization, with regional banks which are fairly autonomous, and a strong retail basis. This makes these banks well suited to the small-business and household markets. In the past the mutual banks have taken advantage of special situations such as a monopoly of certain subsidized loans or certain tax-free savings products. These advantages are less significant today and should be even less important in the future.

It is reasonable to expect that competition between mutual banks and AFB banks will be more even in the future, and that differences between these two types of banks will be less apparent – as is already the case with the Banques Populaires and the AFB banks.

The Sociétés financières

These credit institutions have in common that they do not take short-term deposits, and have a specialist licence. They are quite numerous (approximately 800) and fall into several categories of specialist activities: consumer lending (instalment credit), equipment leasing and renting, real-estate leasing, real-estate finance and mortgage lending, factoring, and securities houses (*maisons de titres*). In terms of markets, they cater mostly to households (consumer and mortgage loans) and to small and medium-size business (leasing and factoring).

Many of the *sociétés financières* are bank subsidiaries. Some are part of industrial or commercial groups. They account for only 10 per cent of the total volume of loans extended by the banking system, but they play a significant role in the specialist areas where they operate, and have very often been the innovators in the banking industry.

As they fund their loans on the money market, they are sensitive to the level of interest rates in competing with banks which have retail deposits: when market rates are high (10 per cent or more), the banks have a lower cost of funds thanks to non-interest-bearing deposits. The future development of the *sociétés financières* is therefore dependent on two factors: (1) the level of interest rates, and (2) the deregulation of interest rates on demand deposits and on savings. Such deregulation may be hastened by competition from foreign banks, and it will clearly put the *sociétés financières* in a much more favourable position relative to retail banks.

The Institutions financières spécialisées *(IFSs)*

These institutions have in common that they are endowed by the state with a specific mission in the public interest. For instance, the Société des Bourses Françaises, which runs the stock exchange, and the CCIFP, which runs the MATIF, are *institutions financières spécialisées*. All the IFSs have a representative of the Treasury on their board. From a banking standpoint, the most active are Crédit Foncier de France, Crédit National, Crédit d'Equipement des Petites et Moyennes Entreprises (CEPME), and the twenty-two *sociétés de développement régional*.

With the exception of Crédit Foncier, which distributes subsidized mortgage loans to households, the IFSs lend primarily to companies and to small business. The funds they lend are raised on the bond market and on the money market, and they receive a state subsidy in order to lend at below market rates. These subsidies have been reduced since 1985, and the IFSs have been led to offer more loans at market rates, thus competing with the banks and the finance houses. The IFSs account for approximately 18 per cent of total bank lending, this being shared in roughly equal parts between mortgage loans (Crédit Foncier) and long-term loans to the corporate sector.

The IFSs will remain a significant player in their specialist areas: they have a competent staff, a strong image, and are used by the government whenever subsidizing a given sector is deemed necessary. Although subsidized loans are currently out of favour, for budgetary as well as conceptual reasons, it is unlikely that they will altogether disappear from the French system after such a long history. In this matter the administrative culture still dominates the marketing culture.

The Caisses d'épargne *and the Caisse des Dépôts et Consignations (CDC)*

There are approximately 390 *caisses d'épargne*, non-profit savings banks, run by locally elected boards which include representatives of the depositors and of the local authority. The savings they offer are regulated in terms of rate (currently 4·5 per cent for passbook savings), and they have a monopoly (together with the Postal savings banks) of the tax-free Livret A. The funds collected are centralized by Caisse des Dépôts, a public agency, and by twenty-one regional agencies (the *sociétés régionales de financement*, or SOREFI). A large share of these funds are used to finance subsidized low-cost rented housing by the Caisse des Dépôts, as well as, to a diminishing degree, to finance local authorities. (This is now done almost entirely by a separate agency, Crédit Local de France, run by Caisse des Dépôts and funded through the bond market.)

Therefore, until recently, the *caisses d'épargne* were purely savings centres, with practically no lending authority. This has changed gradually, and the *caisses d'épargne* have been authorized first to offer cheque accounts, then to lend to individuals, for mortgage and consumer loans, and finally (in 1987) to lend to small businesses. Altogether the Caisse des Dépôts system accounts for 27 per cent of the loans extended by the banking system, mostly in housing finance.

The consumer market remains the main market for the *caisses d'épargne*. They have a significant share of this market, thanks to their local presence and the fact that they have initially underpriced their loans. The future of the *caisses d'épargne* is not clear. On the one hand, they play a key role in raising the funds needed for the low-cost subsidized housing system – which is politically a very influential force, as subsidized housing is run mostly by local authorities; on the other, this system is based on a regulated tax-free, passbook savings account, which has already suffered and will continue to suffer from the competition of other deregulated forms of savings products. A transition is necessary, towards a situation where the *caisses d'épargne* would compete with banks to offer a broad range of retail products, rather than rely almost entirely on the Livret A, as they still do.

Trends in the structure of banking

All the preceding accounts lead to a common conclusion: the banking system should be less and less made up of separate networks with regulatory specialization. The regulatory barriers between types of banks were based on legal monopolies: monopolies for subsidized loans in most cases, or monopolies for savings products with tax advantages. As the importance of subsidized loans decreases, and as competition and deregulation prevail in savings products, these monopolies became meaningless, and their beneficiaries are the first to request their disappearance and to be allowed to broaden their activities.

As regulatory barriers vanish, we may expect to see more voluntary specialization. Banks will recognize that they cannot compete on all products for all customers – and customers will also be more demanding, and willing to use several credit institutions for their various needs.

The products

Payment-related services

The structure of payments in France is peculiar, as shown in table 4.4. A very widespread use of bank cheques, levelling at an impressive 4·5 billion cheques per year, and the rapid development of the bank card, which progresses at almost 50 per cent per year, are the two main features of the scene.

Table 4.4 Structure of payments, 1986

Method	% of number of payments	% of amounts
Cash	77	24·5
Bank cheques	19	63·4
Card	2	3·3
Automatic transfers and drafts	2	8·8

Source: Centre de Recherche Économique sur l'Épargne (Paris, 1986).

Payment-related services have been, until now, an area of interbank co-operation rather than competition. Favoured by the Ministry of Finance and supported by the Bank of France, this co-operation covers every area of payment-related services, with good results in terms of technology and service efficiency, but awkward and unstable economics.

Technology

The cheque clearing system is decentralized in nearly 100 centres, managed by the Bank of France, with the exception of the Paris centre, which is run by the banks themselves. The clearing is still based on the presentation and exchange of the paper cheques but a fully computerized process handling the 'electronic image' of bank cheques has recently been tried out and will be implemented by the banking community before the end of the decade.

Transfers and pre-authorized drafts are also cleared through computerized centres run by the Bank of France. A new system (SIT, Système Interbancaire de Télécompensation), based upon direct electronic transfers from bank to bank, is currently being developed under the control of a specific banking association; it is expected to replace the present system at the beginning of the 1990s.

Cash is put at the disposal of the customers at bank branches and through 11,200 automatic teller machines, or cash dispensers, usually located on the forefront of the branches. These machines, mostly off-line and limited to a cashing capability, are owned, installed, and maintained by each bank, but they may be used, on a fully shared basis, by any customer holding a card of the *carte bancaire* association.

The card industry is by and large controlled by a co-operative organization, the *carte bancaire* group, which gathers not only the various categories of banks (AFB banks, mutual banks, farmers' banks) but also the Post Office financial services and the local savings banks (*caisses d'épargne*). With more than 16 million cardholders, 420,000 licensed retail outlets and a 163 billion fr. annual payment volume, the *carte bancaire* dominates the market of the 'debit' cards, leaving little room to its competitors American Express (370,000 cardholders) and Diners' Club (160,000). The main reason for this success stems from the co-operative nature of the card, which makes it a very convenient product for the customers.

From a technical viewpoint the architecture of the card system is rather complex. Banks have contracted most of the back office (control, clearing, billing, data collection) to a bunch of software companies, using intensively on-line point-of-sale equipment, and they retain the commercial relation with customers and merchants, while the association has been given the marketing of the label and institutional relations with public authorities, retailers' organizations, and the international structures of Visa and Mastercard. Both brands are accepted in the *carte bancaire* retail and cash dispenser network, but Visa (6 million holders), supported by AFB banks, overnumbers Eurocard-Mastercard (1·5 million), marketed by Crédit Agricole and Crédit Mutuel.

Economics

From an economic viewpoint, the situation of payment-related services is not as bright. The prices of these services bear little, if any relation to their costs, and as a whole they are a net charge on the banking industry, while the counterparts, founded on regulations, are unlikely to survive in the long run.

Owing to history, political and regulatory constraints, and also to the self-binding policy of the banking community, the price structure of payment-related services is widely divergent from the cost structure. Payment instruments which are the most expensive to manage, namely cash and bank cheques, are provided free of charge to the customers. The average cost of processing a cheque being estimated at 3·50 frs., the annual expense to the banking system is approximately 13·5 billion frs. The banking community has repeatedly tried to introduce a charge on cheques, but so far consumer associations have successfully opposed the move. Transfers and pre-authorized drafts, which are fully computerized and cost the banks very little, are charged either to the customer or to the company which receives the draft.

As regards the *carte bancaire*, the situation is far more complex but equally awkward. The cardholder is charged an annual fee which is among the lowest in the world (95 frs. for a domestic use, 135 frs. for an international use); the retailer pays a commission on sales, which has been sharply reduced owing to interbank competition and at present ranges from 0·40 per cent or less for the largest stores to 1 per cent for the smallest, with an 0·8 per cent average, well below the market percentage in the UK or the USA. Furthermore, the retailer's bank often gives up the float generated by the largest stores and provides the point-of-sale terminal free or at a bargain rental.

As a result, the *carte bancaire* system generates an annual loss estimated by the association at 1 billion frs. in 1987, with a better balance for the banks which have large numbers of cardholders than for those which have focused on retailers. Recent attempts to raise the annual fee charged to the card's holder and to adapt the retailer's commission to the cost have failed under the pressure of public opinion and the government.

According to the analysts of the banking system, the management of payment services as a whole generates a net loss of approximately 40 billion frs. per year. But the cost/revenue balance of payment-related services is only a part of the story. It has economic counterparts in other areas of banking services, namely the legal prohibition of interest on demand deposits and the practice of 'value dates'.

Since 1967 banks have been forbidden by law to pay any interest on demand deposits and cheque accounts, whatever the balance. An additional regulation forbids daily automatic transfers between a deposit account and a saving account. These regulations, initially aimed at curbing the money supply, have survived until now at the banks' request, though they have been abolished in most developed countries. As demand deposits account for 40 per cent of liabilities, this regulation generates sizeable profits for the depository institutions, especially when interest rates are high.

The other main problem area lies in the traditional practice of lagged value dates. Household customers are usually credited with two to five business days' lag and debited with a one-day advance. Business customers usually get better terms, depending on their bargaining power.

These two sources of revenue can hardly be regarded as stable, relying on obsolete regulations or practices and fluctuating with the level of short-term interest rates. There is little doubt that, in forthcoming years, French banks will have to unbundle these packages and sell every service at a profitable price, while paying the deposits at their market price.

Short-term savings products

Passbook savings account for an unusually high share of total savings; their structure is shown in table 4.5. These products have some peculiarities:

Table 4.5 Structure of passbook savings, 1987 (billion frs.)

Type of saving	Total outstanding (end 1987)	New savings (in 1987)
A passbooks	702	25
Blue passbooks	86	3
CODEVIs	77	2
LEPs	62	6
Banks' passbooks	223	6

All kinds of passbook provide the same regulated interest, currently 4·5 per cent, but some of them (A and Blue passbooks, CODEVIs, LEPs) enjoy very favourable tax treatment, interest being tax-free for the depositor, and then earn higher net interest than many long-term savings, though they are as liquid as cheque accounts.

The most attractive products for the average residential depositor, namely A and Blue passbooks, cannot be offered by commercial banks, being an exclusive advantage given to savings banks and Post Office branches, in the case of A passbooks, and to the mutual banks in the case of Blue passbooks.

Savings collected on tax-favoured passbooks are channelled to specific uses said to be in the 'public interest'. Until mid-1988 CODEVI deposits were shared by the collecting institutions and the Caisse des Dépôts, the former to grant corporate loans at a below-market regulated interest rate, the latter to fund equipment loans granted by the administration. New money will now be used by banks to fund short-term corporate lending below the base rate. The A passbook funds and at least 50 per cent of Blue passbook funds come to the Caisse des Dépôts to fund long-term (up to thirty-five years) low-interest loans for low-rent housing institutions (*habitations à loyer modéré*).

This circuit can be regarded as risky, in terms of liquidity and interest rate matching, and unstable, as the regulation of bank deposits can hardly survive in a unified European financial market. However, it holds, owing to its political and social implications, and stands as the cornerstone of the regulatory corset which in France rules the liabilities side of the banks' balance sheet.

Term deposits and T notes

This corset has been relaxed since 1983, but for institutional and corporate depositors only. Besides term deposits, which were and still are regulated (and heavily taxed when they are in bearer form), a new instrument has been introduced: certificates of deposit, which can be issued by any bank and bought by any investor, with a range of maturities from ten days to seven years, a minimum amount of 1 million frs., and – last but not least – market-driven interest rates. Investors and issuers have responded, so that the value of certificates of deposit outstanding has reached 250 billion frs. as at mid-1988.

Despite the rapid growth of CDs, Treasury notes remain the major product of the money market, with over 420 billion frs. outstanding at mid-1988 and an average monthly issue of 35 billion frs. The quality of the issuer, the wide range of maturities (from thirty days to five years), up-to-date issuing techniques (predetermined calendar, auction procedure, primary dealers), and a future contract traded on the MATIF: it is not surprising that Treasury notes are the most liquid instrument on the money market. Nevertheless it is used by institutional investors and banks much more than by customers, even corporate ones.

Mutual funds

The mutual funds industry has experienced dramatic growth in the last decade, managing, at the end of 1987, 160 billion ECU, i.e. more than the total of Britain, Germany, Italy, and Benelux. This development, which is the market answer to the tight regulation of deposits and savings accounts, presents three main characteristics:

1. Banks, allowed to distribute and manage mutual funds, are the predominant player in the market, though performance-wise, insurance companies often do better than banks.

2. The regulation is tighter than in most European countries, i.e. the structure of assets has to comply with specific rules: minimum percentage of liquidity, maximum percentage invested in one security, minima invested in bonds, etc. The tax treatment is sophisticated, with an incentive for funds invested in French securities (funds called 'Monory CEAs'), and a deterrent for funds generating capital gains rather than income.

3. Money-market funds make up more than half of total assets, and their rate of growth is consistently higher than that of other mutual funds.

Short-term lending

Short-term funding of business customers

The funding of working capital is provided by various products, some of which have been in use for a long time, others being more recent. Besides short-term credits used in all countries (advance or overdraft facilities), French banks frequently use discounting, either in its traditional form, i.e. discounting of bills or promissory notes, or in its more recent form, called the 'Loi Dailly', which allows a company to sell its receivables to a bank through a simple and cheap procedure. The total volume of working capital finance, which exceeded 600 billion frs. at the end of 1987, is equally divided into these three categories of products: overdraft facilities, discounting, Loi Dailly. Two points should be outlined:

1. The large and undoubtedly excessive amount of trade credit, or 'suppliers' credit'. Estimated at 240 billion frs. in 1984, it is generated by business practices and by the balance of power existing between traders and manufacturers and between manufacturers

themselves. This exceptional situation accounts for the role of discounting, as well as the rapid growth in use of the Loi Dailly and the high annual growth rate of factoring, with a volume of 30 billion frs. in 1987.

2. The recent trend towards disintermediation resulting in the launching of the commercial paper market (*billet de trésorerie*) in 1985. In fact this financial instrument, which can be issued by companies of any size, since the minimum denomination is only 1 million frs., and bought by any investor, is used only by the largest companies and, in practice, mostly bought by the banks themselves. Banks can provide a swing-line in case issuers are unable to roll over maturing commercial paper and, since July 1988, can even guarantee commercial paper issues. At mid-1988 the amount of commercial paper outstanding reached 60 billion frs.

This still recent commercial paper market provides issuing companies with very cheap funding (roughly at the same rate as Treasury bills of the same maturity and with very narrow spreads between issuers); but it should be pointed out that up to now major companies alone have benefited from this innovation and that the spread in cost of funds between the largest companies and the small and medium-sized companies has thus widened. However, the proportion of loans linked to money-market rates has increased substantially (approximately two-thirds of working capital funding), while there has been a decline in the proportion of loans linked to the base rate established by the banks jointly with the Finance Ministry.

Short-term lending to households

Recently, consumer credit in its various forms (instalment loans, car loans, revolving credit, credit cards) has undergone sizeable growth. The total outstanding, as measured by the Bank of France, increased from 60 billion frs. at the end of 1980 to 180 billion frs. at the end of 1986 and to 240 billion frs. at the end of 1987. Admittedly, consumers' indebtedness in France, with a debt to disposable income ratio of 6·5 per cent, is still low compared to a ratio exceeding 15 per cent in English-speaking countries. Competition is fierce and margins, compared to money-market rates for the same maturities, are among the lowest in Europe.

While short-term business funding and consumer credit are governed by market mechanisms, matters are not yet quite the same as regards the financing of capital expenditure, and even less as regards housing finance, both remaining heavily regulated.

Business equipment finance

As French banks were traditionally short-term lenders, the government introduced in the 1960s and 1970s a number of incentives to encourage banks to finance corporate equipment:

1. *Liquidity incentives*, banks being allowed to fund equipment loans complying to specific rules from state-owned specialist institutions, CEPME for the small and medium-size borrowers, Crédit National for the large ones.

2. *State subsidies*, to lower the rate of equipment loans, to some categories of borrowers ('arts and crafts, cottage industry', farmers, small firms).

3. *Tax advantages* given to deposits on the CODEVIs, the funds having to be used for medium-term corporate loans with a below-market regulated interest rate.

Since 1985 these incentives, and their related regulations, have lost their importance, and market products have vastly increased their share (table 4.6). Among market products, leasing shows the most rapid growth (20 per cent a year on average from 1984 to 1987).

Table 4.6 Subsidized corporate equipment loans: new loans, 1984–7 (billion frs.)

1984	1985	1986	1987
87	84	57	44

Housing credit

Housing has always been and still is the area of banking services where the government has been most heavily involved. A complex set of regulations, tax incentives, and direct or indirect subsidies rules this business, which was totalling 1,500 billion frs. outstanding at the end of 1987 and, for the same year, 286 billion frs. of new loans. Leaving aside credit to developers, either private or public, and focusing on credit to owners, the various products can be grouped under four headings:

1. *State-subsidized loans (prêts à l'accession à la propriété, or PAP)*. Under some strict conditions of personal income, price, and characteristics of the house, these loans, granted mainly by a public institution, Crédit Foncier de France are subsidized by the government to bring the rate below the market. The total outstanding at the end of 1987 was 244 billion frs. The volume of new loans is decreasing: 45 billion frs. in 1984, 29 billion frs. in 1987.

2. *Housing savings plans or accounts (plan – ou compte –*

d'épargne–logement) offered by all the deposit-taker institutions. These products have two phases: (*a*) a *saving* period, with a regulated tax-free interest rate (2·75 per cent for the account, 6 per cent for the plan) and regulated minimal – and maximal – amounts; (*b*) a *credit* period, with a regulated subsidized interest rate (2·75 per cent for the account, 6·32 per cent for the plan and a regulated amount (cumulated lending interests cannot exceed 1·5 times for the account – or 2·5 times for the plan – cumulated deposit interests).

These products, very attractive for the customers, are of course very popular: 8 million plans, 5 million accounts, a total outstanding of 443 billion frs. deposits and 156 billion frs. credits at the end of 1987. But they could be a financial bomb in the banking system if the proportion of depositors using the credit facility, at present below 40 per cent, were to rise rapidly, which could occur if market interest rates went up.

3. *'Contractual loans' (prêts conventionnés).* This product has a regulated ceiling on interest rate (mortgage in interbank market + 1·5 per cent), though it does not receive any benefit from the government, either in tax or in direct subsidy. Low-income borrowers are entitled to receive a 'personal allocation' (APL) covering a part of the interest charges. This is a typical example of useless regulation, as competition in the market place has brought the interest rate below the official ceiling. The amount outstanding at the end of 1987 was 281 billion frs. and new loans were 69 billion frs. in 1987.

4. *Market mortgage loans.* In the first three categories above, products are standardized: long-term (ten to twenty years) and fixed-rate. Market mortgage loans are more diversified. If, until recently, most of the loans were also long-term fixed-rate, some institutions – finance companies more often than banks – have recently introduced variable-rate products with success. The two main characteristics of this market are: (*a*) fierce competition which brings the rates quite often below the Treasury bonds of similar maturity; (*b*) a consumerist regulation called the 'Loi Scrivener', which allows the borrower of a fixed-rate loan to repay it early, whatever the time and the conditions, for a forfeited 3 per cent pre-payment fee.

As regards the funding of these loans, four main sources may provide the long-term money, namely:

(*a*) *Discount facilities* offered by Crédit Foncier.
(*b*) *The bond market*, which is deep and liquid.
(*c*) *Mortgage certificates*, which can be issued by lenders and bought by banks.

(*d*) *Bonds* issued by the Caisse de Refinancement Hypothécaire (CRH), backed by the mortgages and, until the end of 1988, by government guarantee.

Securities

Banks play a major role in the securities business in France and have always played this role, as they have both the distribution network through their branches and access to the issuers through their corporate finance departments. The weak structure of the brokerage industry has reinforced the banks in this role: until the 1986–7 reform of the Bourse, stockbrokers were mostly personal firms with very limited equity and no distribution network. Therefore banks had, for all practical purposes, a *de facto* monopoly, with stockbrokers playing a marginal role, limited to trading on the Bourse. The fact that the brokers had a legal monopoly of trading, but not the financial resources to develop this function, accounts for the relative underdevelopment of the Paris Bourse until the early 1980s.

The growth of the bond and equity markets has been spectacular in recent years. Bond issues increased from 112 billion frs. in 1980 to a peak of 350 million frs. In 1986, while the volume of trading on the secondary market reached 2,427 billion frs. in 1987. Equity issues increased from 3·5 billion frs. in 1982 to 62·5 billion in 1986, thanks to the privatization programme.

The most important events in the bond market were the deregulation of primary issues following the Tricot Commission report in 1985, the creation of *spécialistes en Valeurs du Trésor* (SVTs), or primary dealers, in 1986 and the creation of an interest-rate futures market, the MATIF, also in 1986. The Treasury has developed a modern issuing policy (planned issuing calendar, auction bidding, product diversification). In a few years France has caught up with the English-speaking bond market and developed an active and liquid market in government bonds. For the banks, this has had several effects:

1. The Tricot report has opened the primary bond market to competition. Commissions have dropped as banks lost the carefully controlled positions they had, taking turns to lead bond issues for each corporate or public customer, and sharing the management and placement of these issues according to negotiated syndicates. Competition has not yet reached the degree it has on the Eurobond market, but it has seriously eroded the profitability of the primary bond market.

2. At the same time, trading in bonds has become a significant

part of bank activities. Securities held by banks now account for 15·2 per cent of their loan and assets portfolio, a doubling over the level of ten years ago. This activity has been very profitable during the period from 1982 to 1986, with regularly declining interest rates and a bull market in bonds and equities. It is less so now.

3. Financial innovation has found a fertile ground in the bond market; many new formulas have been used, mainly aimed at professional investors.

The development of quasi-money market funds (in fact they are unit trusts invested in bonds but yielding short-term rates without risk through repurchase agreements), the so-called *SICAV de trésorerie* has also contributed to the development of the bond market. These unit trusts are usually managed by the banks, which use them to offer a return on short-term deposits, and they are an outlet for bond issues, especially for variable-rate bonds.

In the equity markets, banks have traditionally been very active in the primary market, through their relationship with corporate customers. Two significant developments must be noted:

1. The creation of the *second marché*, similar to the unlisted securities market, where shares in over 250 medium-size businesses are now traded. Banks have played a significant role in finding companies suitable for this market. While a highly visible activity, and a useful one, listing new companies on the *second marché* has remained a marginal contributor to bank profits. The *second marché* suffered more than the regular stock market after the October 1987 crash, and the rate of new listings has been significantly reduced.

2. The privatization programme: in a very short period of time, between the March 1986 elections and the October 1987 crash, a substantial privatization programme has been carried through. Banks played a key role, and a profitable one, as advisers to the government or to the privatized companies, and as sellers of the stock to their customers. On the other hand they now have to handle several million small accounts with little or no fees, which are, however, very stable and marginally profitable.

The reform of the Bourse

A law passed in 1987 has allowed banks to acquire stockbroking firms, and most large banks have done so, ususally buying a majority or controlling interest. With this step the range of financial services that banks can offer in relation to securities is complete. All large banks offer the full range of such services, including portfolio management and unit trust management. This raises several questions for the future.

In terms of profitability, significant investments have been made in trading rooms, the acquisition of stockbrokers and in bank office systems (including systems for customer accounts). To what extent can these instruments be profitable in a market that is becoming more competitive at a time when volumes and prices are not growing as quickly as in previous years? Clearly, some specialization will occur, and not all the businesses started will remain profitable.

In terms of marketing and customer service, how will banks integrate this new range of services into their branch network? They have been very successful so far in using their network to sell securities and unit trusts, but this was in a booming market, where money was easily made. How will the bank customer react to poor performance on the part of the bank unit trusts or of a security sold by a bank? One customer has recently won on appeal a suit against his bank, which had failed to inform him of the impending failure of a company the bonds of which the bank had sold him well before any problem. Even if this judgement is overturned by the High Court, the degree of risk involved for the banks is significant.

There will therefore be opportunities for new entrants, or for existing banks, to approach specifically the retail securities business, and solve the problems of cost and investment performance that bigger banks may face.

Another question is the relative weight of the French securities markets in the European Community. The recent development of the bond and equity markets, the deregulation of the Bourse, and the entry of a number of foreign institutions that have acquired French brokerage houses should allow the French financial market to keep up with the development of the French economy. For banks there is the challenge of playing a significant role on the Bourse without hindering its development. To the extent that capital will be required to develop securities trading in France, there is a danger that the business may become an interbank affair rather than an open market with active independent operators. In the long run it is in the banks' interest to maintain an open securities market, with foreign and non-bank-owned brokers. The success of the financial futures market, MATIF, with a diversified membership ranging from banks to brokers, both French and foreign, may serve as a model for the development of the securities markets.

An assessment of the products

Coming from a highly regulated financial environment, French banks have had some difficulty in adjusting to a deregulated market-oriented one. In practice, many of the financial innovations have been possible only through regulation rather than by private initiative. This was the case, for example, with commercial paper and certificates of deposit. On the other hand, the banks have been innovative in the securities area, with the development of unit trusts, of new bond products, of new services such as the cash management account offered by CORTAL (a Compagnie Bancaire subsidiary). Innovation has also been effective in lending, with the development of a great variety of loans for business and individual customers.

The major obstacle to further product innovation is the regulation of savings. Unlike in most developed countries, demand deposits cannot pay interest, and most other forms of liquid savings are regulated, and may in addition have special tax treatment. This has resulted in a relatively rigid system, where banks cannot adjust their product offering to consumer demand. So far it has been a profitable system, but it is becoming increasingly fragile. Disintermediation is eroding this regulated savings basis, with the growth of money-market funds. More dangerously, there are great imbalances in the profitability of the retail business, with large savers accounting for the bulk of the profits, while a costly branch network has to be retained to service the mass of other customers. There is therefore room for many changes yet, in the products offered and, as a consequence, in the structure of the banking industry.

Chapter five

Bank profitability in France

Philippe Szymczak

Over the last decade, in France as in most other major industrial countries, financing and payment systems have undergone dramatic changes. Unprecedented international macro-economic developments, such as the counter-cyclical behaviour of interest rates during the period of disinflation and the less developed countries' debt crisis, drastically transformed the macro-economic environment in which banks operate. Moreover a series of systemic changes, brought about by financial innovation and deregulation, altered the banking market structure.

So far, however, in spite of the recent disintermediation process, commercial banks have remained the centrepiece of the financial system. Notwithstanding macro-economic and structural developments, they have managed to improve their profitability dramatically since 1985. However, since the timing of this improvement coincided roughly with major structural and macro-economic developments, considerable uncertainties persist as to the nature and the durability of the recent strengthening in banking profitability. Furthermore the recent structural changes have raised questions about the viability and profitability of certain types of traditional banking activities. Yet, whether they are private or state-owned, commercial banks must remain profitable in order to perform smoothly their essential role in the payment and financing systems.

As a prerequisite for judging the prospects of this crucial dimension of banks' operations, the performance of the banking industry over the past two decades has to be traced and explained. Therefore, this chapter[1] assesses the recent trends in commercial banks' costs, margins, and profits, proposes an international comparative analysis of bank performance, and examines the various causative factors of these developments. For that purpose it uses consolidated figures on the operations and profitability of French commercial banks over the last two decades. However, owing to database limitation, it will be restricted to the traditional commercial banks, the currently so-called 'Banques AFB' (i.e. the members of the Association Française des Banques, or the former 'registered banks') and will exclude mutual and co-operative banks.

This chapter concludes that, traditionally, cost minimization and profit maximization were not the dominant guide to economic behaviour in significant segments of the French banking industry. Weaknesses in actual and potential market pressures and extensive economic regulation have shaped the traditional features of bank performance in France. This explains why, although the country's top banks were among the largest in the world in terms of total assets, they generally appeared poor performers in terms of return on assets and in terms of capitalization, compared with their foreign competitors.

The chapter also shows, however, that owing to significant macro-economic, behavioural, and structural changes, the general picture of the banking industry improved dramatically in 1985 and 1986. Nevertheless, even though part of the improvement is structural in nature and may be due to a successful adjustment of French banks to a new market environment, banks have also benefited from an exceptional set of circumstances since 1984. Consequently recent improvements are potentially partially reversible. In this regard, the drop in banks' operating income experienced in 1987 gave rise to concern, with many analysts considering that profits peaked in 1986 and that a flattening-out period in the industry's profitability may now be ahead.

The first section outlines the main developments in the banking industry's costs, margins, and profits between 1972 and 1984, and shows how the various indicators of costs and margins are related to the traditional nature of the financial system. The second analyses the dramatic improvement in bank profitability and the strengthening of commercial banks' balance sheets experienced in 1985 and 1986, as well as the setbacks encountered in 1987.

Traditional features of bank profitability

In this section bank profitability is assessed at various levels of analysis. Bank income and profit formation are broken down in consecutive stages, in order to evaluate costs and margins on the basis of the balance sheets and profit-and-loss accounts. Relevant aggregates are systematically calculated and divided by business volume indicators, in order to allow historical and international comparisons. In order to provide a broad picture of the traditional features of costs and margins in French banking, two complementary sources of data are used. On the one hand, the data collected and compiled by the French Banking Commission is used to assess the major developments over the period 1972–84. On the other, the international comparisons of costs and margins rely mainly on bank accounting series compiled and harmonized by the OECD (1985, 1987).

Since most of the analysis is undertaken in terms of ratios, and since bank costs and margins can be constructed as interest rates, the choice of business volume indicator is crucial. For this purpose the balance sheet total is no doubt the standard indicator, and will therefore be used extensively in this chapter. However, the balance-sheet total includes all interbank transactions. Therefore it introduces a systematic bias, especially in international comparisons. Indeed, French commercial banks have experienced a relatively atypical balance-sheet structure. During the early 1980s more than 45 per cent of their assets consisted of interbank loans, against 25 per cent for the London clearing banks, 23 per cent for all German universal banks, and 11 per cent for all American banks. (For more details on international comparative analysis of bank costs and margins, see J. Revell, 1980; P. Szymczak, 1987b).

In order to correct this bias, a second business volume indicator, the funds committed to non-financial entities, is used to supplement the balance-sheet total. This aggregate is obtained by deducting from the balance-sheet total all self-contained interbank transactions unrelated to a net funding requirement or capacity generated by transactions with non-financial entities. As such, the new aggregate constitutes a more accurate indicator of the volume of final intermediation carried out by banks, which is of primary importance from an analytical standpoint. International comparisons of costs and margins are made systematically at two separate levels of aggregation in each country: for all banks as well as for the largest banks alone. Finally, since international comparisons aim at highlighting major structural features of bank profitability as compared with other major industrical countries, only the average ratios calculated for the years 1980–4 are listed below.

In what follows, the chapter successively analyses the banks' gross margins, their operating costs, the burden of provision for risky loans, and finally their profitability and capitalization.

Wide, distorted, and vulnerable gross margins

Traditionally, gross margins in France had three major characteristics: a high level of interest spread, a peculiar structure of net banking income, reflecting over-reliance on the interest margin, and finally, vulnerability of the interest margin to disinflation and to changes in the level and structure of interest rates.

Wide interest margins

One of the most unusual indicators of intermediation cost is the interest margin, i.e. the difference between interest received and interest paid by the banks.

If the balance-sheet total is chosen as an indicator of banks' volume of activity, the traditional interest margin of all French banks appears much wider than that of Swiss, Japanese, and German banks, but compares favourably with that of US, Italian, and Spanish banks (table 5.1). Using the same indicator, the largest French banks had an interest margin comparable to those of major Italian, US, and German banks, but significantly lower than those of British clearing banks and the largest Spanish banks.

Table 5.1   Interest margin: average ratios, 1980–4

All commercial banks				Top commercial banks			
Interest margin/ FCNFE		*Interest margin/ balance-sheet total*		*Interest margin/ FCNFE*		*Interest margin/ balance-sheet total*	
Switzerland	1·6	Switzerland	1·3	Japan	1·5	Japan	1·2
Japan	1·8	Japan	1·5	Switzerland	1·8	Austria	1·2
Canada	2·9	Belgium	1·8	Austria	2·0	Switzerland	1·3
Belgium	3·1	Germany	2·3	Italy	2·8	Italy	2·6
Germany	3·3	Canada	2·5	USA	3·2	USA	2·7
USA	3·7	France	2·7	Germany	3·8	Germany	2·7
Italy	3·8	USA	3·2	France	4·7	France	2·7
Spain	4·8	Italy	3·2	UK	4·7	UK	3·4
France	4·9	Spain	4·1	Spain	5·7	Spain	4·9

FCNFE: funds committed to non-financial entities.

Source: OECD (1987).

However, this ranking is distorted by the atypical proportion of interbank transactions in French banks' balance sheets. This can be corrected by assuming that the volume of banks' activity is best reflected by the restricted aggregate 'Funds committed to non-financial entities'. Use of this new indicator suggests a substantially different picture. It now appears that French banks' interest margin outranked that of all the other major banking systems. The same, apparently, applied for the largest banks' margin, London clearing banks and the largest Spanish banks being the only ones to outperform their French competitors during the early 1980s.

If the interest margin is undeniably an important indicator, its significance should not be overstated in comparative international analysis, since the structure of gross margins did vary significantly from country to country.

The peculiar structure of gross margins

Historically, as a result of the regulatory environment and because of the nature of competition prevailing in each country, the various national banking systems did not adopt the same pricing policy. This influenced in turn the structure of gross margins and the interest margin relative level.

In France, as well as in many other industrial countries, commercial banks were the subject of extensive regulations and price controls that gradually shifted the locus of competition in the banking industry. Because they forced banks to suspend explicit pricing of payments and ancillary services in an attempt to retain their deposit base, price controls and interest-rate regulation (especially the prohibition of interest payments on demand deposits imposed since 1967) thrust competition into various forms of implicit interest payments (see L. White, 1977; P. Szymczak, 1986; Conseil National du Crédit, 1987). Thriving non-price competition took the form of free financial services, such as free cheques, underpriced capital-market transactions on behalf of customers, and particularly in the late 1960s and 1970s, additional branches to provide customers with free convenience services. Furthermore, banks themselves had generally a poor knowledge of the sectoral net income generated by their various types of operations, since analytical accounting systems were long neglected.

In order to compensate for the underpricing of numerous ancillary and payment services, and to achieve an overall operating equilibrium, French banks systematically overcharged for intermediation operations. This led to extensive cross-subsidization between various types of operations and between different types of customers (G. Faulhaber, 1975; H. Lévy-Lambert, 1980; Conseil National du Crédit, 1987). Allocating costs and revenues between various types of operations in order to estimate sectoral net income would yield useful insights. But in France, no survey equivalent to the Functional Revenue and Cost Analysis carried out by the Federal Reserve Board in the USA is available. Therefore estimating functional profitability is not possible at present. However, partial information is available, since the Banking Commission published useful data based on a very broad categorization of bank activities. According to these analytical accounting data, payment services and various ancillary financial services generated 48·8 per cent of overheads and depreciation, but directly generated only 8·5 per cent of net banking income. Consequently, these activities generated a net operating deficit estimated at 17·9 billion frs. in 1983, which had to be supported by the interest margin (Commission Bancaire, Annual Reports; P. Szymczak, 1986; Conseil National du Crédit, 1987). Consequently, traditional pricing carried out by French banks imposed an over-pricing of intermediation services estimated at more than 30 per cent of what would have been charged if each type of operation had been priced proportionally to its costs of production.

Such pricing patterns drove a wedge between prices and marginal costs, and were reflected in the structure of gross margin and in operating costs. An international comparison of the share of fee and commission income in net banking income (i.e. the sum of the interest margin and of net fees and commissions received) shows that the structure of French banks' gross margin was relatively atypical in the early 1980s, since fees and commissions accounted for only 15 per cent of net banking income. During this period the Japanese banks were the only ones to rank at a comparable level, whereas fees and commissions accounted for 24 per cent of net banking income for American banks, 27 per cent for German banks, 32 per cent for UK clearing banks, and 46 per cent for Swiss banks.

In order to take into account distortions induced by extensive cross-subsidization, the overall margin, defined as the ratio of net banking income to an indicator of volume of bank activity, must be

Table 5.2 Overall gross margin: average ratios, 1980−4

All commercial banks				Top commercial banks			
Net banking income/ FCNFE		Net banking income/balance-sheet total		Net banking income/ FCNFE		Net banking income/balance-sheet total	
Japan	2·1	Japan	1·8	Japan	1·9	Austria	1·5
Switzerland	3·1	Belgium	2·2	Austria	2·4	Japan	1·5
Canada	3·7	Switzerland	2·5	Switzerland	3·6	Switzerland	2·5
Belgium	3·9	Canada	3·2	Italy	4·3	France	3·2
Germany	4·5	Germany	3·2	USA	4·6	Germany	3·8
USA	4·9	France	3·2	Germany	5·4	USA	3·8
Italy	5·2	USA	4·2	France	5·5	Italy	3·9
France	5·8	Italy	4·5	UK	6·9	UK	5·0
Spain	5·9	Spain	5·1	Spain	6·9	Spain	5·9

FCNFE: funds committed to non-financial entities.

Source: OECD (1987).

considered. Again, if balance-sheet total is used as volume indicator, the overall margin of French banks occupies a median rank (table 5.2). But if funds committed to non-financial entities alone are used as an indicator of bank activity, the overall margin was higher for all French banks than for banking systems in other major OECD countries, except Spain.

Such a level and structure of gross margins was undeniably linked to the nature of competition in the French banking industry. As stressed earlier, the degree and nature of competition were partially shaped by the regulatory environment. Furthermore, barriers to entry and imperfect contestability[2] of French oligo-polistic banking markets may have promoted excess profit and/or productive and allocative inefficiencies. This point will be investigated later. For the moment, a last major feature of gross margins deserves consideration: the vulnerability of interest margins to macro-economic developments.

Endowment effect and vulnerability of interest margin

Because changes in market interest rates used to induce changing spreads between assets and liabilities, the general level and structure of interest rates had an important impact on bank profit-ability. During the late 1970s and early 1980s, as the market rates shot up, so did spreads. Consequently the profitability of traditional intermediation activities was boosted. But since 1981 rapid disinflation and the associated gradual decline in interest rates have imposed a squeeze on banks' interest margin, further impairing bank profitability (figure 5.1).

This rate sensitivity resulted from the existence of an indexation differential between bank assets and liabilities. Indeed, when the money-market rate moved by one percentage point, the average yield on loans moved – in the same direction – by 0·57 per cent, but the average cost of deposits moved – also in the same direction – by only 0·4 per cent. Consequently, during the period 1972–84, when the money-market rate changed by 1 per cent, the spread moved in the same direction by 0·17 per cent on average.

Since this indexation differential was the major feature of the rate sensitivity profile of the French banking system, the underlying balance-sheet characteristics that accounted for such a repricing gap must be identified. In this regard, it is possible to construct a somewhat crude but useful indicator of the degree of mismatch on banks' balance sheets. Commonly referred to as the one-year repricing gap, the difference between assets and liabilities scheduled to be repriced or to mature within a year constitutes a

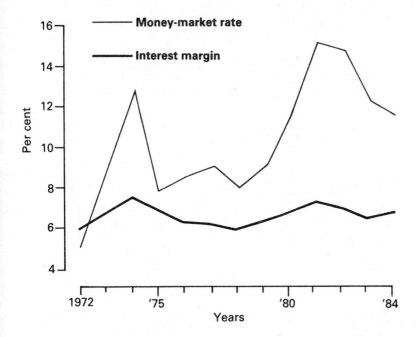

Figure 5.1 Sensitivity of interest margins to changes in the money-market rate.

usual proxy for both the direction and the order of magnitude of the banks' near-term interest-rate sensitivity.

Such an indicator, based on the transactions with non-financial entities and denominated in French francs, shows that in 1984 commercial banks' balance sheets were characterized by a significant repricing gap which resulted from a structural disequilibrium between short-term (in terms of repricing or maturities) assets and short-term liabilities (E. Sautter, 1981; E. Deval-Guilly and F. Renard, 1984; P. Szymczak, 1987a). Figure 5.2 shows that, within a year, a change in money-market rates could alter the yield of 57 per cent of banks' assets but modify the cost of only 42 per cent of their liabilities.

To provide a more accurate insight into the traditional dynamics of interest margins in French banking, a small-scale model has been built (P. Szymczak, 1987a). It stimulates the changes in yields and interest costs triggered by moves in base lending rate and in capital-market interest rates. Thus it shows the implications of the inertia

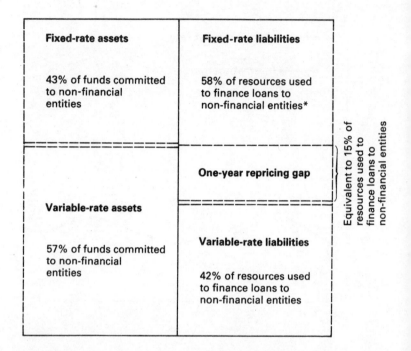

Figure 5.2 Balance-sheet structure and indexation gap, 1984. (Excludes all self-contained interbank operations and all operations not denominated in French francs.) *This aggregate encompasses demand deposits, 75 per cent of savings deposits, fixed-rate time deposits, fixed-rate subsidized rediscounts, and fixed-rate bonds issued by banks.

that used to characterize the costs of resources in France. It shows, on the one hand, that if only changes in money-market rate are taken into account, a 0·39 per cent increase in the base lending rate was adequate to compensate for a 1 per cent increase in the money-market rate, which had a leading role in setting the price of bank resource. On the other hand, if, in addition to changes in the money-market rate, the associated changes in other rates affecting the cost of resource are taken into account, then a 0·47 per cent move in the base lending rate was required to compensate for a general increase of interest rates associated with a 1 per cent increase in the money-market rate. Between 1978 and 1981 any 1 per cent increase in money-market rate was matched on average by a 0·69 per cent increase in base lending rate; therefore the intermediation margin on transactions denominated in French francs improved markedly. The margin increased from 5·8 per cent in 1978 to 7·2 per cent in 1981. By contrast, during the period 1982−4 the base lending rate declined more rapidly than would have been required to leave the interest margin unchanged, since any 1 per cent decline in the money-market rate was accompanied, on average, by a 0·56 per cent decline in the base lending rate. Consequently the interest margin declined during this period from 7·2 per cent in 1981 to 6·6 per cent in 1984.

Such a sensitivity pattern was a result of the nature of the intermediation operations undertaken by French banks (S. Maisel, 1981). Duration mismatch and mismatch between the repricing frequencies of assets and liabilities were substantial, and both shaped the repricing gap which appeared above. These mismatches were themselves related to other major features of the French banking and financial systems. First of all, the commercial banks were funded by a significant amount of low-cost and rate-regulated accounts (non-interest-bearing demand deposits or savings accounts bearing low, regulated nominal interest rates), even though the core of regulated fixed-rate funding had been eroded since the late 1970s, with a shift towards longer-term liabilities. With a significant proportion of deposits bearing a fixed rate of interest, more assets than liabilities were on a *de facto* variable-rate basis. In a period of accelerating inflation and rising interest rates such a balance-sheet structure generated significant 'endowment profits' which were partly regulatory-induced. But since 1982 disinflation has engendered a gradual decline in interest rates which has squeezed these endowment profits and has exerted downward pressure on the profitability of intermediation operations.

The banking industry was characterized by a notable heterogeneity (V. Lévy-Garboua and G. Maarek, 1977; C. Joffre and M.O. Strauss-Kahn, 1980; P. Artus, 1986; P. Szymczak, 1987b). According to the structure of their balance sheets, various banks displayed contrasting patterns of vulnerability. Deposit banks – particularly the Big Three (BNP, Crédit Lyonnais, and Société Générale), and, to a greater extent, the regional banks – received larger endowment profits as interest rates rose, but suffered from the steady downward trend of interest rates, which induced a significant squeeze on their interest margin. This is not surprising, since deposit banks relied on a large retail network for their deposit base, and had by far the highest proportion of zero-interest rate demand deposits. On the contrary, banks which essentially relied on wholesale capital-market funding had an inverted vulnerability profile. Their interest margin was squeezed when money-market rates rose, but improved with the gradual decline in interest rates which accompanied disinflation since 1982 (H. Sterdyniak, 1986; P. Szymczak, 1987a).

Besides extensive regulation, which explains the size of endowment profits in French banking, the dynamics of interest rates in France is also an important explanatory element. The limited variability of market interest rates was indeed a further incentive for undertaking or allowing unhedged repricing mismatches. Furthermore the base lending rate was an administered price set by the major players (essentially deposit banks) in the banking oligopoly under the supervision of the authorities (the Treasury and the Bank of France) in order to allow the banks to break even (V. Lévy-Garboua, 1982; C. de Boissieu, 1985; P. Szymczak, 1987a). Such a characteristic further reduced the uncertainty facing the banks, which could secure a minimum interest margin covering their comparatively high operating costs.

High operating costs

From an accounting standpoint, international differences in the level of gross margin reflect the respective levels of operating costs and of gross profits, the relative importance of which differs significantly from one country to another. As regards comparative level of operating costs, French banks were once again in a median position, and the largest banks ranked very favourably when balance-sheet total is used as a volume indicator (table 5.3).

By contrast, in terms of funds committed to non-financial entities, French banks traditionally appear as burdened with higher

Table 5.3 Operating costs: average ratios, 1980−4

All commercial banks				Top commercial banks			
Operating costs/ FCNFE		Operating costs/ balance-sheet total		Operating costs/ FCNFE		Operating costs/ balance-sheet total	
Japan	1·5	Japan	1·3	Japan	1·3	Japan	1·0
Switzerland	1·7	Switzerland	1·4	Austria	1·8	Austria	1·1
Canada	2·3	Belgium	1·9	Switzerland	2·1	Switzerland	1·5
Germany	3·0	Canada	2·0	USA	3·2	France	2·2
Belgium	3·2	Germany	2·1	Italy	3·3	Germany	2·6
Italy	3·4	France	2·2	Germany	3·7	USA	2·6
USA	3·4	USA	2·9	France	3·8	Italy	3·0
France	3·9	Italy	2·9	Spain	4·4	UK	3·5
Spain	3·9	Spain	3·4	UK	4·8	Spain	3·8

FCNFE: funds committed to non-financial entities.

Source: OECD (1987).

operating costs than their foreign counterparts, except for Spanish banks. The largest French banks had operating costs comparable with those of the largest German banks and lower than those of their British and Spanish counterparts. But still, these costs were higher than those of Japanese and American banks.

Since banking is traditionally a labour-intensive industry, the ranking by operating costs reflects in large measure the ranking by staff costs. The staff costs of French banks used to represent two-thirds of total operating costs, and in terms of funds committed to non-financial entities they have been far higher than in the other industrial countries, again with the exception of Spain. For the largest banks these costs were comparable to those of German and Italian banks, but still far higher than for Japanese and American banks.

From an historical standpoint, operating and staff costs increased unevenly during the 1970s, and declined marginally in the early 1980s. During the period 1972–5 operating costs increased by more than 10 per cent a year. This increase reflected the aggressive growth policy implemented by major French banks, in an attempt to expand or at least retain their market share. This policy implied extension of their branch network, which increased by 18 per cent during the period 1972–5, and a 14 per cent increase in the staff during the same period. However, as a consequence of the very poor profits made in 1974, commercial banks adopted a new approach to domestic competition and tried to decelerate the growth in their previously burgeoning costs. Since then the overall number of branches and employees has remained in the same range, i.e. 9,500 branches and 230,000 employees. In terms of loans, operating costs increased from 4·8 per cent in 1972 to 5·6 per cent in 1975, and gradually increased to 5·9 per cent in 1981. Then, with the onset of disinflation, banks had to intensify their efforts in cutting the growth of their costs. As a result, operating costs as a proportion of loans fell slightly, from 5·9 per cent in 1981 to 5·5 per cent in 1983.

Finally, high spreads reflected the heavy overheads incurred by the major commercial banks. In turn, various structural features of French banking explain, at least partly, the high level of operating costs. First of all, differences in operating costs are a result of deep-rooted functional specificities of each national banking system. They reflect differences both in branch network density and in the nature of the payment systems. In this regard, in the mid-1980s, France ranked third, after Belgium and Switzerland, in terms of banking density, with one branch for only 1,524 inhabitants, against one for 2,283 in the UK, 2,310 in the USA, and 2,780 in Japan.

As regards payment systems, such functional differences tend to prevail as well. The largest commercial banks are traditionally heavily involved in operating the national payment system, and provide extensive payment services. Because free chequebooks were the rule, no incentive to reduce the use of cheques was embedded in the system. Since it was dominated by the use of cheques as the prime payment instrument, the French payment system proved very costly. Banks had to sustain the cost of this payment system, and therefore relied on extensive cross-subsidization which induced, in turn, productive and allocative inefficiencies. However, until the mid-1980s such cross-subsidies were sustainable, as banks enjoyed a monopolistic position on the credit market and could determine – in agreement with the authorities – the base lending rate on the basis of their costs.

More generally, the degree and nature of competition prevailing in French banking shaped costs and margins. As a consequence of extensive regulation, of significant public ownership, and of a traditional oligopolistic structure, which allowed on certain occasions the occurrence of collusive behaviour, banking markets were imperfectly contestable (W. Baumol *et al.*, 1982; R. Gilbert, 1984; W. Baumol and R. Willig, 1986). To a certain extent the method of monetary management (the so-called *encadrement du crédit*) and other regulations discriminated against new entrants. Furthermore the very structure of the industry, dominated by an oligopoly of four major banking groups which could benefit from significant economies of scale in their retail banking operations, also protected these banks from entry. Indeed, for a new entrant it would have required an inportant quasi-irreversible outlay of capital, i.e. significant sunk costs, in order to create from scratch a branch system sufficiently widespread to imply effective competition in retail banking. Hence, in this concentrated industry, the threat of entry was not a strong constraint on pricing. Banks could charge monopoly prices, and gross margins were probably higher than would have been sustainable in a perfectly contestable industry. In this context, because firms' market power relieved them from some pressures to minimize costs, certain patterns of expense preference behaviour (O. Williamson, 1963; T. Hannan and F. Mavinga, 1980; M. Smirlock and W. Marshall, 1983; F. Edwards, 1987) and of X-inefficiency (H. Liebenstein, 1966) were likely to emerge and to become pervasive. In this regard, besides possible risk avoidance (F. Edwards and A. Heggestad, 1973), imperfect competition allowed overstaffing, excessive extension of branch networks, slack organizational structures, and as a consequence inefficient resource use in significant portions of the industry. All this contributed to maintain intermediation costs at a high level and implied a reduction in consumers' surplus.

A dramatic increase in provision for risks

During the period 1972–84, actual and anticipated loan losses contributed to put downward pressure on bank profitability and to raise base lending rates. Like their foreign counterparts, French banks were hit hard during the early 1980s by the sharp deterioration in the quality of their assets. Worldwide recession and the very unusual counter-cyclical behaviour of interest rates reduced the ability of debtors to service their bank debt. Besides increasing difficulties for domestic borrowers, the onset of the LDC debt crisis led to unprecedented levels of loan losses. In France non-performing assets rose throughout the period, from 1·4 per cent of total loans to non-financial entities in 1972 to 2·6 per cent in 1980 and 4·1 per cent in 1984.

Consequently, banks strove to build up loan loss reserves, especially on sovereign debt. Annual appropriations to provision accounts increased from 0·2 per cent of total credits in 1972 to 1 per cent in 1980 (after 0·5 in 1979), and to 1·4 per cent in 1984. Loan loss reserves increased steadily from 0·9 per cent of total loans in 1972 to 1·7 per cent in 1980 and 2·2 per cent in 1984. In order to finance their provisioning effort, banks allocated an increasing proportion of their gross earning to provision. In 1972 provision absorbed 12·3 per cent of net operating income, but they absorbed 36·8 per cent in 1980 and 50·5 per cent in 1982 and 1983. In 1984 loan loss provision totalled 25·5 billion frs. for the commercial banks, against 7·7 billion frs. of net profits. For the Big Three the ratio was even more marked: 18·3 billion frs. in provision, against 1·5 billion frs. in net profits.

But in spite of this effort banks barely managed to stabilize their risk-provision ratio. In 1981 this ratio reached 62·1 per cent, against 66·5 in 1972. Later on, owing to further deterioration in debtors' solvency and to the rapid appreciation in the dollar, non-provisioned non-performing assets rose slightly. By the end of 1984 corresponding reserves represented only 16 per cent of commercial banks' sovereign risk.

In building up loan loss reserves the banks have undeniably participated in a general move towards higher provision in industrial countries, especially since the onset of the LDC debt crisis. However, certain features tend to particularize the French experience.

On the one hand, normal accounting practices tend to inflate non-performing assets and loan loss reserves, so that they appear, *ceteris paribus*, higher in France than, say, in the USA or the UK. Usually French banks do not write off doubtful loans immediately but only when every effort, particularly bankruptcy proceedings, has failed. In the meantime, loan loss reserves are posted and left on the balance sheet, so that reserves tend to appear for a long time on the balance sheet before being charged against. Furthermore, French bankers accrue interest on non-performing loans as if it had been paid, and build up reserves against this fictitious interest income.

On the other hand, several structural features account for the high level of loan loss reserves. Since the late 1970s, a consensus has emerged with respect to the need for higher bank provision. French banks became increasingly involved in international credit and capital markets. They managed to build an extensive network overseas, and they had to play a prominent part in financing balance-of-payments deficits in the early 1980s. Consequently, protecting their credit rating and their international reputation by strengthening their balance sheets soon emerged as a priority for the bankers and the authorities as well. This proved all the more necessary since French banks were widely regarded as undercapitalized by international standards, and their already meagre capital position was seen as potentially impaired by extensive sovereign risk exposure.

Therefore, as early as 1979, the state urged the banks to reinforce the level of their provision. Such pressure proved all the more effective in that, in this process, the state played a triple role. As regulatory authority, especially through the Banking Commission, it urged continuously higher provision. As tax collector it permitted commercial banks to build up reserves from pre-tax profits, allowing them to claim large tax deductions on the basis of their provision against sovereign risks. Finally, and more particularly from 1982 onwards, the state intervened also as shareholder of all the major commercial banks. As such the authorities were faced with the urgent need to strengthen banks' balance sheets. But budget constraints have been such since the early 1980s that the state considered this strengthening politically easier to achieve by increasing reserves than through a capital injection. As a matter of fact the state-shareholder provided the healthiest banks with next to nothing in the way of fresh capital. Sparse state budgetary aid was reserved for the weakest banks nationalized in 1982 and for the industrial companies whose needs were seen as more pressing. Then, as owner of all the main banking groups, the state proved to be a complaisant shareholder, taking much smaller dividends than the stock markets have demanded of, say, their American competitors.

This in turn left the state with lower dividends and less tax revenue from the banks, but this adverse outcome was accepted as the price of effecting a much-needed recapitalization of the major banking groups, and of achieving broader macro-economic and industrial goals at the same time.

Finally, in the French context of the early 1980s, posting higher reserves appeared as a sustainable second-best solution to help off-set capital inadequacy and deterioration in the quality of assets. This helped stabilize the capital-adequacy ratio as loan loss pro-visions are eligible for inclusion in calculating banks' capital. More-over the fact that the French commercial banks devoted such a con-siderable proportion of their gross income to building up provision explains why, despite the widening of gross margins, profitability declined at the commercial banks during the period 1972–84.

Low and stagnant profitability

Traditionally, French banks were considered far less profitable than their foreign competitiors. Analysis of the data compiled by the OECD tends to corroborate this general opinion broadly, but not fully. Indeed, it appears that the banks' return on assets (i.e. after-tax profits as a ratio of the balance-sheet total) was fairly meagre in the early 1980s, outranking only those of the Belgian and Japanese banks (table 5.4). The largest banks as well had a very low return on assets, outranking only the largest Austrian banks. How-ever, calculated as a ratio of after-tax profits to funds committed to non-financial entities, French bank's return on assets appear some-what higher, while the largest banks still come out in the lower half of the sample, with a return on assets comparable with that of Japanese banks, but much lower than that of their German, American, British, and Spanish competitors.

Analysis of the return on equity (i.e. ratio of after-tax profits to equity capital) yields a complementary picture, in so far as leverage, i.e. the ratio of equity capital to assets, exhibited sharp contrasts between countries. French, Belgian, and Japanese banks had higher leverage in the early 1980s than German, British, and American banks in terms both of balance-sheet total and of funds committed to non-financial entities. However, use of the latter volume indicator suggests that the conventional view that French banks were unduly and dangerously undercapitalized should be mitigated. It finally appears that, partly owing to higher leverage than in some other countries, French banks' return on equity, even though moderate especially for the largest banks, was not atypical in the early 1980s (table 5.5).

Table 5.4 Return on assets: average ratios, 1980—4

All commercial banks				Top commercial banks			
Post-tax profits/ FCNFE		*Post-tax profits/ balance-sheet total*		*Post-tax profits/ FCNFE*		*Post-tax profits/ balance-sheet total*	
Japan	0·26	Belgium	0·19	Austria	0·08	Austria	0·05
Belgium	0·34	Japan	0·22	Italy	0·17	France	0·13
Germany	0·34	France	0·23	France	0·23	Italy	0·15
Italy	0·37	Germany	0·24	Japan	0·24	Japan	0·20
France	0·41	Italy	0·32	Germany	0·36	Germany	0·25
Spain	0·58	Switzerland	0·48	Switzerland	0·62	Switzerland	0·43
Canada	0·60	Spain	0·50	USA	0·70	USA	0·57
Switzerland	0·60	Canada	0·52	UK	0·90	UK	0·65
USA	0·84	USA	0·71	Spain	0·94	Spain	0·80

FCNFE: funds committed to non-financial entities.

Source: OECD (1987).

Table 5.5 Return on equity and capital-to-assets ratio: average ratios, 1980—4

Post-tax profits/ equity		*Equity/ balance-sheet total*		*Equity/ FCNFE*	
		All commercial banks			
Germany	5·7	Japan	2·4	Japan	2·8
Spain	6·0	Belgium	2·5	Italy	4·2
Belgium	7·2	France	2·6	Belgium	4·4
Switzerland	7·6	Italy	3·6	France	4·6
Italy	7·7	Germany	4·0	Canada	4·8
France	8·0	Canada	4·1	Germany	5·6
Japan	8·7	USA	5·9	USA	7·0
USA	11·6	Switzerland	6·0	Switzerland	7·5
Canada	12·4	Spain	7·7	Spain	8·9
		Top commercial banks			
Austria	2·1	Japan	1·9	Japan	2·4
Italy	4·0	France	2·0	France	3·6
France	5·9	Austria	2·3	Italy	3·6
Germany	5·9	Italy	3·2	Austria	3·7
Switzerland	7·2	German	4·0	Germany	5·8
Spain	8·6	UK	4·7	USA	5·9
Japan	9·7	USA	4·8	UK	6·5
USA	11·5	Switzerland	5·7	Switzerland	8·2
UK	12·4	Spain	8·7	Spain	9·4

FCNFE: funds committed to non-financial entities.

Source: OECD (1987).

These findings, based on data published by the OECD, are corroborated by an analysis of the profitability of the five largest banks in each of the major industrial countries. In terms of return on assets (calculated as a ratio of pre-tax profits to assets less contra-accounts), the largest French banks, at 0·3 percentage points, ranked last but one in 1984, just ahead of Belgian banks (0·26), far behind their Japanese, German, British, and American competitors. But even though they exhibited high leverage (again, French banks ranked last but one in terms of capital to balance-sheet total ratio at 2·25 per cent), the largest French banks still appeared far behind most of their competitors in terms of return on equity, at 13·5 per cent, against 17·2 in the USA, 18·1 in Germany, and 21·6 in the UK. Finally, in terms of pre-tax profits per employee, the largest French banks ranked last at only US$5,110.

The situation described above is the result of the adverse developments which generated a significant slippage in profitability since 1981. In the 1970s, with the exception of the earnings low point of 1974, French banks managed to stabilize their profit margins. Even though at a relatively low level return on assets and return on equity remained remarkably stable. But in the early 1980s, a squeeze on interest margins as well as a deterioration in the quality of assets imposed a drag on bank profits. Return on equity fell to 8 per cent in 1982, against an average 11 per cent during the 1970s. During the next two years, banks profitability barely improved and remained significantly below the average level reached during the preceding decade. After-tax profits rose from a low 6·6 billion frs. in 1982 to 7·4 billion frs. in 1983 and 7·7 billion frs. in 1984.

Various factors account for the traditionally low profitability and the deterioration experienced over the period 1981–4. On the one hand, macro-economic developments were particularly adverse. Domestic disinflation imposed a squeeze on interest margins and impaired the ability of borrowers to service their debt. On the other hand, worldwide disinflation and recession contributed to the advent of the LDC debt crisis, which, alongside a structural intensification of competition in international markets, contributed to an unprecedented slump in the profitability of international operations. Overseas branches' pre-tax profits shrank by about 47 per cent over the period 1982–4.

But, clearly, such macro-economic developments do not account for the traditionally low level of bank profitability. In this respect, two major structural and interconnected factors contributed to what was an integral feature of French banking. Oligopolistic and imperfectly contestable market structures on the one hand, and widespread public ownership and controls on banks on the other, contributed to the low level of profitability, despite the high level of interest margins imposed on customers. Of course, a detailed analysis of economic problems associated with public ownership, and public intervention more generally, in French banking would take us too far afield. However, it is crucial to note that, over the years, close relations between the state and the large banks developed and favoured the management of the banking industry on the basis of an unabashed mutuality of interest. As a dominant shareholder, especially after the 1982 nationalizations, the state did not require a market return on its equity investment. Rate-of-return targets were set relatively low, as the state chose to allow the banks to allocate their intermediation income into high operating expenses and, particularly since the beginning of the 1980s, into boosting their loan loss reserves. Besides, prices as well as operational targets were set in order to allow the industry to break even. Therefore the commercial banks were not under pressure to minimize their costs, and could afford to be more concerned with size than with profitability and capital strength. In this regard, the state umbrella provided an efficient substitute for equity capital with respect to credit ratings on international capital markets.

To be sure, managing interest rates in order to allow the banking industry to break even contributed, on the one hand, to raise the cost of funds, which penalized investment, and on the other, to lower deposit rates, which may have discouraged financial savings. But until the mid-1980s the authorities (as well as some prominent bankers) gave highest priority to preserving banking stability, even though this entailed a degree of inefficiency in the intermediation process.

Finally, cost minimization and profit maximization were not traditionally the dominant guides to economic behaviour in the banking system. As a matter of fact, this appears as an integral part of the French financial system, in which, prior to the recent reforms, market mechanisms played only a minor role.

Bank profitability in a changing environment

Since the mid-1980s, financial innovations and liberalization measures have accelerated dramatically the pace of structural change in the financial system. Assuredly, commercial banks have been at the epicentre of these recent structural changes in the supply of and demand for financial services. Since that period the state has undertaken numerous steps to modernize the financial system in order to bring it more into line with international standards, particularly by opening up the banking system to competition. In fact, one of the main motives of the state was to encourage competition in order to improve the efficiency of the banking system, and reduce the operating costs of financial intermediaries. Therefore the banks have been faced with fresh challenges which have already reshaped their operations, costs, and margins.

To be sure, the process of financial reform has exhibited a remarkable degree of continuity, and the period under review has been a transitional period. Consequently, it is difficult to draw a dividing line as starting point for the second part of this chapter, and any choice is bound to be subject to criticism. The year 1985, however, was characterized by an acceleration in the pace of structural changes and by a significant improvement in bank profitability. Furthermore, the enforcement of the 1984 Banking Act led to the institutional reclassification of a number of financial entities. Some financial intermediaries formerly classified as registered banks (the so-called *banques inscrites*) were reclassified in other institutional categories. But because these institutions were, on average, much more profitable than the other former registered banks (in 1984 they represented 35 per cent of net profits of the whole category of *banques inscrites*, but only 3·6 per cent of its net banking income), the reclassification induced a significant discontinuity in the series published by the Banking Commission. Hence 1985 has been chosen as the dividing line for the purpose of this study.

In order to highlight the major recent developments in bank profitability, the various significant stages in bank profit formation are discussed. Developments in gross margins, in operating costs, in loan loss provision, and in profitability over the period 1985−7 are reviewed in turn.

Improvement and restructuring of banks' gross margins

Since 1984 gross margins have improved and have experienced a dramatic change in their internal structure. Net banking income has increased by 8·6 per cent in 1985 and by 11 per cent in 1986. In real terms, net banking income has increased by 2·6 per cent in 1985 and by 8·3 per cent in 1986, against only 1 per cent in 1984. A significant improvement in gross margins on domestic operations explains this development, since net banking income stemming from overseas branches further declined by 7·8 per cent in 1985 and by 6·8 per cent in 1986.

In 1987, however, the positive trend in gross margins was interrupted. Net banking income declined by 2·3 per cent in nominal terms, and by 5·4 per cent in real terms. Again, this development is entirely accounted for by deterioration in gross margins on domestic operations, with domestic net banking income deteriorating by 2·7 per cent in 1987, while overseas branches' net banking income increased by 1·8 per cent. This setback is unprecedented, as it was the first decline in nominal net banking income since the early 1970s.

Similarly, the changes in the internal structure of net banking income are unique in recent French banking history. Traditionally heavily dependent on their interest margins, the commercial banks experienced a significant improvement in net non-interest income in 1985 and 1986, while in the meantime net interest income stagnated. In 1985 and 1986 net non-interest income increased respectively by 26·2 per cent and 32·3 per cent, and contributed respectively to 88·8 per cent and 99·3 per cent of the improvement in net banking income in each of these years. By contrast, net interest income increased only by 1·4 per cent in 1985 and by 0·1 per cent in 1986, and contributed to only 11·2 per cent in the improvement of net banking income in 1985 and 0·7 per cent in 1986.

In 1987 the decline in net banking income was a result of the continuation of the adverse trend in net interest margin, which declined by 4·6 per cent, and also the result of a quasi-stagnation in net non-interest income, which increased by only 0·9 per cent. As a consequence the internal structure of net banking income experienced an unprecedented shift towards increased reliance on non-interest income. In 1987 net non-interest income accounted for 41·8 per cent of net banking income, against 29·2 per cent in 1984.

The combination of a series of macro-economic and structural developments explains this change. Prolonged disinflation induced a gradual decline in interest rates which squeezed the deposit banks' interest margin, as it did during the period 1982–4. More important, the years of steadily declining interest rates generated a stream of capital gains on banks' growing investment portfolios. This bull market associated with the process of disinflation also benefited profitability by boosting commissions on market operations. In this new interest rate and stock market environment, because of the 'securitization' of banks' portfolios, realized gains and losses on trading account inventories and investment portfolios assuredly became an increasing but volatile component of earnings. Illustrative of this new vulnerability pattern, commercial banks' profitability was dragged down in 1987 by the October stock market crash, which occasioned an estimated 6 billion frs. net loss on banks' investment portfolios. This is mainly the reason why 1987 appears in such sharp contrast with preceding years.

But recent developments in banks' gross margins are also structural in nature. Since the mid-1980s financial innovation and deregulation have induced a process of disintermediation and have increased the contestability of French banking markets. This dual evolution, in turn, may have reduced profitability of the banks' traditional core business. Indeed, suppliers of financial services experienced some squeeze in margins in certain areas of business as their market power weakened. Banks suffered particularly from a decline in volume and profitability in their wholesale lending business, i.e. the market for loans to large, well known, and low-risk corporate borrowers. Changing market structures led to the development of new competitive behaviour, with thriving explicit interest-rate competition. New competitive pressures induced financial intermediaries to offer more competitive rates, which now carry lower spreads – at least for prime borrowers – and vary more closely in line with market rates. In this process the base lending rate has lost some of its former importance. As a consequence the costs of intermediation for large customers has come down over the course of recent years, and interest margins experienced erosion. More generally, banks were forced to price their products more competitively. In this sense, recent structural developments induced a marketization of banking operations (T. Bingham, 1985; C. de Boissieu, 1987).

As banks were confronted with new competition in a number of areas that constituted their core business, they strove to adjust to the new environment by broadening the scope of their activities, and changing the price structure of the industry.

Disintermediation and marketization contributed to a move into personal lending, more sophisticated forms of financing, and ancillary financial services. Banks expanded their activities beyond their traditional fields, in an attempt to compensate for stagnation of activity in traditional areas and in order to exploit potential economies of scale. They made strong marketing efforts to promote new products and services, which were also more aggressively priced than in the past.

Such positive developments proved possible partly because the banks have played a major role in the development of Paris as a financial centre. Unencumbered by regulations such as the American Glass-Steagall Act, the major banks were in a position to play an active – and sometimes dominant – role in the development of new financial instruments and services.

Besides channelling the bulk of a rapidly growing number of orders to brokers who long managed to preserve their monopoly over bonds and equity trading, banks have been extremely active in

123

all aspects of the recent structural changes of the financial system: commercial banking, investment banking, stock placement, management of bond issues, portfolio and mutual fund management, and venture capital.

In this sense, new competitive pressures obliged the traditional financial institutions to shift the focus of their activities, while deregulation and innovation allowed them to do so. But at the same time that they strove to develop a new product mix, banks also tried to change the price structure operative in the industry, by moving towards explicit charges for most services.

Because of the increased contestability of the various banking markets, traditional intermediary activities stagnated in terms of volume and declined in terms of profitability. Consequently, traditional cross-subsidization proved unsustainable. Indeed, it became increasingly difficult to finance underpriced and therefore unprofitable services by overcharging intermediary activities and by levying high interest margins. Gradually explicit interest-rate competition has meant reduced non-rate competition and increased non-interest revenue in the form of explicit service charges. As fees and commissions were progressively deregulated in 1985 and 1986 banks rapidly increased their use of explicit fees to recover the cost of providing services. So far, however, the transaction services have not been significantly repriced, since their prices remained heavily regulated, but also because banks' customers managed to impede the introduction of a new pricing structure in 1987.

Finally, the squeeze on interest margins, the development of new products, and explicit pricing of a larger number of services have affected the internal structure of net banking income. A growing fraction of this income now arises from trading and fee-based activities rather than from traditional intermediary activities. Therefore the recent positive developments in the level and structure of net banking income are partly the result of the banks' structural adjustment to a new competitive environment. However, the magnitude of this positive evolution should not be overstated. As illustrated by developments during the last quarter of 1987, part of the improvement in gross margins was associated with a booming stock market and may prove as reversible as the ascent in the price of securities which marked the mid-1980s.

Reduction in the growth of operating costs

Since 1984 the growth in operating costs has been significantly reduced. In nominal terms the growth rate in operating costs decreased from 11·2 per cent in 1984 to 7·1 per cent in 1985, 5·2 per cent in 1986, and 3·9 per cent in 1987. In real terms, growth declined from 3·2 per cent in 1984 to 0·8 per cent in 1987. This development is primarily the result of a reduction in the growth in personnel expenses, which decelerated from 9·6 per cent in 1984 (1·6 per cent in real terms) to 2·6 per cent in 1987 (i.e. a negative 0·5 per cent in real terms). Here as well, domestic operations largely account for such positive developments.

These developments are the result of the interplay of various factors. But fundamentally, they reflect the cost containment efforts undertaken by banks in order to cope with increased competition and the squeeze in interest margin. In this regard it is important to bear in mind that a significant element of financial innovation and deregulation has been deliberately implemented by the state in order to lower the cost of financial intermediation. The authorities considered this a necessity in order to enhance their success in fighting inflation and to improve prospects for productive investment.

Against this background a general awareness emerged among bankers and the supervisory authorities that the financial benefits of rising banking productivity should no longer be channelled primarily into higher overheads. In order to achieve effective cost containment, banks attempted to limit the rate of growth of staff costs by restricting hiring, except for their then fast-growing and highly profitable investment banking departments. As a consequence the total number of employees declined by 1·1 per cent in 1987 to 226,700, compared with a decline of 0·7 per cent in 1986, and of 0·1 per cent in 1985.

Despite this development, general expenses continued to expand somewhat, since new activities required substantial additional capital outlays. Furthermore, recent technological changes altered the relative cost structure of providing banking services. These have already contributed to changes in the internal structure of operating costs, with staff costs representing only 64·7 per cent of total operating costs in 1987, against 67 per cent in 1984.

Finally, the major banking groups have attempted a rationalization of their organizational structures along more functional lines. Such a move, which allows easier identification of profit centres, is likely to remedy some aspect of the traditional X inefficiency of banking organizations, generated by complex and sometimes overlapping organization charts.

Together with improvements in net banking income, this recent cost containment undeniably helped the 'bottom line'. This is particularly apparent at the level of operating income (i.e. the difference between net banking income and operating costs), which

125

improved by 12·5 per cent in 1985, and by an unprecedented 23·4 per cent in 1986. In 1987, however, owing to adverse developments in gross margins, operating income dropped by 12·2 per cent, to 45·3 billion frs. Domestic operations accounted for the entirety of this overall improvement, as operating income at overseas branches declined by 22 per cent over the period 1985–7.

A further strengthening of loan loss reserves

During the period 1985–7 French banks continued to build up weighty loan loss reserves against foreign debt. Net provision peaked in 1986 when the banks increased loan loss reserves by 30·9 billion frs., against 25·2 billion frs. in 1985. In 1987 this effort was slightly reduced, with provision amounting to about 28 billion frs., essentially for sovereign risk.

Owing to this continuous and important provision effort, French banks managed to improve dramatically the provision level of their domestic and international risks. As a result, by the end of 1986, risky loans, estimated at 306 billion frs. for the forty-four major banks, were globally provisioned to the extent of 40 per cent. Private risks were provisioned to the extent of 57 per cent by the end of 1986. The provision ratio for sovereign risk reached 31 per cent by the end of 1986, against 23 per cent by the end of 1985, while domestic risks were considered heavily provisioned. According to preliminary estimates, the provision ratio for sovereign risk reached 40 per cent by the end of 1987.

This continuing policy proved especially relevant in 1987. Indeed, during 1987 the initiative taken by major American banking institutions substantially to increase allowances against sovereign-risk loans did not trigger off similar action in France as the banks and their regulators considered existing loan loss reserves adequate from a prudential standpoint. Consequently French banks' profitability remained fairly stable at a time when their American and British counterparts experienced an unprecedented deterioration in profitability.

Finally, besides banks' provision effort triggered by the awareness of the relative undercapitalization of French commercial banks, the provision ratio for sovereign loans has also been significantly improved by exchange-rate developments. Indeed, in France, as in other countries outside the USA, the sharp decline in the value of the dollar has tended to raise the value of the existing loan loss reserves (which are generally held in French francs) when measured in relation to the US dollar-denominated cross-border loans. Owing to the combination of these various factors, the major French banks managed to reach high levels of provision compared with their foreign competitors. In a sense, this move was one aspect of a more general strengthening of balance sheets and profitability during the period 1985–7.

Improved profitability and capitalization

French banks have made dramatic strides as regards declared profits. They managed to post hefty gains in 1985 and 1986, with net profits increasing by 66·2 per cent in 1985 to 8·4 billion frs. (against 4·9 billion frs. in 1984), and by 36·5 per cent in 1986 to 11·4 billion frs. Despite adverse developments in operating income, and owing to lighter loan loss provision and to exceptional earnings, banks managed to post further gains in 1987, with net profits estimated at about 13·5 billion frs., i.e. an 18 per cent increase as compared with 1986. As a consequence, profitability increased significantly at commercial banks. In 1986 return on equity reached 10·9 per cent, against 10·3 per cent in 1985 and 7·4 per cent in 1984 for the AFB banks. In 1987 return on equity is estimated to have reached about 10 per cent.

As a matter of fact, return on equity did not improve as significantly as net profit figures because during the period 1984–7 banks strengthened their balance sheets by increasing capital. This gradual recapitalization proved to be a multi-dimensional process. As early as 1984, banks were resorting to financial innovation and issued various quasi-equity instruments such as non-voting shares known as *certificats d'investissement*, perpetual floating-rate subordinated notes, and *titres participatifs*. However, bad debt provisioning and setting aside part of post-tax profits were the major aspect of the recapitalization process. As a consequence, capital (i.e. shareholder capital, reserves, and provision) increased by 15·8 per cent in 1987 to 139·3 billion frs., against an unprecedented 31·8 per cent increase in 1986, and increase of about 16 per cent in 1985.

Despite such positive developments, the usual profitability indicators and capital-to-assets ratios are still low by international standards, with the possible exception of 1987. Compared with the five largest banks in the major industrial countries, in 1986, French banks still performed rather poorly in terms of pre-tax profits per employee, of capital-to-assets ratio, and of return on assets, ranking just ahead of Belgian and Japanese banks. However, owing to their high leverage, the largest managed to post a pre-tax return on capital which ranked in a median position at 17·4 per cent (table 5.6).

In 1987 the picture appears quite different from what it used to

Table 5.6 Ranking of the top five banks of eleven industrial countries, 1986

Capital to assets ratio (%)	Pre-tax return on assets (%)	Pre-tax return on capital (%)	Pre-tax profit per employee (US $000)
Belgium 2·37	Belgium 0·37	Switzerland 11·7	UK 12·16
Japan 2·75	Japan 0·50	Netherlands 13·5	Netherlands 12·54
France 3·00	France 0·52	USA 14·1	Canada 12·83
Germany 3·25	Netherlands 0·53	Canada 14·7	France 12·92
Netherlands 3·94	Germany 0·61	Belgium 15·6	Belgium 13·56
Italy 4·26	Switzerland 0·68	France 17·4	USA 15·25
UK 4·87	USA 0·71	Japan 18·1	Spain 17·34
USA 5·05	Canada 0·75	Germany 18·9	Germany 20·88
Canada 5·10	Italy 0·88	Italy 20·6	Italy 27·13
Switzerland 5·79	UK 1·11	UK 22·9	Switzerland 32·24
Spain 5·82	Spain 1·44	Spain 24·7	Japan 67·39

Source: The Banker, July 1987.

be. American, British, and Canadian banks experienced a sharp drop in profitability because of enormous one-time provision against bad debt. As a consequence, the largest French banks' relative profitability improved significantly. They ranked at a median level in terms of pre-tax profits per employee, of pre-tax return on assets, and were very well positioned in terms of pre-tax return on equity, just behind the largest Spanish and Japanese banks (table 5.7).

Such an improvement in profitability and capitalization became possible but also, in a sense, necessary during the period 1985–7. Recent macro-financial developments, and particularly the bull market of the mid-1980s, contributed to improve significantly

Table 5.7 Ranking of the top five banks of eleven industrial countries, 1987

Capital to assets ratio (%)	Pre-tax return on assets (%)	Pre-tax return on capital (%)	Pre-tax profit per employee (US $000)
Belgium 2·22	USA −0·40	USA −9·1	USA −9·28
Japan 2·59	Canada 0·00	Canada 0·03	Canada 0·03
France 3·18	UK 0·01	UK 0·1	UK 0·1
Germany 3·22	Belgium 0·34	Switzerland 10·6	Belgium 14·71
Italy 3·40	Italy 0·46	Netherlands 12·7	Netherlands 15·79
Netherlands 4·14	Germany 0·46	Italy 13·4	France 16·01
USA 4·46	France 0·51	Germany 14·2	Italy 16·37
Canada 4·89	Japan 0·51	Belgium 15·3	Germany 19·12
UK 5·83	Netherlands 0·53	France 15·9	Spain 21·96
Switzerland 5·88	Switzerland 0·62	Japan 19·8	Switzerland 37·60
Spain 5·93	Spain 1·21	Spain 20·4	Japan 78·78

Source: The Banker, July 1988.

largest banks' operating income. This, in turn, allowed them to boost profits and risk provision simultaneously in 1985 and 1986.

But other changes, more structural in nature, played a significant role in recent developments regarding profitability and capitalization. The major move to privatization, initiated by the Chirac government in 1986 and 1987, undeniably obliged banks to pay more attention to the 'bottom line' and certainly had an impact on profit posting behaviour. As early as 1986 the imminence of privatization led to an unprecedented increase in reported profits, since banks strove to show something approaching foreign standards of post-tax published profits. For example, in preparation for its imminent flotation, Société Générale raised reported profits by 64 per cent, and altogether the big three state-owned banks managed to increase net profits by more than 50 per cent. Privatization imposed an additional constraint on newly privatized banks. As major banks moved out from under the state umbrella, banks' debt became priced according to their profitability and perceived financial strength. This led US rating agencies to downgrade French banks' rating, which could make it more expensive to borrow on international capital markets. In order to preserve their valuable international reputation, French banks had to embark on a process of normalizing their balance-sheet structure and their reported profitability.

However, the role of privatization should not be overstated. Privatization *per se* does not lead to greater productive and allocative efficiency if private monopolies are substituted for public ones. In this regard the French privatization programme has been implemented in a favourable context which eased the extensive divestiture of government shareholdings in nationalized banks.

Since the early 1980s a gradual shift in French attitudes to enterprise and profit has taken place as more social actors have acknowledged their crucial importance. Paralleling this move, as early as 1984, the management and, to a certain extent, the role of state-owned banks was reconsidered. Gradually, decision-makers in state-owned banks were granted more autonomy, and profit became a more important performance criterion and indicator of financial viability. This contributed to better cost control and higher reported profitability as profit-maximizing behaviour tended to assume greater importance.

Furthermore, structural changes in the market place forced, in a sense, such changes in attitudes. Intensification of market pressure meant that banks could not afford anymore to behave as X-inefficient monopolists. Loss of market power associated with increased contestability of banking markets reduced the sustainability of prevailing non-profit-maximizing behaviour.

Finally, recent changes may have contributed to the transformation of the banks into more efficient operating units, able to move forward competitively into the 1990s. So far they have coped fairly well with the drastic changes that have transformed the financial system. But considerable uncertainties still prevail as regards the reversibility of recent positive developments. Undeniably, the decline in bank operating income generated by the sharp drop in equity prices that occurred in October 1987 warrants such uncertainties.

Conclusion

Since the mid-1980s French banks managed to improve their profitability and to strengthen their balance sheets. Such positive developments are partly the result of a structural adjustment of the major banking groups to a new market structure. In a sense the banks succeeded in their attempt to develop new activities, which allowed a diversification of risks across product lines, and which could smooth income streams in the future.

However, the banks also benefited greatly from possibly non-recurrent phenomena such as the bull market that characterized the mid-1980s, and the wave of financial innovation that changed the basic features of the financial system.

In the present environment there are fears with respect to a possible structural squeeze on profit margins, and an erosion of capital ratios. The profit-making capacity of the banks may be jeopardized in the future by tighter competition, financial innovations, and, possibly, increased risks. In addition, the onset of a bear market would impair the profit-making capacity of those banks which derived an increasing proportion of their income from capital-market activities.

Such risks are potentially damaging and should not be underestimated, especially since further provision efforts may be required. Indeed, the banks' ability or willingness to maintain adequate loan loss reserves may be weakened by the 'underpricing' of loans during periods of intense competition in the loan market, or by increased pressure from shareholders for higher dividends in a period of structural squeeze of operating margins.

In this regard, two major developments may induce further changes in banks' behaviour and structure. On the one hand, French banks will be under pressure to increase their capital-to-asset ratio to 8 per cent by 1992, in line with a Bank for International Settlements agreement reached in December 1987. Under the Basle capital convergence accord, the banks will be subject to the same capital discipline as their foreign competitors. Furthermore, the Basle accord will be married to the banking directives of the European Community, which will have full legal force. Major French banks claim that if their loan loss reserves are properly taken into account they should be close to the capital adequacy floor of 8 per cent of assets recommended by the Cooke Committee. But even though reaching the 1992 capital requirement should not prove too difficult for the major French banks, the new standard, in particular the requirement that core capital be 4 per cent of risk-weighted assets, is more stringent than present standards, and at least some banks will have to make significant efforts in order to meet the new requirement.

More generally, major uncertainties remain as to the final impact of the Basle accord. First of all, in the new stock-market environment following the October 1987 fall in equity prices, raising equity may prove very costly to undercapitalized banks, and would significantly reduce their competitive advantage arising from their traditional balance-sheet structure. The new standard could also restrain balance-sheet and off-balance-sheet growth in the future, forcing banks to look for less capital-consuming activities. Therefore the accord would achieve its purpose, but major uncertainties remain as to the impact of the new requirement on the dynamics of financial innovation, and the role of commercial banks in future financial changes. Furthermore, counter-intuitive effects cannot be dismissed at this stage. The enforcement of the new standard could impose further constraints on profit posting behaviour, at least where capital-to-asset ratios are rather weak, and could increase pressure to maximize short-term book profits. More and more, banks' vulnerability to mergers and acquisitions depends crucially on share prices, and the newly privatized French banks will be no exception.

On the other hand, the banks and the authorities are well aware that further operating and organizational rationalization is to be achieved, especially as a result of the completion of the internal European market by 1992. The prospect of a unified banking market in 1992 and the likely intensification of cross-border competition oblige the banks to prepare adequate defences against an assault on market share by foreign competitors. The challenge for French banks is competitors with less organizational inertia and lower costs as well as more sensible pricing – particularly with respect to transaction services – and which will attack the most profitable markets, i.e. implementing a cream-skimming strategy. This would further reduce the largest banks' market power and impose major changes in banking regulation, and behaviour. Therefore, by allowing effective and potential new entrants, the opening up of European banking markets should force French banks to pay close attention to their pricing policies, which should be reviewed and streamlined in the forthcoming competitive environment. More generally, in order to avoid cream-skimming of their most profitable markets and to retain market shares, French financial institutions will probably have to phase out the still prevalent cross-subsidies over the next few years. Furthermore, they will have to raise their efficiency and cut costs so as to be in a position to compete efficiently in an increasingly open European market.

In this sense the banks will have to rely on further productivity gains and on innovation to remain competitive in terms of price and quality in the forthcoming European markets for financial services. Such efforts will have to be matched by further regulatory changes, since, from a regulatory standpoint, the corollary to an explicit pricing of transaction instruments would be to remove the prohibition of explicit interest payment on demand deposits. Together with harmonization of value-added tax rates, this would contribute to the broad behavioural and regulatory convergence process that should stem from the completion of the European internal market.

Notes

1 The views expressed in this chapter are those of the author and do not necessarily represent those of the IMF or the Ministry of Finance.
2 'A contestable market is one in which entry is absolutely free, and exit is absolutely costless' (W. Baumol, J. Panzar, and R. Willig, 1982). In such a perfectly contestable market the entrants suffer no disadvantage and no cost discrimination. Because of its vulnerability to hit-and-run entry, a contestable market has the same welfare characteristics as perfectly competitive markets, even with a very small number of incumbent firms.

References

Artus, P. (1986) 'Hétérogénéité des banques et des circuits de financement et régulation monétaire', Banque de France, June.
Bailey, E.E. and Friedlander, A.F. (1982) 'Market structure and multi-product industries', *Journal of Economic Literature* 20, September.
Banker, The, 'World top 500', July 1984, 1987, and 1988.
Barroux, Y. and Chauveau, T. (1985) 'La determination des taux d'intérêt en France', unpublished, Paris: Banque de France.
Baumol, W.J., Panzar, J.C., and Willig, R.D. (1982) *Contestable Markets and the Theory of Industry Sector*, San Diego: Harcourt Brace Jovanovich.
Baumol, W.J. and Willig, R.D. (1986) 'Contestability: developments since the book', in D.D. Morris, P.J.N. Sinclair, M.D.E. Slater, and J.S. Vickers, *Strategic Behaviours and Industrial Competition*, Oxford: Clarendon Press.
Bingham, T.R.G. (1985) *Banking and Monetary Policy*, Paris: OECD.
Boissieu, C. de (1979) 'Taux du marché monétaire, taux de base bancaire et conditions débitrices effectives des banques', *Revue Banque* 380, January.
——— (1985) Eléments d'analyse de la rigidité à la baisse des taux d'intérêt', *Economie Apliquée* 38, 1.

—— (1987) 'La banalisation de l'intermédiation financière', *Eurépargne* 11–12, August–September.

Commissariat General du Plan (1984) *Quels intermédiaires financiers pour demain?* Paris: La documentation française.

—— (1987) *Perspectives du financement de l'économie française*, Paris: La documentation française.

Commission Bancaire, Annual Reports.

Conseil National du Crédit (1987) 'L'incidence des technologies nouvelles sur l'activité des intermédiaires financiers', Paris: CNC.

Deval-Guilly, E. and Renard, F. (1984) 'Une maquette du système financier français: le cas des banques inscrites', *Economie et Prévision* 63.

Edwards, F.R. (1987) 'Managerial objectives in regulated industries: expense-preference behavior in banking', *Journal of Political Economy* 85, 1.

Edwards, F.R. and Heggestad, A.A. (1973) 'Uncertainty, market structure, and performance: the Galbraith–Caves hypothesis and managerial motives in banking', *Quarterly Journal of Economics* 87, August.

Faulhaber, G. (1975) 'Cross-subsidization: pricing in public enterprises', *American Economic Review* 55, December.

Fort, J.L. (1983) 'Comportement des banques face à l'encadrement du crédit et conséquences pour celles-ci d'une telle réglementation', *Cahiers Economiques et Monétaires* 18, Paris: Banque de France.

Gilbert, R.A. (1984) 'Bank market structure and competition: a survey', *Journal of Money, Credit and Banking* 16, 4, Part 2, November.

Hannan, T.H. and Mavinga, F. (1980) 'Expense preference and managerial control: the case of the banking firm', *Bell Journal of Economics* 11, 2, autumn.

Joffre, C. and Strauss-Khan, M.O. (1980) 'Quelques implications de l'hétérogénéité des banques françaises quant à la politique monétaire', *Cahiers Economiques et Monétaires* 11, Paris: Banque de France.

Lévy-Garboua, V., 'Note sur les taux d'intérêt dans une économie d'endettement', in C. de Boissieu and J.L. Guglielmi (eds) *Formation et rôle des taux d'intérêt*, Paris: Economica.

Lévy-Garboua, V. and Maarek, G. (1977) 'Le comportement des banques et la politique monétaire', *Cahiers Economiques et Monétaires* 5, Paris: Banque de France.

Lévy-Garboua, V. and Renard, F. (1977) 'Structure et rentabilité des banques', *Revue Banque* 363, September.

Lévy-Lambert, H. (1980) 'La vérité des prix bancaires', *Revue Banque* 392, February.

Liebenstein, H. (1966) 'Allocative efficiency v. X-efficiency', *American Economic Review* 56, June.

Maisel, S.J. (1981) *Risk and Capital Adequacy in Commercial Banks*, NBER.

Métais, J. (1990) 'Towards a restructuring of the international financial industry: some preliminary empirical and theoretical insights', in E.P.M. Gardener (ed.), *The Future of Financial Systems and Services*, London: Macmillan.

Organization for Economic Co-operation and Development (1985) *Costs and Margins in Banking: Statistical Supplement* (1978–82), Paris: OECD.

—— (1987) *Bank Profitability*, Paris: OECD.

Pastré, O. (1986) *La Modernisation des banques françaises*, Paris: La Documentation française.

Revell, J.R.S. (1980) *Costs and Margins in Banking: an International Survey*, Paris: OECD.

Sautter, E. (1981) 'Résultats des banques et taux d'intérêt', *Revue Banque*, December.

Smirlock, M. and Marshall, W. (1983) 'Monopoly power and expense preference behavior: theory and evidence of the contrary', *Bell Journal of Economics* 14, spring.

Sterdyniak, H. (1986) 'Des conséquences patrimoniales de la désinflation', *Observations et Diagnostics Economiques* 17, October.

Szymczak, P. (1986) 'La réforme de la tarification bancaire', Paris: Direction de la Prévision, December.

—— (1987a) 'Taux d'intérêt et système bancaire', *Economie et Prévision* 77.

—— (1987b) 'Eléments de comparaison internationale des coûts et marges bancaires', *Revue d'Economie Financière* 1. (This paper has also been published in English: 'Costs and Margins in Banking: some International Comparisons', research papers, Institute of European Finance, Bangor, Gwynedd, RP 87/12.)

White, L.J. (1987) 'Price regulation and quality rivalry in a profit-maximizing model: the case of branch banking', *Journal of Money, Credit and Banking* 8, 1, November.

Williamson, O.E. (1963) 'Managerial discretion and business behavior', *American Economic Review* 53, 5, December.

Chapter six

International strategies of French banks

Joël Métais

From their origins the major French banks have been strongly committed to international activities. Between 1860 and 1905 they had already settled a strong foreign presence, mainly through branches, primarily in Europe, in the French colonies and in the Far East (where the 'ancestors' of Indosuez and of BNP were well represented). This network of ninety-six offices abroad in 1914,[1] slowly increased during the inter-war period, which recorded only twenty-nine new offices, among which eighteen were also established in the colonial territories and the remaining ones mainly in Europe. After the Second World War foreign expansion retained a low profile until the turn of the 1970s where a mere eighty-three new offices (in broad terms) were established before 1968 and some former ones were closed or had to change their status – mainly from branch to subsidiary – especially in the newly independent countries. It was only in the early 1970s that the pace of their international expansion started to gather momentum again.

From the 1860s to the early 1970s three main forces drove the international activities and shaped the network of the French banks: the direction and intensity of French international trade flows, the investment of long-term capital abroad, and political connections. These are indeed very conventional factors which they largely shared with their main competitors in the international arena, especially the British clearing and overseas banks before the First World War.

Since the '70s their international activities have undergone two different successive regimes. The first lasted through the whole decade of the 1970s up to the debt crisis of 1982. The second has been slowly emerging since the mid-1980s. In view of the aims of the book, the latter move will be analysed in greater depth, to enable us to point out the major issues for the years ahead. Section one summarizes the main features of the wave of international expansion during the '70s and outlines the similarities and peculiarities of the French banks' strategies compared to those of their major foreign competitors. Section two is concerned with the analysis of the new framework for international financial activities since the mid-1980s, particularly at the domestic level. But the new international environment which is likely to emerge from measures such as the regulatory provisions of the Cooke Committee, the achievement of the single European market in 1992, and some further liberalization of trade flows in financial services as a possible outcome of the current round of multilateral trade discussions, will also be examined at some length. Section three elaborates, from a theoretical point of view, the major factors which are now likely to give a competitive edge to a financial institution in the international field before assessing the situation of French banks in this respect. A major conclusion is that they now need to define their strategies very tightly as competition will probably get tougher and as a new balance between domestic and international activities has to be reached. More precisely, an international offensive strategy will certainly have to be supported by a defensive domestic one as new competitors, foreign or domestic, will try to encroach on their respective traditional turf for many reasons, especially those related to the internal European market.

The main theoretical arguments will often be drawn from recent developments in the field of industrial economics. Such an approach is all the more sustainable in that banking and the financial services sector more generally seem now to be involved in a process which is transforming them into a global industry just as the automative, aircraft manufacturing, oil refining, and many other industries were transformed some years ago. Although such theoretical premises are not yet commonly agreed upon among all the economists involved in the study of financial systems, they seem to be fruitful enough to be successfully applied in a growing number of research studies in this field.

International growth in the 1970s up to the debt crisis: an empirical and analytical summary appraisal

We can probably consider the twenty years from the mid-1960s to the mid-1980s as the second most significant wave of foreign expansion of French commercial banks after the first, experienced from 1860 to 1905. And the decade starting around the first oil shock probably witnessed their most tremendous ever foreign involvement. As such this period needs detailed investigation. So we first trace a condensed empirical record of their international activities during this time. Then we try to outline the main features of the most suitable analytical model to explain their rapid foreign expansion.

The empirical record

The number of offices abroad may appear as a very rough indicator of the international involvement of a banking system. It nevertheless has to be considered, for three main reasons at least: it has been available for many years on a quite consistent basis; it allows of reasonably reliable international comparisons; its evolution in respect of its geographical extension and in terms of the respective shares of the different vehicles abroad may provide significant information about the banks' strategies. We shall thus start with some figures on the evolution of the foreign network before looking more closely at the volume and types of international activities. Some information about the performance of French banks abroad will also be given. But as a general preliminary remark it must be stressed that empirical information about the international activities of French banks was rather scanty during this period. This raises some difficulties when international comparisons are needed for the sake of the analysis.

According to a study by C. Michalet and C. Sauviat (1981), during the years 1968–73, French banks set up abroad twenty-seven representative offices, twenty-three branches, and thirty-seven subsidiaries; their respective performance for the five following years 1974–9 is: eighty-one representative offices, forty-eight branches, and sixty-three subsidiaries. In other words, the pace of foreign expansion markedly gained momentum after the first oil shock, and this was no accident. Figures released since 1977 by the Association Française des Banques (French Bankers' Association) also confirm that the build-up of the network still went on after the turn of the 1980s at a sustained pace.

Whereas, according to table 6.1, by the end of 1977 thirty-two banks could rely on 562 offices[2] in eighty-four countries, in 1983 forty-five banks were established in 104 countries through 801 offices. When taking into account the own network of their foreign subsidiaries and affiliated banks, French banks were generally thought to own the third or the second most extensive foreign network in the world after the American and British ones, according to whether representative offices are included in the figures or not.

The 1960s had witnessed a tremendous geographical restructuring of this network. The major trend was then the retreat from the former African colonial territories, where many branches and

Table 6.1 Foreign network of French banks, 1977–86

	1977	1979	1982	1983	1984	1985	1986
Number of French banks abroad	32	37	46	45	49	48	n.a.
Number of foreign host countries	84	91	104	104	102	104	n.a.
Total number of foreign 'vehicles'*	562	665	765	801	809	810	824
of which: Branches	177	213	237	251	284	283	286
Subsidiaries	68	71	88	96	98	102	110
Geographical breakdown							
Europe							
Branches	71	83	103	110	119	n.a.	114
Subsidiaries	29	33	33	35	37	n.a.	48
Africa							
Branches	42	41	3	4	5	n.a.	5
Subsidiaries	16	15	22	22	22	n.a.	22
America							
Branches	23	33	53	55	66	n.a.	66
Subsidiaries	12	13	19	21	20	n.a.	21
Asia							
Branches	18	29	42	46	58	n.a.	65
Subsidiaries	3	0	8	10	10	n.a.	10
Middle East							
Branches	17	19	24	24	24	n.a.	24
Subsidiaries	8	6	2	2	2	n.a.	2
Oceania and other							
Branches	6	8	12	12	12	n.a.	12
Subsidiaries	0	0	4	6	7	n.a.	7

* Include branches, subsidiaries, affiliated banks (minority stakes in), and representative offices.

Source: Statistical releases of the Association Française des Banques.

subsidiaries had to be given up after independence, leaving French banks with a minority stake in affiliated banks now controlled by national interests, private or public. Europe, Asia, and Latin America benefited most from this restructuring of the network. From the 1960s onwards, foreign expansion of the French banks may be considered as entering into a new era of international involvement after cutting some privileged ties with the former colonial territories so as to compete more openly in the emerging and fast-growing Euro-currency markets with banks from the major industrial countries.

Michalet and Sauviat show that during the period 1968–73 35·6 per cent of the new outlets (representative offices plus branches plus subsidiaries) were set up in Europe, 11·5 per cent in the United States and 19·5 per cent in Asia, with a mere 4·6 per cent in Africa. These results confirm the trend observed in the 1960s. Table 6.1 also shows that between 1977 and 1983 Europe, the Americas, and Asia still accounted for an undisputed majority of the new offices of French banks around the world. However, we can get another picture of the relative importance of the different areas by considering their respective amount of foreign direct investment, as such figures are generally related to the volume and type of activities performed by the offices through their capital requirements. These statistics were released in 1985 by the Commission Bancaire[3] and are summarized in table 6.2.

During the decade 1974–84 foreign direct investment by French banks grew sevenfold, from an amount outstanding of 2,824 million frs. to 20,780 million frs.[4] Europe stands out as the primary investment area – with a 9,963 million fr. figure in 1984 – although its share has been steadily declining, from 56·3 per cent to 47·9 per cent, throughout the decade. This trend mainly benefited North America and Asia, which also gained 'market share' at the expense of Africa and Latin America so as to represent 18·1 per cent and 14·6 per cent of total stock figures respectively at the end of the period.

As a main conclusion of tables 6.1 and 6.2, during the 1970s and early 1980s French banks were able rapidly to redirect their foreign network and to build a strong international presence at a time when the banking industry in the major industrial countries was looking precisely for new growth opportunities outside its traditional areas.

However, such global figures may still be misleading as regards the real involvement of the whole banking system in international activity. Although forty-five banks were said to have a foreign presence in 1984, the seven major banking groups of the time[5] controlled 98·2 per cent of French banks' foreign direct investment.

Table 6.2 Foreign direct investment of French banks: geographical breakdown, 1974–84

Region	1974		1978		1981		1984	
	(1)	(2)	(1)	(2)	(1)	(2)	(1)	(2)
Europe	1,588·4	56·3	3,832·9	56·4	7,122·9	53·1	9,963·5	47·9
North America and Caribbean	296·5	10·5	1,065·8	15·7	2,316·3	17·2	3,769·2	18·1
Latin America	269·0	9·5	449·8	6·6	1,269·4	9·5	1,614·1	7·8
Asia	181·6	6·4	443·7	6·5	1,055·7	7·9	3,030·9	14·6
Africa	300·4	10·6	601·2	8·8	911·0	6·8	1,051·0	5·1
Middle East	126·5	4·5	288·1	4·2	437·0	3·3	812·0	3·9
Oceania	61·2	2·2	121·9	1·8	299·9	2·2	529·0	2·6
Total	2,823·6	100	6,803·4	100	13,412·2	100	20,769·7	100

Notes: (1) Gross amount outstanding at year end (million frs.). (2) as a percentage of total foreign investment.

Source: Commission Bancaire, Annual Report, 1986.

Moreover the 'big three' (Banque Nationale de Paris, Crédit Lyonnais, and Société Générale) alone accounted for two-thirds of the total figure. It should be noticed here that, as in the other leading industrial countries, international banking is handled mainly by the major institutions. This fits perfectly well with one of the major conclusions of the multinational enterprise theory, which also applies to multinational banking.

Although we lack precise statistical information about the share of international activities in the total business of French banks for the beginning of the 1970s, these were estimated at 36 per cent in 1976 and 47 per cent in 1981.[6] Figures relating the business of the sole foreign branches to the total activity of their parent banks[7] can also provide another partial insight.[8] In 1978 they stood at 18·1 per cent of the total business of the twenty-four banks which actually owned foreign branches,[9] and in 1980, 1982, and 1984 at 25·4 per cent, 38·1 per cent, and 41·5 per cent respectively. This confirms the important weight of international business and its rapid growth until the year 1982, which appears as the heyday of the movement.

The analytical interpretation

The economics of international banking had been for many years concerned essentially with its international financial intermediation aspect. Only after the mid-1970s was research undertaken with attention focused on industrial economic analysis of this fast-growing sector of the international economy. Its main conclusions were summarized in 1984 in a critical survey by Robert Z. Aliber (1984). The latter partly provides the analytical framework needed to explain French banks' foreign expansion in the 1970s and early '80s. The factors which underlay their internationalization process can be classified according to whether they are of international or domestic origin.

The influence of the international context

The 1970s was a decade of tremendous growth for international banking. The Euro-currency market gross size, which can give an appropriate indicator of this growth, was only US$111 billion in 1970. It stood at US$524 billion in 1980 and passed the US$2,000 billion benchmark in 1982 at US$2,057 billion.[10] The main forces underlying such an unprecedented growth rate are well known and we shall only recall here that they relate to:

1. The expansion of international trade, foreign direct investment, and ensuing growing openness of major economies, despite some slowing-down after the second oil shock of 1979.

2. The huge imbalances in current-account balances of payments after the two oil shocks and the need to recycle funds from surplus to deficit countries, especially the developing world – and more particularly the newly industrializing countries. It must be stressed here that, according to the traditional distinction by Gurley and Shaw (1960) between institutional financial intermediation and financing through securities markets, the former took the main part of the burden of the recycling process, owing to the portfolio preferences and constraints of the surpluses' owners and of the borrowers respectively.

Regulatory constraints on financial activities in many countries and various impediments to the free movement of capital enhanced this bias towards an institutionalized intermediation process through Euro-currency markets. This created enormous growth opportunities for the deposit banks of major industrial countries. They were able to cope with the problems raised by the recycling process itself through some financial innovations like the medium-term syndicated Euro-credits. American commercial banks were prompt to exploit these opportunities but banks from other countries were also eager to share the cake!

One uncontroversial conclusion of international banking theory states that banks follow their domestic customers expanding abroad to finance their international trade flows, and their foreign investments, and to provide them with various financial services in their foreign host countries. Their comparative advantage against foreign competitors in such activities is related to the ownership of some special intangible assets such as information about the true creditworthiness and specific needs of their customers. This factor is of course especially relevant to explain the growth in the international activities of French banks. But this first category of factors tells only part of the story. French banks also wanted to capture a share of the fast-growing Euro-market activity.

Of course, they were in an unfavourable position as regards American commercial banks, owing to the dominant role of the US dollar in the Euro-credit markets. But they were on an equal footing in this respect with their competitors from other major industrial countries. As long as Euro-credits – especially medium-term roll-over ones – were the leading sector of international banking activities, the ability to secure regular access to huge amounts of dollars at the lowest cost represented a major competitive edge. For banks mostly relying on the international inter-bank money market such an ability was roughly associated with their size and their national origin. There seems to have been an inverse relationship between this size and the spread over the cheapest funds in the interbank market. Banks from countries with capable supervisory systems and lender of last resort facilities incurred lower risk premiums in this interbank market. Rather than solely tapping international money markets, some banks decided, as a complementary approach, to acquire a retail deposit base in the United States through the take-over of US commercial banks, as they probably expected that the predominant model of international financial intermediation at the time was here to stay.[11]

Table 6.3 Ranking and size (US$ billion) of major French banks

Bank	1974		1979	
	Rank	Size	Rank	Size
Crédit Agricole*			1	105
BNP	4	35	4	99
Crédit Lyonnais	6	33	6	91
Société Générale	10	28	7	85
Paribas	58	12	50	32
Banque Indosuez†			94	16

* In 1974 Crédit Agricole was not ranked, owing to its mutual character.
† Formed in 1975, through the merger of the Banque de Indochine and the Banque de Suez et de l'Union des Mines.
Source: *The Banker*, June 1975 and June 1979.

Considering the position of French banks in the light of these factors, it can be argued that the 'big three' enjoyed a particularly favourable position in respect to the size criterion, as evidenced from table 6.3. More generally, French banks certainly benefited from positive externalities due to the resilience of the banking system, which had remained unaffected by any crisis or significant failure since the Second World War. Of course, they were often criticized, especially the three major ones, for their weak capital ratios. But this does not seem to have hampered their involvement in international lending, as their public ownership status probably more than compensated for the risks presumably attached to their lower capital ratios. On the contrary, it can even be argued that their relatively lower costs of capital gave them a decisive competitive edge through higher leverage.[12]

At a time when participating in and lead-managing medium-term Euro-currency credits was, for whatever reasons, considered as an index of competitive strength in the international banking market, the ranking of French banks in international league tables is of some interest. Table 6.4, based on the *Euromoney* magazine

Table 6.4 Ranking of French banks as lead and co-lead managers of syndicated Euro-credits, 1973–82

Bank	1973	1974	1975	1976	1977	1978	1979	1980	1981	1982
BNP	9	7	9	29	>50	23	56	20	18	29
Crédit Lyonnais	6	8	11	24	23	27	11	7	17	31
Société Générale	n.a.	n.a.	n.a.	12	>50	38	21	14	32	49
Crédit Commercial	7	8	22	n.a.	>50	42	29	30	44	>50
Indosuez*	—	—	—	89	>50	>50	88	>40	>50	38
Paribas	13	10	25	69	34	>50	57	23	38	23

* Formed in 1975 (see note, table 6.3).

Source: Euromoney, various issues.

reporting system for Euro-credit activity, displays such information for the period 1973–82. Owing to some breakdowns and inconsistencies in the time series, the comparability of performance for the successive years must be interpreted carefully. During this decade five of the six internationally most active French banks generally managed to be among the fifty most active lead and co-lead managers of medium-term Euro-credits. This performance might be considered satisfactory, allowing for the fact that the highest rankings were generally achieved by the major American commercial banks, which drew their competitive edge from their domestic dollar base – after the relaxation of controls on capital movements in January 1974 – and from their sheer size. Nevertheless it also appears from *Euromoney* computations that at some time the biggest German, British, Japanese, or Canadian banks were able, at least temporarily, to break into the upper end of the league tables, notwithstanding the fact they were not dollar-based banks. Comparable in size with French banks, they often got higher rankings than their French competitors, except for Crédit Lyonnais.

The performance of French banks may then appear' all the more modest in that the foreign borrowing requirements of France might have provided them with a lot of mandates for lead-managing syndicated credits. But it can also be argued that the net external debtor position of France and its consequence on the French franc exchange rate did finally more than cancel this advantage. Moreover their moderate profile in this field of Euro-currency business may also have been the result of a more cautious approach towards a sector where rapidly growing competitive pressures soon shaved out the profit margins. In the neighbouring Euro-bond sector, except for Indosuez lagging always behind the fortieth position, the five other major banks performed better on average than in the syndicated Euro-credit sector, at least until 1979 (see table 6.5). But this may be partly due to the fact that French banks were given the monopoly of managing the Euro-bond issues of French borrowers. It should also be mentioned here that until the turn of the 1980s Euro-bond business was largely dominated by the leading universal German and Swiss banks and some prominent London merchant banks. French banks themselves performed as well as American investment banks and brokerage houses or Japanese securities houses, whereas American commercial banks were not really concerned with this sector of activity except for Citicorp and Manufacturers' Hanover. However, after 1980 their position seems to have deteriorated. But these broad rankings based on all types of Euro-bond business may have then become more and more

Table 6.5 Ranking of French banks as lead and co-lead managers of Euro-bond issues, 1975–82*

Bank	1975	1976	1977	1978	1979	1981	1982
BNP	17	12	15	9	9	16	28
Crédit Lyonnais	18	17	14	20	11	38	17
Société Générale	15	16	18	14	6	12	10
Crédit Commercial	13	29	41	22	8	7	31
Indosuez	70	88	79	>40	>40	>40	>40
Paribas	11	10	11	34	40	36	29

* All notes and bonds, including floating-rate notes but excluding New York issues. Starting from 1978, rankings are based on sole lead managers receiving full amount of the issue and joint lead managers equal amounts.

Source: *Euromoney*, various issues.

misleading as new types of more sophisticated instruments (convertibles, non-dollar-denominated FRNs, etc.) found their way on to the market. Looking at the records in these new specialist sectors may be more informative. For example, in 1982 Paribas was the fourth lead manager in the emerging convertible bond market. But it is also to be noted that, at the same time, French banks were second only to the powerful Credit Suisse First Boston in the French issuers' sector after some relaxation in the rules protecting their position in this area.

The domestic influence

As for industrial multinational companies and banks from other countries – especially the United States – domestic economic factors played a significant role in the expansion of French banks abroad during the 1970s. Two of them are of outstanding importance: the new competitive framework established by the Banking Acts of 1966–7 and the quantitative credit ceiling system (*encadrement du crédit*) which was to become the major instrument of monetary policy after 1972.

The Banking Acts of 1966 and 1967 (known as the 'Debré Acts'), inspired by the need to give the banking system a larger role in financing the economy, aimed at three main objectives: blurring the old distinction between the deposit banks (*banques de dépôts*) and merchant banks (*banques d'affaires*); some levelling of the playing field in term and savings deposit-taking activity through the partial removal of the privileges of some institutions; enabling banks freely to establish new branches and offices. These new rules enlarged the scope of growth opportunities for the banking sector whereas, at the same time, they began to dismantle the former cosy cartel which had been the normal framework of their activities for so many years. The decade following these reforms witnessed increased competition, particularly through the opening of new branches and offices, which culminated in 1972 before slowing down until a new Act in July 1982 reinstated restrictions.[13] As a result, a major restructuring occurred: between 1967 and 1977 the number of deposit banks fell from 201 to 184[14] and that of merchant banks from twenty-eight to eighteen. Beyond these rough figures it should also be mentioned that seven major universal banking groups emerged which controlled smaller regional banks and specialist financial service subsidiaries (mortgage finance, leasing, mutual funds, merchant banking).

During the decade following the Debré Acts, the banking system enjoyed satisfactory domestic growth through the broadening of its customer base and a diversification of its activities. But competition grew and profit margins soon started to shrink. By the mid-1970s domestic growth opportunities were more and more severely impaired by the credit ceilings and the system was dominated by non-price competition. Faced with such a context, the banks became all the more inclined to look for new growth opportunities in the international field in that the slowing down of domestic economic activity induced by the first oil shock still hardened competitive pressures, and that profitability and growth at home worsened.

The previous paragraph showed that the pace of expansion of the foreign network accelerated during the second half of the 1970s. Moreover between December 1975 and December 1982 cross-border claims in foreign currencies – which of course do not reflect all the international activities – of the banking sector grew from 178,350 million frs. to 830,430 million frs. at an average compound annual rate of 24·6 per cent, far exceeding the growth rate of domestic credit activity.

In this turn of events, French banks behaved in a rather similar way to their American counterparts, which had had to circumvent by international expansion the consequences of a restrictive regulatory framework on their growth and profit rates at home. Although much empirical work may be required to elaborate this argument further, it does appear that 'follow my leader'-type strategies, induced by the oligopolistic interdependences in the domestic market, played their role in the foreign network-building strategies of the major banks and of their second-tier rivals. In some respects we may question whether this did not result in some sort of 'over-shoot' in the number of foreign offices.

The latter argument has to be interpreted in the light of the higher profitability of their international banking activities during the late '70s and early '80s. According to research by the Commission Bancaire,[15] based on the sole foreign branches of twenty-four banks, for the years 1978–84, their net profits grew at a rapid rate from 340·9 million frs. in 1978 to 1,262·5 million frs. in 1981, so as to represent 19·4 per cent and 53·7 per cent of the global profits of these banks for the two respective years. Afterwards profits fell sharply to 380·9 million frs. (or 18.3 per cent of global profits), mainly as a consequence of heavy provision for doubtful assets. However, the rate of return on assets of these foreign branches steadily declined from 1978 to 1984, reflecting stiffening competition in the international arena, especially in interbank business, which at the end of 1984 represented 72 per cent of foreign branches' total activities (as against 66 per cent in 1978). In other words, global profits reaped from the foreign network until 1982 grew only as a consequence of a very rapid increase in assets, and of higher leverage, as already mentioned.

During the 1970s and up to the early '80s the major banks expanded rapidly abroad, according to a rather simple model which relies on a few explanatory variables: the growth of international trade and foreign direct investment by French companies and the expansion of Euro-currency markets, on the one hand; the slackening of the growth rate and the decline in profitability at home which hampered the strategies of the major players in the domestic oligopoly, on the other. Strategies relying on this model could go on as far as international activities could fuel the overall growth rate and help maintain overall profitability despite some deterioration at home.

After a decade and a half this model was largely impaired by the rather radical turn-round in its underlying premises following the international debt crisis of 1982 and the new macro-economic and financial environment at the world level which emerged afterwards.

A new framework for international banking activities after the 1982 debt crisis

Although the Mexican debt crisis of August 1982 is commonly regarded as the immediate cause of a major breakdown in the process of expansion of international banking activities it may be questioned whether it played such an important role as it is generally credited with. During the past five years the international banking scene has been witnessing a sizeable shift of activity from the traditional intermediation between deposits and credits to the securities markets and the markets of derivative products such as

futures, options, and swaps. Meanwhile, deposit banks have lost
some ground in the international market to the benefit of investment banks, merchant banks, securities brokers, and dealers. More
precisely, some transformations occurred in the environment of
international financial activities and they entailed a redistribution
of respective comparative advantages for the various types of
financial institutions and markets. Although some of these
evolutions may be reversed or have already entered a vanishing
phase, many of them will certainly have long-standing effects.
French banks, like their major foreign competitors, have had to
redefine their international strategies and commitments in order to
be able to compete more effectively with the new players in the
international field.

We shall first review the most significant developments in the
international and domestic fields which account for the new
directions, shape, and volume of international financial activities.
We shall then discuss, in a theoretical perspective, their influence
on the comparative advantages and sources of competitive edge in
the international market for different types of financial institutions.

Developments at the international level

These are economic, financial, institutional, and technological. On
the economic and financial scene three factors deserve special
mention. Since the mid-1980s the world economy has been experi-
encing a tremendous shift in the imbalances of current account
payments. Whereas, notwithstanding severe adjustment policies,
many developing countries still face huge deficits, the United States
is now by far the major deficit country while Germany and Japan
are piling up their largest-ever surpluses. Beyond their sheer size
and their influence on the functioning of the world economy, these
imbalances, through their compensating financing flows, are
largely responsible for the emergence of a new model of international financial intermediation.

On one hand current-account surpluses in Germany and Japan
reflect domestic excess savings of the household and business
sectors. These savings are channelled and managed primarily
through institutional investors – insurance companies, pension
funds, mutual funds, and the like – which invest them mainly in
negotiable financial assets. On the other hand, the United States'
current-account deficit can be traced back to the federal budget
deficit, and the US Treasury is a major borrower through bills and
bonds. Such patterns of savings and borrowings in these countries

have resulted in a capital recycling process which relies much more on securities markets. This differs greatly from the model of financial intermediation of the '70s, which essentially relied upon the international deposit banking system as OPEC surplus countries had a strong liquidity preference and preferred bank deposits to long-term portfolio investments, while many second-tier quality borrowers – particularly from the LDCs – had no access to the securities markets and had to borrow from the multinational banks.

1. This is one of the main factors underlying the move towards 'securitization' in international as well as in domestic finance during the past five years. Another impetus to this move came from the steady decline in nominal interest rates which accompanied the disinflation process in OECD countries until 1987.

2. Following the October 1979 decision of the US monetary authorities to monitor more strictly the growth of the monetary base, interest rates on dollar assets, after a sharp rise, entered a period of higher volatility. Those on assets in other currencies also soon experienced larger swings, although to a lesser degree. Moreover the exchange rates between the major currencies became more unpredictable. Combined with greater financial sophistication of financial and non-financial agents, the ensuing uncertainties fed a fast-growing demand for hedging instruments and were responsible for the emergence and development of many markets for derivative financial products (futures, options, swaps).

Not only did markets for financial assets grow in importance and sophistication, they also achieved higher integration between them all round the world. This has been labelled the 'globalization' of finance.

3. Institutional reforms combined with these macro-economic and macro-financial developments to support the move towards 'securitization' and 'globalization' in the international financial field. These reforms pertain to the general process of deregulation of financial systems which aims at improving their efficiency through stiffer competition and innovation. The relaxation of exchange controls, since the turn of the 1980s, in some major industrial countries – the UK (1979), Japan (1981), etc. – was also an important step in the 'globalization' process.

4. The latter also received a strong impetus from rapid changes in computer technology – hardware and software – and in telecommunications which helped to design many new financial products and to improve productivity in the financial sector.

5. Finally and in a quite different respect it must be stressed that, after 1982, banks entangled in the troubles of the debt crisis became

considered a bad risk by some large investors. The ensuing higher cost of their resources, *mutatis mutandis*, deprived them of a part of their comparative advantage against securities markets in the process of channelling funds. In other words, more investors and borrowers were induced to short-circuit the banking system and use direct finance procedures. This represented another impetus to the disintermediation process and to the development of direct finance through short-term and long-term financial assets. It also involved banks in the risk of being trapped in an adverse selection process which worsened their situation as better risks resorted to the securities markets and they were left with the poorer ones.

Some important preliminary conclusions may be drawn from this short survey of the transformations of the international financial scene during the recent years. First, the framework of competition in the international arena for the major banks from industrial countries is no longer the same as during the 1970s. Competition then occurred mainly in the limited area of the Euro-currency business. More traditional international activities and domestic business remained largely protected, essentially through foreign-exchange rules and domestic regulations. In a few countries like the United States, the United Kingdom, Belgium, and to a lesser extent France, foreign banks nevertheless partially succeeded in encroaching on some segments of activities like credit to large industrial and commercial firms. Nowadays the banking systems of the main industrial countries are much more vulnerable to direct foreign competition in many areas of domestic and international business following deregulation and the relaxation of controls on capital movements. Such a tendency could be strengthened in the EC at least by the enforcement of directives on financial and banking activities to achieve the single European market after 1992. The current round of multilateral GATT negotiations might also result in freer international trade in financial services and a consequently greater scope for direct competition between the major financial institutions of the world.

Second, during the 1970s, the expansion of international banking activities, especially through the Euro-markets, led to the emergence of overcapacity in the supply of bank intermediation services. This hypothesis has been explored through a theoretical framework[16] which can be summarized as follows. Banks are unique among financial intermediaries, as they offer their customers deposits with an insurance service attached. More precisely, the latter can be seen as consisting of two components: explicit insurance in countries with institutionalized deposit insurance schemes; implicit insurance – which includes the former – at least for the biggest banks, derived from the fact that the insurance company or the lender of last resort will never let them go bankrupt. They pay fixed premiums – whatever the riskiness of their overall portfolio – for the explicit insurance and the implicit insurance is free but has an opportunity cost related to the regulation and supervision designed to ensure the soundness of the banking system. In a framework where banks can offer two types of loans – loans in the domestic market representing an unsystematic risk, and loans in the international competitive market, which are a systematic risk – it can be shown that explicit and implicit insurance acts as a subsidy which distorts actual interest-rate margins and credit volumes from their purely competitive equilibrium values. More precisely, these subsidies create an incentive for banks to overextend themselves on the international lending scene.

Starting from identical premises, the argument can be developed along slightly different lines[17] which distinguish at the conceptual level the pure intermediary role of a bank from its insurance role. The latter, associated with the supervision of activities and the enforcement of capital requirements (indirect insurance), and with the existence of deposit insurance schemes, enable banks to reap an extra profit wholly independent of their activities as intermediaries. This extra profit can then be used to cross-subsidize other activities and so to expand preferred activities beyond the equilibrium point of a purely competitive situation, for example in the international lending area. It follows that, whereas a large part of bank activities remains justified on purely economic grounds, other ones – those benefiting from the subsidy element – will rather be developed according to purely managerial objectives. As a consequence 'the latter business may be changed very rapidly quite independently of changes in supply and demand conditions' (I. Bond and C. Briault 1983).

Finally, this assertion of overcapacity in bank intermediation services can gain further support from oligopoly theory, which stresses the build-up of overcapacity as an outcome of the international growth strategies of firms reacting to oligopolistic interdependences.

Although it may prove difficult to provide direct empirical evidence of this overcapacity hypothesis, it seems to explain accurately the behaviour of commercial banks in their LDC lending policies during the 1970s and their sudden withdrawal from this business in the aftermath of the 1982 international debt crisis, followed by their rapid redirection towards new activities such as investment banking and securities markets. Similarly agressive

153

price-cutting policies in the area of spreads and fees on medium-term Euro-credits during the late 1970s and the first half of the 1980s fit perfectly well in this framework. And it may also be asked whether the overcapacity is not already responsible for some over-shoot of activity and the associated misjudged pricing policies in many sectors of the securities and new financial product markets.

So for the years ahead, banking, at least among the major industrial countries, appears an industry impaired by overcapacity which will entail stiff competition through product differentiation or through agressive pricing in particular market segments – depending on the circumstances and the type of activity involved; rapid strategic moves by some players and, sooner or later, a restructuring at the world level alongside the growing globalization of the industry.

Developments at the domestic level

Major banks in industrialized countries are now all faced in much the same way with the consequences of the international developments outlined above. Nevertheless, their international strategies cannot afford to ignore developments in their own domestic markets precisely because the boundaries between domestic and international banking have been blurred and direct (straight?) competition between different national banking systems has been steadily growing. Such an explanation seems also all the more sustainable in the case of French banks in that the changes in the domestic financial scene during the five past years have been tremendous.

In this respect it must be stressed that the authorities which played a leading role in these developments were anxious precisely to improve the efficiency of the financial system and keep its competitiveness in line with new international standards. Although it is not our aim in this chapter to discuss this point in depth,[18] let us recall for the sake of argument the main features of this transformation. They can be summarized in five main headings:

1. Innovations with the introduction of new short-term and long-term assets: certificates of deposit; commercial paper; shares in mutual funds; the growing sophistication of existing assets, especially in the bond sector, with floating rates, zero coupons; the emergence of derivative products and their associated markets.

2. Enhanced competition between various types of financial institutions through the removal of some privileges – for example, in the field of subsidized loans – and the introduction of a new uniform Banking Act in January 1984 which encompasses a much

larger variety of institutions than the former commercial banking sector.

3. A greater role for market mechanisms in the channelling of funds and the pricing of financial assets with the introduction of new markets, like commercial paper, the indexation of loans and bond rates to various market rates, like PIBOR, and the use of auction procedures for state and public-sector agencies' borrowing.

4. New techniques for monetary policy – after the removal of credit ceilings – which relies on interest rates and open-market techniques to control monetary conditions in the economy.

5. Deregulation and modernization of the Paris stock exchange, where the former *agents de change* (stockbrokers) will have to give up their protected status by 1992 after their transformation into *sociétés de bourse*, already effective since 1 January 1988. After 1989 banks and other financial institutions – French as well as foreign – are also allowed to take stakes in or control of these newly formed companies in order to strengthen their capital resources and financial capacity. This is required by the introduction of new market-making procedures especially for Treasury securities, with the licensing of primary dealers, and the larger scope now allowed in dealing – not just broking – in shares and bonds through block trading. Moreover, futures and option markets are now available and have been diversifying their contracts since the first appeared in February 1986.

As in foreign countries and at the international level, macro-economic factors – like public-sector deficits, or larger swings around a declining trend in interest rates – have compounded the influence of rapid technological change and of institutional framework revamping to explain such a radical transformation of the financial landscape.

As a result the banks are now given the freedom to use domestic techniques and instruments which were formerly available only in some foreign financial centres. They are in a position to build up expertise in these new areas and, given a greater innovative capacity, can compete more effectively with foreign players. Following the relaxation, since May 1986, of many foreign-exchange constraints they are now able to offer a broader range of products and services from France rather than from their foreign offshoots. But at the same time the domestic market has also become more open to outside influence and competition as foreign operators have, sometimes for long, become accustomed to use the same instruments and techniques and as the foreign-exchange control can no longer play its protective role. It follows that for the years ahead international and domestic strategies will have to be carefully articulated. More important, the factors which formerly influenced the competitiveness of banks have to be reassessed in the light of all the developments briefly summarized here.

The competitiveness of financial institutions: the need for a reappraisal

In the protected and tightly regulated environment which defined many national financial systems, at least until the mid-1970s, the competitiveness of financial institutions was not really a major concern and this may explain the backward state of economic theory in this field until very recently. Moreover, earlier studies concerned with the American commercial banking system are of very little help, owing to the peculiarities of the US regulatory framework at that time. Nowadays, on the contrary, with deregulation and enhanced competition being the major features of the financial scene in many advanced countries, a clear understanding is needed of the factors actually underlying the competitiveness of the financial institutions.

1. Banks are now typically multi-product concerns which along with traditional intermediation of deposits into credits also offer a wide range of services in fields as diverse as dealing and brokerage of negotiable assets, risk management, financial engineering, custody, etc. In fact these latter services are no longer the preserve of investment or merchant banks that they traditionally used to be.

2. As a result, economies of scope may be as important as economies of scale in determining the structure of the industry. Unfortunately, empirical evidence remains as scant as it is as controversial to support these two important hypotheses. In particular the results of former American empirical studies on economies of scale must be questioned in the light of the demise of their underlying premises following the deregulation of the US financial system.

3. Notwithstanding deregulation and the growing openness of financial systems, the distinction between wholesale banking and capital-market activities on one hand and domestic retail banking on the other retains much of its validity in respect to the factors underlying competitiveness and the competitive behaviour of actors. But the latter generally undertake these types of activities, whether as universal banks or through the conglomerates which emerged in the early 1980s.

Starting with such premises in mind, a growing number of economists now agree that standard industrial economics — relying on the three pillars of market structure, behaviour, and performance —

can no longer offer the sole sustainable theoretical framework for the understanding of financial institutions' competitiveness.[19] This approach, indeed, is a short-term, static one where structure is assumed to determine performance, not vice versa, and which ignores both the effects of potential competition and the possible endogeneity of industrial structure to the activities of firms.[20] As a more fruitful alternative it is proposed to address these questions with the recent developments in contestable market (W. Baumol, J. Panzar, and R. Willig, 1982) and strategic competition theories (J. Vickers, 1985; G. Yarrow, 1985).

Potential entry is central to the idea of the contestability of a market. For potential entry actually to induce competitive behaviour by participants in an already oligopolistic market three conditions must be met: lags betwen the decision to enter a market and actual entry are short; demand responds very rapidly to changing prices, and there ar no sunk costs for entrants when they have to leave the market. As a corollary, economies of scale are no longer a barrier to entry, and potential entrants are able to enter according to 'hit and run' strategies aimed at reaping part of the excess profits in a sector. More precisely they may adopt 'cream-skimming' strategies towards the most profitable segments of activity in an industry subject to widespread cross-subsidization by multi-product firms. Finally, it seems that entry in these industries is easier for firms operating in related industries when economies of scope are important.

Although many authors argue that this theory fits quite well with current deregulated financial systems, these do not exactly fulfil the required conditions for contestable markets. In particular customer relationships and reputation, which are important features of their functioning, lower the responsiveness of demand to changes in prices.

Therefore some authors suggest taking into account some elements from recent developments in the theory of strategic competition, in order to arrive at a better understanding of the industry's dynamics. A key element in this field is the notion of firms' discretion, which is especially relevant for multi-product firms in oligopolistic markets where they earn excess profits. These can be devoted to deterring entry by potential competitors, establishing dominance in the market, or entering new markets through temporary subsidization of unprofitable activities. We have already mentioned that such a situation seemed to prevail in the banking industry, where excess profits reaped from the insurance content of deposits were responsible for the emergence of overcapacity in Euro-currency lending followed by a rapid retreat after 1982 and a redirection towards capital-market activity.

Among the ways of deterring entry by potential competitors, predatory pricing, overcapitalization, a high level of research expenditure, the setting of high wage rates in the industry, pre-emptive patenting, advertising, product differentiation, brand proliferation, and a reputation for innovation or trustworthiness are commonly cited.

After this brief summary of the main features of the seemingly most relevant framework for analysing the industrial dynamics of current financial markets and systems what are the main factors likely to influence the competitiveness of financial institutions? A subsidiary question pertains to the most suitable organizational form and to the optimal size of the successful players in the years ahead. The most obvious factors for new capital-market activities are the following.

1. Capital resources are growing in importance, for many reasons. The first relates to the regulatory requirements of the Cooke Committee in its recommendation of December 1987. More generally the importance of capital-market activities – which were not really impaired by the crash of October 1987 – and the recent evolution of some of their techniques require huge capital commit-ments on the part of successful players. The 'bought deal' on the primary bond markets, market-making with tightly priced com-missions on the secondary markets, or bridging finance in leveraged buy-outs are among the most capital-draining techniques. Moreover, capital needs are also growing to cope with fixed investment in new technologies and to hire teams of highly skilled professionals.

2. Placing power can no longer be restricted to a clientele of large institutional investors, whatever their newly acquired strength in the international field. It must also rely on a large retail investor base. Macro-economic factors, of course, play a role, since aggregate savings and the current account of balance of payments largely determine the amount of funds available for foreign invest-ment. Investors' preference for foreign diversification of their port-folio and the regulation of investments abroad – as, for example, solvency ratios for institutional investors – cannot be dismissed in this respect. There has been a clear tendency during past years towards greater international diversification by institutional investors from the main industrial countries, especially Japan, the United States, and Great Britain, etc. Simultaneously the array of financial assets directed towards such investors has been steadily enlarging, from Euro-bonds to Euro-equities, whereas government bonds are now sold and negotiated abroad through specially

designed packages. This is now the case with French Treasury bonds, which are available to foreign investors in Paris but also in New York through American depository receipts.

3. Perhaps the most important competitive edge will be derived from the capacity to innovate. Financial innovations, major as well as minor ones, have become a major weapon in a competitive process which relies more and more on diversification and growing sophistication of products and services. Process innovation not only plays a role through lowering production costs but also through locking in some customers for particular financial products and services. In such instances new processes appear as a way of circumventing some of the drawbacks associated with the fact that financial innovations – through products and services – cannot be patented. None the less the best way for innovating firms to reap profits from their innovations seems largely to derive from their ability to innovate on a regular basis and – maybe more important – from their reputation for implementing successful innovations. Moreover being the first to achieve rapidly a strong position in the market for a new product also seems important in this respect, as experience shows that although new entrants will soon be able to offer very similar products and services they often face greater difficulties in really challenging the innovator. All this explains why a growing number of financial institutions, following true industrial logic, are building up a research capacity so as to be able to generate new products and services on a regular and reliable basis. All this, of course, is expensive and brings us back to the importance of capital resources in competitiveness.

As a conclusion from the preceding paragraph it appears that whatever the new importance of capital markets and investment banking activities, traditional wholesale banking and retail banking will still play an important role for most institutions. But they can no longer be handled along the same lines as in the 1970s. The time is over when banks were essentially driven by market-share motives in a protected domestic market. They have to become more profit-oriented in a deregulated and competitive market with more sophisticated customers and with foreign competitors on their own turf. In such a context the price as well as the quality of the financial services must deserve more careful attention in the competitive process. Once again, the reputation for ability to provide high-quality products – as financial products are essentially 'experience goods', according to the Nelson distinction – is of first importance. But production at lower costs will also certainly give a more visible competitive edge than before.

It is dubious whether the branch network, domestic and

international, will play as important a role as during the 1970s. At the domestic level rationalization is already on its way through the massive introduction of electronic banking for the delivery of some elementary products and services. At the international level we need to know whether a branch network which was designed for the supply of traditional banking products and services still fits the requirements of capital-market activity and of investment banking. The latter question has two aspects. Don't capital market activities imply concentration on a few larger financial centres for reasons of liquidity and economies of scale? Isn't a wide international network necessary for a better placing power? This would certainly imply a reshaping of the existing network.

This discussion by no means exhausts every aspect, in some respects still highly controversial, of the various means of achieving a competitive edge by the successful international banks. Let us now consider the position of French banks according to these criteria. Along with those presented above, other factors of secondary importance must also be mentioned.

International strategies of French banks for the years ahead

Maybe the most striking difference between the 1970s and the years ahead lies in the fact that international expansion can no longer provide a substitute for slackening domestic growth for a protected oligopoly more concerned with growth and international ranking than with profitability. The latter will on the contrary become the benchmark of international success, especially in the single European market after 1992, whereas the relative scarcity of capital resources will certainly represent a major constraint requiring strict arbitrage between the international and domestic sectors. However, these two sides of banking activity will have to be jointly developed, since domestic strength will certainly represent a major factor in competitiveness abroad and in overall success.

Nevertheless it does not seem realistic to aim at being a universal bank in every country. More exactly, activities at home and abroad and the vehicles for undertaking them will probably have to be selected according to a logic of product lines and of customer segmentation. This will be particularly true in the single European market, where the relatively high degree of financial development of many countries will entail costly barriers to entry for newcomers.

The international position of French banks today

Recent empirical research[21] provides some enlightening information about the international activities of French banks since the mid-

1980s. Between September 1985 and December 1987 their total cross-border claims grew from US$255·4 billion to US$315·7 billion (i.e. an 11 per cent compound annual growth rate), according to the consolidated figures released to the Commission Bancaire by all the domestic banks and the foreign network of the eleven French banks most active abroad. Following the reporting standards of the Bank for International Settlements, between September 1985 and March 1988 the international claims of French banks and of their network inside the BIS reporting area (seventeen countries) rose from US$221 billion to US$377 billion, i.e. a nearly 25 per cent annual compound rate.

Therefore they could maintain their overall ranking and market share in the international banking arena: in September 1985 they held a 8·9 per cent share of all international claims of the BIS reporting banks, third after Japanese and US competitors (with 25·7 per cent and 23·4 per cent respectively) and ahead of British and German banks, with 7·3 and 6·6 per cent respectively. In March 1988 they still rank third, with a slightly reduced market share, at 8·6 per cent. The Japanese banks skyrocket at 36·8 per cent, the US ones have dropped to 14·1 per cent (the dollar – yen exchange-rate slide-down of course played an important role in widening the gap betwen their respective market shares during these two and a half years), whereas the German banks now lead the British ones, with 7·8 and 5·6 per cent shares respectively (exchange-rate movements played their role in this case too).

Other interesting features of these international activities can be gained through this data analysis, which are summarized in table 6.6. According to the statistics of the Commission Bancaire, claims in French francs grew only modestly during the period under review, from 9·3 per cent to 11·1 per cent. The dollar-denominated claims fell sharply, from 58·6 per cent to 47·2 per cent. The yen-denominated assets, benefiting most, rose from 3·4 to 8·4 per cent. It is also noticeable that, with a 4·6 per cent market share, ECU-denominated claims are now challenging Swiss franc and sterling claims.

According to the type of activity breakdown, claims on foreign banks always led their share growing from 55 per cent to 62 per cent, at the expense of non-bank customers, which retreated from 40 per cent to 36 per cent, probably as a consequence of the aftermath of the international debt crisis of the early 1980s. This is to some extent confirmed by the evolution of the geographical breakdown: claims on industrial countries rose significantly, from 62 per cent to 68·6 per cent, while those on the East European countries fell from 5 per cent to 3·9 per cent and those on the developing

Table 6.6 Breakdown of cross-border assets of French banks, 1985 and 1987 (%)

	30 September 1985	31 December 1987
Currency		
US dollar	58·6	47·2
Deutschmark	8·2	8·5
Yen	3·4	8·4
Pound sterling	4·8	5·9
Swiss franc	4·0	5·4
ECU	3·2	4·6
French franc	9·3	11·1
Other	8·5	8·9
Activity		
Commercial banks	55	62
Foreign central banks	3	2
Non-bank customers	42	36
Geographical		
Industrial countries	62	68·6
East bloc countries	5	3·9
LDCs	33	27·5
of which (% of LDC):		
Asia	18	17
Africa and Middle East	45	48
Latin and South America	36	34
Other	1	1

Notes: Foreign-currency activity with French residents is not included. Cross-border assets are those of the whole domestic banking system (including foreign banks in France) and of the foreign network of the eleven most internationally active French banks.

Source: Computations by Jean-Luc Menda, using statistical releases of the Commission Bancaire.

world from 33 per cent to 27·5 per cent. Within the latter the share of South American countries receded from 36 per cent to 34 per cent, and that of Africa and the Middle East rose from 45 per cent to 48 per cent. In conclusion to this point we can note that significant portfolio restructuring seems to be on the way among French banks, which have already managed to lower their exposure to non-bank borrowers in LDCs. This restructuring also reflects changing French international trade flows, as evidenced in table 6.7, which shows that trade with OECD countries has risen significantly during recent years. A few other details about interbank activities are also interesting: around two-thirds of them are conducted from the French domestic network and they are concentrated on banks from six countries: Japan, the United Kingdom,

Table 6.7 Geographical breakdown of French international trade, 1981–7 (%)

Region	1981	1982	1983	1984	1985	1986	1987
Exports							
EEC	52·0	52·7	53·1	52·9	53·7	57·9	60·4
Other non-EEC							
OECD countries	16·0	16·0	16·9	18·8	20·1	19·4	18·8
Other countries*	32·0	31·3	30·0	28·3	26·2	22·7	20·8
of which OPEC	*10·8*	*11·0*	*9·6*	*9·8*	*7·4*	*5·5*	*4·3*
Imports							
EEC	48·3	51·0	53·8	54·3	55·8	59·7	61·1
Other non-EEC							
OECD countries	18·0	18·1	18·1	18·4	18·9	19·9	19·9
Other countries*	33·7	30·9	28·1	27·3	25·3	20·4	19·0
of which OPEC	*18·4*	*15·9*	*12·7*	*11·5*	*9·7*	*5·5*	*4·4*

* Including French overseas territories.

Source: *Comptes de la nation, 1987*, vol. 2, Institut National de la Statistique et des Etudes Economiques, Paris, 1988.

the United States, Italy, Belgium, and Germany (in declining respective shares).

The international activities of French banks also exhibit some peculiarities, revealed by the BIS figures. In March 1988 around 62 per cent of international claims and liabilities originated from the domestic offices. For American banks the figure was only 33 per cent and for the German ones 46·5 per cent. Only the Japanese now show a similar pattern, with a 59·8 per cent share after a rapid rise from 43·5 per cent in September 1985, probably as a consequence of the deregulation of the Japanese financial system.

Finally the major foreign financial centres where French banks handle much of the rest of their international assets are essentially five: the United Kingdom (10·3 per cent), Belgium (5·4 per cent), Japan (5·2 per cent), Luxembourg (5·2 per cent), and the United States (3·6 per cent. A rough indicator of their competitive position in these important places is provided by table 6.8. The first column refers to their share of the gross international assets of all banks in these centres; the second to their share of international assets handled by the sole foreign banks (including the French ones) in these places. While they seem to have strengthened their position in international activities conducted from the other European centres, the French banks lost considerable ground in Japan, where they formerly seemed firmly established.[22]

As a general outcome of this empirical analysis the position of

Table 6.8 International assets: market share of French banks in foreign countries, 1985 and 1988 (%)

Country	September 1985 (1)	March 1988 (2)	September 1985 (1)	March 1988 (2)
UK	3·3	3·5	4·1	4·2
USA	2·4	3·1	5·2	5·8
Japan	4·0	1·9	35·5	26·8
Luxembourg	7·6	8·8	8·2	9·6
Belgium	10·7	9·7	16·5	16·9
Germany	1·7	2·4	8·2	12·3
Switzerland	4·2	4·5	13·7	16·2

Notes: (1) Share of gross international assets. (2) Share of international assets held by foreign banks.
Source: Jean-Luc Menda, op. cit.

French banks is rather paradoxical. Not so much that, with the third most extensive foreign network, they control a rather modest share of international banking assets: after all, British banks are in a rather similar position and the paradox in this instance may come from the Japanese, with undisputed first place for the international assets, around a third of the total, despite a still limited foreign network. In fact the question that may be raised for French banks pertains to the volume of business of the major part of this foreign network: it carries only around 40 per cent of total international activities, and five host countries alone account for about 30 per cent, with only sixty-four branches[23] and twenty subsidiaries (at the end of 1987). An explanation may be that this foreign network is quite deeply involved in the domestic activity of its host countries. Unfortunately, empirical evidence is still too scant to sustain such a hypothesis.[24] A more realistic explanation may be that during the 1970s and early '80s French banks were eager only to set up maximum international coverage at a rapid pace. Nowadays many branches show a poor record as they are too new or in already over-banked markets to generate a sufficient volume of business.

Competitive strengths and weaknesses of French banks

Quite apart from the already mentioned low profitability (after 1982) of the network, it is now questioned whether a dense inter-national presence yields 'network externalities' (in activities such as correspondent banking, financial services to multinational cor-porations, ancillary services linked with financing international trade). Moreover this network was originally designed to meet the requirements of traditional commercial banking at a time when deposit intermediation for granting loans was the dominant activity of multinational banks.

Foreign networks

As shown in section two, capital-market activities now represent a major and dynamic business area and are here to stay in the foreseeable future, although they will not crowdout traditional banking. So French banks (like many of their foreign competitors) are faced with the necessity of redesigning their foreign network so as to be able to participate fully and competitively in these new activities. Many bankers agree that it will be a long and difficult haul before branches formerly involved in ordinary international banking services are transformed into successful capital-market units. And it seems that capital-market activities, by their nature, by the way they are handled – through computerized systems and information networks – and by the liquidity requirements of assets, need to be concentrated in a limited number of financial centres. It implies that the international network does not need the same type of coverage as before. Does this mean that French banks will have to cut back their foreign branch network? Although the latter has not grown since 1984 and some restructuring of its geographical coverage has already occurred, it does not seem that they will behave in this instance in the same way as American banks (for example) have recently done. It is quite commonly agreed that a new network of subsidiaries for undertaking capital-market activities has to be set up to supplement the former commercial banking network. This will be costly, as many capital-market activities such as market-making of their nature require strong capital backing. The need to comply with the Cooke ratio by 1992 will also reinforce the already noticeable tendency in the foreign investment of French banks towards capital endowments for specialist subsidiaries in these new fields of activity.

As the international financial scene is far from being stabilized as regards the respective roles and importance of the major financial centres of the world, it is still difficult to ascertain whether the major French banks can yet rely on a network tailored to compete efficiently and successfully in the securities and investment banking business. Nevertheless as New York, London, and Tokyo at least already appear as the main anchors of the emerging global financial services industry it may be of some interest to look at the involvement of French banks in capital-market activities in these places. After some deregulation foreign competitors were indeed allowed to start fully fledged capital-market subsidiaries or to buy existing ones.

Moreover, capital-market activities are now global, and following the transformation of the Paris stock exchange to bring it into line with its rivals we must also consider the French banks' capacity in their own domestic market. As evidenced by table 6.9 they are already active in the four financial centres through quite well established vehicles which sometimes own foreign subsidiaries or agencies. It should be stressed here that strategies to enter the securities and investment banking business differed among banks and according to the host country. In Paris they all bought existing stockbroking firms. In London, where the perspective of the 'big bang' had also provided an opportunity to participate in existing domestic firms, they all took route to the stockbroking business and the gilts market, to raise their placing ability and customer base rapidly.[25] But whereas two banks (Paribas and BNP) took the option of transferring the bulk of their other capital-market business to London by starting powerful subsidiaries from scratch in the City, the other four considered that the new financial scene in Paris offered sufficient opportunities to maintain there the major part of business. As mentioned in the previous sections the sophistication in techniques and instruments available in Paris is now often as high as in the other major financial centres. Moreover the liquidity of the secondary markets for the new instruments has generally reached satisfactory levels, although it may sometimes seem costly to ensure for some market-makers and may as such appear precarious.[26] Some banks clearly intend to enlarge the capacity of the French stockbroking firms in which they have invested towards investment banking services and to develop the synergies with their capital-market divisions at their Paris headquarters.

More generally, strategies seem to differ among them as regards their commitment to these four financial centres and their activities there. For example, in Tokyo three of them own licensed securities houses and among the latter the subsidiaries of Indosuez and Société Générale already belong to the restricted circle of foreign members of the Kabuto-cho. According to statistics released by the Tokyo stock exchange, W.I. Carr, a subsidiary of Indosuez, ranked sixth, with a 6 per cent market share in equity trading in the last two months of 1988, among its twenty-two members. As such it appeared a rather strong competitor while Sogen was lagging far behind. This, of course, reflects the fact that W.I. Carr has long had a presence in the Pacific region while Sogen has only recently been established. Moreover Indosuez is also strong in the futures and currency options industry and aims at strengthening synergies in capital-market activities all over the ASEAN area.

Table 6.9 Subsidiaries of the major French banks in capital-market activities (end 1987)

Bank	London	New York	Tokyo	Paris
BNP	BNP Capital Markets Ark Securities[a]	BNP-IFS New York[b]	Securities house	du Bouzet[c]
Crédit Lyonnais	Alexander Laing & Cruikshank[d] Astaire[c]	GL Global Partners	Securities house with ALCH	Cholet-Dupont[c]
Société Générale	SG Merchant Bank Strauss Turnbull[c]	Sogen Securities	Sogen Securities Pacific[e]	Delahaye-Ripault[c]
Crédit Commercial	Laurence Prust[c,h]			Wolff-Goirand[c]
Indosuez	W.I. Carr[c,f]	W.I. Carr[c]	W.I. Carr[c,e]	Chevreux-de Virieu[c]
Paribas	Paribas Capital Markets Quilter Goodison[c]		Securities house[g]	Courcoux-Bouvet[c]

[a] Securities house.
[b] BNP International Services has subsidiaries in Singapore and Hong Kong.
[c] Stockbroker.
[d] ALCH Ltd is also established in Hong Kong, Singapore, Japan, and Australia. It is licensed as a primary dealer in gilts in London.
[e] Member of the Tokyo stock exchange.
[f] W.I. Carr is also present in Hong Kong, Malaysia, Korea, and Taiwan.
[g] This securities house is also present in Sydney.
[h] Laurence Prust has recently developed a significant investment banking capacity.

Source: Annual reports of the banks for the year 1987.

In New York, where Paribas sold its Wall Street investment bank, A.G. Becker, in 1984, Crédit Lyonnais decided on the contrary to leave its joint operation in Europartners and start its own securities business arm, CL Global Partners, in March 1988. The latter soon originated the new sector of American depository receipts in French Treasury bonds in September 1988.

It is, of course, debatable whether this network – with outposts in Hong Kong, Singapore, Sidney, or Chicago – is by itself a sufficient cushion for successfully operating in capital-markets activities. Strong capital backing and innovative capacity are certainly as important as good placing power through a large individual and institutional customer base. This is all the more true in that entry costs are generally high and initial losses common for many participants, who may quickly be forced to give up. Only long-term backing on the part of the parent bank may overcome these initial starting-up difficulties. The problem of capital resources stands out as a major one for all French banks –although in varying degrees – and as it does not pertain only to the backing of capital-market activities we shall discuss it later in more depth.

Placing power and customer base

Although information about the placing power and the customer base are scant because banks do not disclose the clientele connections on which they rely, two fields of activity provide good indicators of the strength of an institution in this area as well as of its underwriting capacity in the international bond and international equity markets. As a general point, it is no wonder that both the latter had been dominated for so long by the Swiss and German universal banks, which recently gave up their leading position to the four most powerful Japanese securities houses. In such a context how did the French banks perform?

Tables 6.10 and 6.11 provide information about their ranking and market share in the overall Euro-bond market as well as their performance in some of its sub-sectors since 1984. Except for Indosuez – which does not seem much concerned with this business area – the five other major banks continued to perform as satisfactorily as during the 1970s and early '80s, with Paribas showing by far the best and most regular record at around tenth place, with a market share of the global volume of issuing business near 3 per cent, far ahead of the 'big three'. It should be recalled here, however, that the market shares of the leaders (Crédit Suisse First Boston until 1987 and Nomura thereafter) stayed in the range 11–13 per cent, far ahead of their nearest followers (around 5·5–7·5 per cent).

Looking at particular sectors of this market, the situation reveals

Table 6.10 French banks as book runners in the overall Euro-bond market, 1984−8

Bank	1984 (1)	(2)	1985 (1)	(2)	1986 (1)	(2)	1987 (1)	(2)	1988 (1)	(2)
BNP	10	2·2	26	1·4	25	1·16	45	0·39	47	0·28
Crédit Lyonnais	32	0·8	31	0·3	36	0·55	46	0·38	32	0·69
Société Générale	14	1·6	21	1·5	15	1·72	28	0·77	29	0·82
Crédit Commercial	30	0·9	23	2·2	26	1·03	27	0·79	26	1·05
Indosuez	>50		>50		>50		>50		>60	
Paribas	12	1·9	10	2·5	8	3·8	12	2·65	11	3·20

Notes: (1) Rank. (2) Market share (%).

Source: *International Financing Review*, 7 January 1989 (for the year 1988); *Euromoney*, annual financing reports (for the other years), March issues.

far more contrasts. In areas such as floating-rate notes (which were so buoyant in 1984−6) three French banks fared rather well. The same is true of the US dollar Euro-bond sector. But the French position is especially strong in the ECU bond sector, where four banks (Paribas, BNP, Société Générale, and Crédit Lyonnais) have always ranked among the top ten book runners.[27] Paribas stands out as the undisputed leader, with a market share since 1985 in the range of 18−20 per cent after a peak of 35 per cent in 1986.[28] In 1988, however, German, Swiss, and American challengers stepped into the league table to break up the leading French group, with Paribas still in first position (with 19·6 per cent) but all the others coming only after seventh rank. And the Japanese securities houses are also showing some interest in this sector.

According to a regulation much criticized by foreign banks, they still retain the monopoly of the French franc sector whose CCF stands ahead of its four French rivals, with a market share above 40 per cent since 1986. Finally, a few banks seem at times to have developed a special expertise in some specific field: Société Générale in the Canadian dollar sector (and more recently in the New Zealand dollar sector), Paribas in Swiss franc issues.

Since 1985 international equity primary markets have reached some maturity and are expected to develop further after their slow recovery from the 1987 October crash. Paribas was the only one to enter the league table of the twenty most active leading and co-leading managers as early as 1985: it then already stood in seventh place with a 4·5 per cent market share. In 1986 it performed still better, in fourth place, whereas BNP entered the league table at fifteenth (fifth when lead managers only are considered). This of

Table 6.11 French banks as book runners in specialist sectors of the Euro-bond market, 1984–8 (rank in brackets)

Sector	1984	1985	1986	1987	1988
Floating-rate notes	CCF (16) Société Générale (25)	CCF (15) Société Générale (18) Paribas (19)	Paribas (5) Société Générale (9)	n.a.	n.a.
of which Banks' FRNs	Société Générale (9) CCF (15)	Société Générale (10) CCF (14)	Société Générale (5)	n.a.	n.a.
ECU Euro-bonds	BNP (3) Crédit Lyonnais (4) CCF (5) Paribas (6) Société Générale (11)	BNP (2) Crédit Lyonnais (4) CCF (7) Paribas (1) Société Générale (10)	BNP (2) Société Générale (3) Crédit Lyonnais (6) Paribas (1)	Crédit Lyonnais (3) Société Générale (8) CCF (9) Paribas (1)	CCF (8) Crédit Lyonnais (9) Société Générale (10) Paribas (1)
French franc Euro-bonds		CCF (1) BNP (2) Société Générale (3) Crédit Lyonnais (4) Lazard (5)	CCF (1) BNP (2) Société Générale (3) Paribas (4) Crédit Lyonnais (5)	CCF (1) BNP (2) Indosuez (3) Société Générale (4) Lazard (5)	CCF (1) Crédit Lyonnais (2) Société Générale (3) BNP (4) Paribas (5)
US$ Euro-bonds	Paribas (10) Société Générale (12)	Paribas (16) Société Générale (17)	Paribas (12) Société Générale (18)	Paribas (14)	n.a.

n.a.: Not available.

Source: 1984–7: *Euromoney*, annual financing report, March issues. 1988–9: *International Financing Review*, various issues.

course is partly attributable to the French government's denationalization drive. In 1987 Paribas was still in eleventh place, with Indosuez being ranked eighteenth and Crédit Commercial de France twentieth. It remains to be seen whether the French banks have managed to build a sufficiently strong capability in this area to overcome the drawbacks of the end of the privatization process in France after May 1988.

After a receding phase in the aftermath of the 1982 international debt crisis, the syndicated Euro-loan market retrieved some growth potential through innovative devices such as note issuance facilities and fungible or Euro-commercial paper programmes, for which they provide the backing facilities. This has been particularly clear since 1987.

The positions in the league tables of lead and co-lead managers now bear a quite different meaning from the 1970s: activity may be driven by the ability to win borrowers' mandates as well as by underwriting capacity and placing power for the Euro-notes. Since 1984 Société Générale, Paribas, BNP, and Crédit Lyonnais have regularly found their way into the group of the first fifty lead managers, as summarized in table 6.12.

Table 6.12 Ranking of French banks as lead managers of syndicated Euro-loans, 1984–8

Bank	1984	1985	1986	1987	1988
BNP	24	38	19	34	24
Crédit Lyonnais	37	39	29	24	13
Paribas	22	29	27	38	41
Société Générale	69	22	26	46	15

Source: *Euromoney*, annual financing report, March issues. For 1988, *International Financing Review*, 7 January 1989.

Note issuance facilities, which once appeared a major innovation in international capital markets, have recently been displaced by much more sophisticated techniques such as multi-option facilities, which draw on sharper skills than plain 'vanilla' loans. In this new area, largely dominated by the British clearers, which are able to outperform their American rivals, French banks have already established a respectable position: Crédit Commercial de France, Crédit Lyonnais, Banque Nationale de Paris and Société Générale were among the twenty-five top MOF managers in both 1986 and 1987, as evidenced in table 6.13.

Further insight into the innovative capacity as well as into the customer base and placing power of French banks can, finally, be

Table 6.13 Ranking of French banks as arrangers of multi-option facilities, 1986−7

Bank	1986	1987
BNP	17	21
Crédit Lyonnais	25	18
Société Générale	13	23
Crédit Commercial	23	17

Source: Euromoney, op. cit.

derived from their performance in the areas of Euro-commercial paper, Euro-certificates of deposit and medium-term notes, which are now among the most commonly used marketable instruments in international capital markets. In the fast-growing sector of Euro-commercial paper only Société Générale appears, at twenty-ninth and thirtieth places in 1987, in the league tables of top arrangers and top dealers respectively, which are largely dominated by the most powerful Wall Street firms, the US commercial banks, and the British clearers − both through their investment banking subsidiaries − and some London merchant banks. Société Générale was also the sole French bank to appear in the league table of twenty top dealers in medium-term notes, ranking seventeenth for the year 1987. But in retrospective rankings from the origins of this recent market it does not appear among the first twenty.

Finally, French banks are also involved in the funding of corporate acquisitions through syndicated loans, which exploded after the equity market crash of October 1987 to reach US$88 billion in 1988. In this new and until now very 'juicy' − but high-risk − business area, US commercial banks are the undisputed leaders as deal arrangers, largely because they reap the benefit of their very large customer base. Nevertheless Crédit Lyonnais found its way to fifteenth place in the ranks of top arrangers in 1988. As participants committing funds in these financing techniques Société Générale ranked first, Crédit Lyonnais fourth, and BNP twentieth. It must also be stressed that some of them are now promoting similar activities in the French domestic market.[29] So they are gaining valuable experience which may prove especially rewarding with the opportunities in corporate restructuring entailed by the prospect of the single European market.

Interest-rate and currency swaps are now a necessary complement to arranging deals in the Euro-bond and Euro-note markets. Although many of them are standardized, some require very expert skills. There are currently many players in the field but only a few have achieved a strong position and a reputation for expertise. French banks, of course, are present in this area but only Paribas seems to have reached any prominence in the world league table, claiming a volume of business amounting to US$10 billion in 1985, US$20 billion in 1986, and US$34 billion in 1987. In 1986 it ranked between tenth and fifteenth in a league table based on new contract volumes for the year – where the first ten were all American.

To conclude, French banks are often among the major players in many sectors of international capital markets. Nevertheless they never manage to outperform such powerful players as the Swiss and German universal banks, the Japanese securities houses, or American investment and commercial banks. Maybe this is a consequence of their lack of strong specificity as regards the intangible assets which are responsible for the comparative advantage required today of any bank aiming to be among the leading contenders in these fields. Unlike their competitors, which had for long been strongly endowed in one or other of these assets – placing power in the case of the Swiss and German banks and Japanese securities houses, investment banking and securities business expertise in the case of some American and British houses – French banks very often had to build such a capability, especially in the wake of the deregulation of the financial system after 1983. However, the statistics presented above are too broad in scope to give an accurate assessment of their true competitive position and performance. As markets become more and more segmented banks are looking for niche strategies, which seem to be more profitable for those able to be first in a field and to rapidly build a strong expertise and reputation in it. Unfortunately there cannot be statistical releases on all such niche activities. But evidence available in certain segments of the Euro-bond markets – as for the ECU and French franc sectors – suggests that French banks are sometimes able to perform very well when following such a niche approach.[30]

Capital ratios

For many years French commercial banks have been criticized by their foreign competitors for their lower capital ratios. The latter were partly a consequence of their high proportion of interbank activities, especially at the international level. Moreover at times when there were as yet no commonly agreed standards for measuring those ratios the question of their level remained largely disputable. This is no longer true, with the guidelines issued by the Cooke Committee in 1988, which are to be enforced in 1992 and then applied to all the international banks.

Banking in France

Before looking at the position of French banks confronted with the Cooke ratio issue let us discuss their actual situation during recent years. Table 6.14 depicts the evolution between 1983 and 1987 of the capital ratios according to two different definitions. During these five years, notwithstanding the pressures on their profitability,[31] the banks managed to strengthen the structure of their balance sheets. This was all the more necessary in that in 1985 they were lagging behind most of their competitors and their position had been worsening between 1981 and 1985, as evidenced in table 6.15.

Table 6.14 Capital resources and ratios: year end, 1983−7 (billion frs.)

Resources	1983	1984	1985	1986	1987
A = Capital + Reserves + General provisions	99·6	127·0	143·4	186·1	205·9
B = Capital + Reserves	60·9	69·5	80·4	104·2	119·9
Total balance sheet	3,292·5	3,737·4	4,039·1	4,238·4	4,628·3
Ratios (%)					
A/Total balance sheet	3·02	3·24	3·55	4·39	4·45
B/Total balance sheet	1·85	1·86	1·99	2·46	2·59

Source: Association Française des Banques, Annual Report, 1987.

Table 6.15 Capital ratios of banks in industrialized countries: internal funds, 1981 and 1985 (%)

Country	1981 Internal funds		1985 Internal funds	
	Total assets	Partial assets	Total assets	Partial assets
France	2·21	3·72	1·91	3·20
Germany	3·99	5·54	4·42	5·98
Italy	2·50	2·70	3·57	3·99
Japan	1·91	2·35	1·95	2·41
Netherlands	3·15	4·61	3·74	5·32
Spain	9·66	10·27	8·86	9·64
Switzerland	5·78	7·81	5·90	8·25
UK*	5·66	7·70	3·62	4·74
USA	4·63	5·24	5·35	5·77

Notes: Internal funds: capital + reserves. Partial assets: total assets − interbank assets.
* Consolidated figures, including subsidiaries.

Source: Computed from OECD data, Association Française des Banques, Annual Report, 1986.

As underlined in the 1986 annual report of the French Bankers' Association, such comparisons do not weight the relative riskiness of the different types of assets – a drawback which the Cooke ratio tries to overcome – and overlook their provision for doubtful assets on indebted countries. Such controversial points need all the more to be resolved in so far as the rating of international banks and the ensuing cost of their funds borrowed on the international capital market depends on their situation in this respect. More generally it has also been argued that the poor quality of some cross-border assets on the balance sheets of major multinational banks was responsible for their loss of comparative advantage in the international channelling of savings into investment and for the ensuing rise of the assets markets. The latter soon compelled them to engage in assetless banking to regain some of their former business and profits through fee earnings. This may explain why they are now all trying hard to clear their balance sheets of these poor assets through higher provisions before taking their losses. In this field French banks early adopted a very cautious stance and took the opportunity of favourable tax treatment to raise their provisions for sovereign risks to levels which are among the highest in the industrialized countries, as shown in table 6.16.

Table 6.16 Provisions against doubtful assets: comparative evolution, 1981–5 (%)

Country	1981		1985	
	Total assets	Partial assets	Total assets	Partial assets
France	0·68	1·14	0·66	1·10
Germany	0·49	0·68	0·33	0·45
Italy	2·55	2·75	0·42	0·45
Japan	0·02	0·02	0·01	0·01
Netherlands	0·80	1·17	0·36	0·51
Spain	1·02	1·08	1·06	1·15
Switzerland	0·32	0·43	0·52	0·73
UK	0·37	0·50	0·75	0·98
USA	0·26	0·29	0·65	0·70

Source: Computed from OECD data, Association Française des Banques, Annual Report, 1986.

The individual situations of the major banks for 1987 look even more favourable. According to their 1987 accounts statements, provision for doubtful assets in their portfolios of sovereign lending looked as follows:[32]

175

BNP	50%	CCF	46%
Crédit Lyonnais	43%	Indosuez	32%
Société Générale	50%	Paribas	39·5%

This remains above the average of most of their foreign competitors, even after the heavy provisions of American and British banks in 1987.

So, whatever the outcome of the international debt problem, the major French banks, which have frankly retreated from sovereign lending – except for funds committed in debt rescheduling agreements – will not have to divert high provisions from their operating results. Such provisions make them look even more in line with their international competitors when considering the larger concept of free equity rather than shareholders' funds alone. However, the only reliable benchmark in this field will be the Cooke ratio, which sets common international definitions for the diverse components of capital and commonly agreed minimum weights to be attached to balance-sheet and off-balance-sheet activities.

Despite the qualification of general provisions as supplementary capital – which cannot exceed 50 per cent of total capital – French banks still have quite a long way to go to meet the 7·25 per cent risk-weighted capital ratio required in March 1991 before it is raised to the target level of 8 per cent in March 1993. It is, of course, difficult to know precisely how far from the target they actually stand. Only BNP has disclosed, in its 1987 annual report, that it already meets the required 1992 ratio. The only sure thing is that they will all need to raise capital, be it of the first or of the second-tier category. Recently BNP suddenly withdrew a US$500 million offering of subordinated perpetual FRNs intended to raise its capital resources, as it was no longer sure that they could qualify as first-tier capital. In October 1988 Crédit Lyonnais had already raised US$350 million through a similar structure. A more general problem nevertheless arises from the fact that two major international French banks are still state-owned: all depends on the willingness and ability of the State to play its shareholder role at a time when banks will certainly have to attract capital resources far beyond the Cooke ratio requirements to finance their internal and external growth in the wake of the emergence of the European single market.

The single European market: what kind of challenge for French banks?

The financial services industry is expected to be one of the fields most affected by the advent of the single European market. Lower prices for financial services, a broader array of services available to customers, and significant structural changes in the production and distribution aspects of the industry will be the most likely outcome.

Following the approval in June 1985 of the EC White Paper which proposed around 300 measures to unify the European market, in 1987 the Single European Act was passed by the national parliaments, which laid down the founding principles of the single European market: (1) mutual recognition of respective national regulations, rather than trying to unify national regulations and procedures along the lines of common EC-wide standards too difficult to reach; (2) qualified majority decisions for approval of Commission proposals by the Council, except in some particularly sensitive fields such as the hamonization of taxation.

In the financal sector, the Commission has already drafted and circulated in early 1988 its second banking directive (the first one dated back to 1977), which, according to the general framework of the Single Act, will create a single banking licence enabling banks from whichever EC country freely to open branches and provide services across frontiers throughout the Community without prior approval from the host countries. Moreover, banks will be allowed to carry on abroad any of a wide-ranging list of activities as long as they already perform them in their home country. The list is wide enough in scope – in particular, it includes securities business – to provide for the possibility of universal banking, which might so become the European standard.

On the regulatory and supervisory front, banks will mainly be regulated and supervised from their home country, which implicitly means that the Commission has opted for the idea that competition between respective national jurisdictions may be the best and most rapid way to achieve a unified European regulatory framework. The Commission is aware that such a process might entail an uncontrollable deregulatory drive likely to threaten the stability of the financial system. So the directive also provides for some minimal harmonized regulatory requirements, especially in the fields of capital adequacy and failure liquidation. Capital adequacy standards will largely fit the international framework recently phased out by the Cooke Committee in Basle.

The directive also considers the very important question of the European policy to be adopted towards non-EC financial firms which may look to EC-wide operation from an initial foothold in the least regulated EC country. This raises the important issue of reciprocity for banks from the EC, which may not always be allowed to set up shop in some foreign countries. On this point divergences may also arise between EC countries themselves, some of them being likely to look to bilateral rather than European agreement. The United Kingdom is especially concerned about this latter point.

Other directives have already been adopted in specific fields such as consumer credit, mortgage credit, and securities business which are of great interest for banks in some European countries.

Before examining the response of the French banks to the prospect of the single European market and their likely European strategies, it is necessary to discuss in more general terms the potential impact of such a deep institutional change on the actual activity of banks in the European Community.

The single European market in banking services: what are the actual prospects?

Banking is not a homogeneous activity. Today a distinction is to be drawn between wholesale banking, capital-market activities, and retail banking. These three areas will not all be affected in the same way by the advent of the single European market.

Wholesale banking – with large multinational corporations and financial institutions – has for long been a truly international and competitive activity, as it has mainly been conducted through the Euro-currency markets. It is therefore questionable whether the single European market will induce significant changes in this area.

Capital-market activities appear to be the sector with greatest potential in the wake of the securitization and globalization processes which are driven by international forces even more powerful than the perspective of the single European market itself. Without waiting for the directives of the EC Commission, major players in this field have already made pre-emptive strategic moves alongside the deregulation process in countries like the United Kingdom (with 'Big Bang') France, The Netherlands, Italy, Spain, or Germany. The main question relates to the respective roles and importance of the major financial centres of Europe and especially London as compared with some Continental centres (Paris, Frankfurt, Switzerland, Amsterdam). We mentioned in the previous section that French banks had established significant footholds in London while investing in Paris stockbroking houses along the same lines as some of their most powerful foreign competitors like Morgan Guaranty, S.G. Warburg, or Barclays.

As much depends on broking and market-making capacity as on the ability to provide the related investment banking services or the institutional savings products – through vehicles like UCITSs, now also covered by recent EC directives. Successful players will have to be able to combine these segments of activity efficiently. An early lesson to be learned from the immediate aftermath of the 'Big Bang' is that establishing a stockbroking and dealing business is not a sufficient condition for profitable operation in capital-market activities. After the initial massive entry in the newly deregulated markets which we have been witnessing, major restructuring has begun to occur.

Finally, *retail banking* appears the only field where the impact of the single European single market is likely to be greatest while still the most difficult to assess. Some preliminary questions must be tackled before outlining possible outcomes.

First, retail banking encompasses many segments of activity, some of which are rather specialized and are also sometimes covered to a large extent by non-banking institutions – mortgage credit and consumer credit, for example.

Second, recent technological advances now allow new distribution facilities for financial products and services, for example through home banking. In recent years we have witnessed a reorganization of the production and distribution of financial services with the entry of insurance companies and of retail chain stores on the traditional turf of banks. This is an all the more important issue in that the single European market will allow freedom of provision of financial services across frontiers.

More generally, as evidenced by banks' internationalization during the last twenty years, two main alternative strategies have been used to enter the retail banking sector, depending on the characteristics of the host country market such as its growth potential, the sophistication of its financial techniques, its degree of protection. In advanced countries such as those of the European Community a selective approach may prove more suitable than looking for overall 'downstreet' banking in a host country. It must none the less be underlined here that EC countries are far from homogeneous in this respect. In broad terms, northern countries appear more sophisticated, open, and competitive, and their market growth potential looks rather poor – as they are often already overbanked except in some specialist fields. Southern countries, on the contrary, are more protected, less competitive, and offer brighter growth prospects. Considering moreover the absolute size of the respective markets and their arbitrage potential (defined as the efficiency gains likely to be reaped when entering less competitive markets) it seems that the degree of attractiveness of the individual countries varies to a broad extent. Spain often appears the most attractive market, with Italy and France also ranking high. But owing to their overall absolute size the German and British markets are also favourably considered, while Denmark, Portugal, Greece, and Ireland look unattractive.[33]

In advanced economies, entering the overall retail banking market in a foreign country entails high entry costs, as the only strategy likely to be successful is the acquisition of an established institution. But it should be recalled here that whatever their 'European outlook', governments will certainly bar any foreign attempt to take over a major national bank. So only small or medium-size institutions, especially those with a selected customer base – such as wealthy individuals or medium-range companies – remain potential targets. Banks which choose a selective approach, looking for segments such as mortgage or consumer credit, leasing, placement advice, etc., can also try to acquire established foreign concerns as the most rapid way of overcoming barriers to entry. In some instances they may prefer to start up their own subsidiaries from scratch.

It is, finally, difficult to assess the strategies which will actually be followed and their effects on the structure of the banking industry in the European Community. However, there are already some indications concerning French banks' behaviour.

French banks' attitudes to the single European market

In general, protecting market share and profitability at home are certainly as important as trying to establish profitable operations in other EC countries.

In the field of investment banking services, except for Paribas and (on a much smaller scale) Crédit Commercial de France – through the strengthening of the capacity of its subsidiary Laurence Prust in London – French banks which had no real tradition in this area seem to lag behind the British merchant banks and the Wall Street houses. These have already set up shop in the main European financial centres to reap the benefit of the opportunities in such fields as bond or equity fund raising, or as mergers and acquisitions, which are likely to see their growth boosted after the advent of the single market and the industrial restructuring it may induce. More important, foreigners are already established in Paris, and defending the domestic market appears a first priority.

We have mentioned that the French retail banking market was ranked as attractive by foreign institutions. Looking more especially at the competitive strengths and weaknesses of French banks, one of the major problems they have to overcome lies in their overall cost level and structure. Research by P. Szymczak (1987) shows that the major banks occupy a mean position in terms

180

of the ratio of operating costs to total assets net of interbank claims when compared with their competitors in the main industrial countries, especially Britain and Germany. Their ratio of interest margin to these partial assets remains in roughly the same position. Another international comparison released by the French Bankers' Association[34] for the years 1986–7 also looks reasonably satisfactory. Last, the individual situations of the leading banks compare favourably, in terms of their return on assets, with the twenty other top European banks, including the Swiss ones. Paribas performs as well as the leader, Crédit Suisse, with a 0·53 per cent ratio. Société Générale ranks ninth (0·34 per cent), BNP tenth (0·32 per cent), and Crédit Lyonnais twelfth (0·27 per cent).[35]

Nevertheless, when looking at some tendencies, such as the trend of operating costs related to total income, the picture does not look so bright. For example, whereas between 1981 and 1985 the British clearing banks managed to reduce this ratio from 72 to 66 per cent, French banks saw the figure stay at 68 per cent.[36] Furthermore, French banks are burdened by the cost of operating the payments system free of charge and by some specific taxes, some of which, however, are soon to be removed. Perhaps the most important problem lies in the mixture of their revenue sources: despite their rapid growth, commissions from service activities still – according to the standards of major international banks – contribute too little of their operating income.[37] This is closely related to the more general problem of the structure of their costs and their pricing policies. Insufficient knowledge of the former and too much cross-subsidization of markets and activities need to be rapidly corrected in order to remove the threat of foreign entrants looking only for the most lucrative segments of activity in the domestic market.

Capital resources will undoubtedly represent the major constraint on the European strategies of French banks. While it seems that even the largest ones cannot afford a universal-bank approach to the European market, the question is which segments of activity and which vehicles to choose. Some activities need more capital backing than others, and in a given activity the entry ticket varies greatly as between countries. Whatever their routes to the European market, French banks will have to raise more capital, not to mention the necessity to strengthen the capital structure of the privatized banks if foreign take-over attempts are to be avoided.

Considering now their actual presence on the European scene, the picture does not seem so bad. Table 6.17 shows that foreign direct investment by French banks roughly doubled in 1987, compared with the annual trend of the previous years, to reach 13,407 million frs. Looking at its geographical breakdown, the

Table 6.17 Direct investment of French banks abroad and of foreign banks in France: annual gross (G) and net (N) flows, 1984–7 (million frs.)

Country	French banks abroad								Foreign banks in France							
	1984		1985		1986		1987		1984		1985		1986		1987	
	G	N	G	N	G	N	G	N	G	N	G	N	G	N	G	N
OECD	4,835	4,454	3,305	2,631	4,685	3,664	11,656	10,456	3,200	2,905	2,424	2,063	4,362	4,067	6,965	5,061
USA	1,480	1,245	1,293	1,122	344	316	1,288	1,097	632	534	386	373	396	389	393	392
Japan	1	1	1	1	3	–4	32	31	185	185	0	0	315	315	323	323
Switzerland	1,295	1,271	70	–5	678	609	895	396	163	148	188	144	752	710	535	461
EEC	1,822	1,716	1,408	1,008	2,880	2,054	9,043	8,590	2,039	1,865	1,802	1,516	2,858	2,677	5,571	3,787
Belgium–Luxembourg	303	231	312	177	606	564	579	470	351	320	520	373	691	587	1,213	936
Germany	167	163	89	80	397	84	106	103	283	154	311	240	19	14	120	114
Italy	176	176	80	–2	514	317	819	622	534	534	102	94	942	942	744	744
Netherlands	967	951	134	130	321	274	3,821	3,754	751	751	644	604	443	398	1,835	772
Spain	104	104	60	60	202	30	561	558	0	0	16	16	56	56	89	89
UK	135	122	383	216	784	729	2,806	2,769	50	36	212	193	693	687	1,569	1,135
Total	5,485	4,956	4,581	3,722	6,315	4,864	13,407	11,580	3,473	3,178	3,118	2,695	4,815	4,479	7,931	6,005

Note: Figures do not include direct investment financed through reinvested earnings and foreign borrowings.

Source: Ministry of Finance, Treasury Department, Paris.

European Community is responsible for this burst of activity, its share standing at two-thirds of the total figure, whereas it always stayed between 35 and 45 per cent before. More precisely, two countries were the recipients of the bulk of these investments: the United Kingdom, where French banks completed their acquisitions of brokers and capital-market subsidiaries after Big Bang, and The Netherlands, where the figure was temporarily boosted by the acquisition of a local bank by Crédit Lyonnais. But Italy and Spain also appear as new targets, as some French banks – Compagnie Bancaire, or Société Générale, for example – want to take advantage of their growth potential. Table 6.17 also shows that other EC countries banks' have also been strengthening their presence in France since 1986, especially British, Italian, Dutch, and Belgian ones. The British in particular made significant acquisitions of stock exchange brokers after the deregulation of the Paris Bourse.

Looking at some individual situations, Paribas has long had a strong presence in the Benelux countries and Switzerland, Société Générale in Germany, Switzerland, and Luxembourg through Sogenal, Crédit Lyonnais in Spain and more recently in The Netherlands, where it merged its two acquisitions – Slavensburg and Nederlandse Crediet – to form the sixth bank in that country. BNP acquired a Spanish bank some years ago – which has now been reshuffled – and is looking to specialist segments in other countries, such as mortgage lending in the UK, where it has bought a mortgage subsidiary from Chemical Bank. Compagnie Bancaire and Crédit Agricole had already made such moves in the British mortgage banking market, which is of great interest, owing to the sophistication of its techniques. In some instances Société Générale is also looking for specialist fields, especially leasing, where it now appears to be the world leader while retaining second position in the European market. Indosuez is also strongly committed to the European single market: apart from the take-over of the Société Générale de Belgique by its parent company, Compagnie Financière de Suez, Indosuez is the sole French bank to have set up in the whole of Scandinavia, expecting that the latter will certainly benefit from the advent of the European single market. It is also very interested in capital-market activities in countries likely to modernize their financial system further, like Spain.

In conclusion, French banks still appear in a mixed position *vis-à-vis* the single European market. While it is difficult to foresee the extent of the restructuring of the banking sector likely to follow '1993' it is certain that competition will get stiffer in a still more deregulated environment. This may lead to consolidation of national markets, with countries formerly more tightly regulated and protected such as France, Italy, and Spain more likely to witness some radical reshaping of their financial landscape. Will there be mergers among banks or between banks and insurance companies? There are already some signs of the latter move, not only in France. After such a phase of domestic consolidation, European manoeuvres may well follow to select the ten or so big players on the European scene. How many French institutions will succeed in gaining admittance to the club?

Notes

1 Forty offices were in Europe and thirty-five in the French colonies. For further details about this abridged historical survey of the foreign expansion of French banks, cf. C. Michalet and C. Sauviat (1981).
2 Foreign offices included in the French Bankers' Association's statistical releases include branches, subsidiaries, minority stakes in affiliated banks, and representative offices. So they are not fully comparable with those of the Banking Commission (Commission Bancaire), which will also be cited in further developments.
3 Cf. 'L'implantation des banques françaises à l'étranger' (Commission Bancaire, 1985: 217–58).
4 This figure includes 1,374 million frs. invested abroad by French-registered subsidiaries of foreign banks in France.
5 i.e. Banque Nationale de Paris, Crédit Lyonnais, Société Générale (the 'big three'), Paribas, Indosuez, Crédit Commercial de France, Crédit Industriel et Commercial.
6 According to P. Masson (1982).
7 More precisely this figure covers only the sole activities of branches abroad. The foreign-currency business of their domestic offices, activities of foreign subsidiaries, and the cross-frontier business of domestic offices are not considered. So the ratio underestimates the international involvement of these banks.
8 Cf. Commission Bancaire, op. cit.
9 Nevertheless this ratio is more accurate than a ratio based on the total business of the whole French banking system. As the seven major banking groups are by far the leaders in international banking among these twenty-four banks, it may be considered as a mean estimate of the weight of the activities of their foreign branch network.
10 According to statistics released in *World Financial Markets* of the Morgan Guaranty Trust Company of New York.
11 Similar reasons also explain why in the aftermath of the first oil shock many banks set up in the Middle Eastern countries to capture the petro-dollars. When it subsequently appeared that the OPEC surplus had vanished, whereas international lending to developing countries and other borrowers was still going on, it became clear that new sources of funds needed to be tapped, among them some domestic money markets.

12 According to computations the results of which may be considered highly tentative, nationalized French banks seemed to have a typical average cost of capital around 0·35 per cent (akin to that of the Japanese banks), whereas their British, Canadian, and US counterparts were more likely to pay around 1 per cent. Cf. N. Saade (1981).

13 4,345 offices and branches (in net terms) were created between 1967 and 1973. During the four following years, 1974–7, this figure stood at 836 only.

14 It should be recalled here that at that time Comptoir National d'Escompte de Paris and Banque Nationale pour le Commerce et l'Industrie were merged to form the Banque Nationale de Paris.

15 Cf. Commission Bancaire, op. cit.

16 Cf., for example, A. Penati and A. Protopapadakis (1986).

17 Cf., for example, I. Bond and C. Briault (1983).

18 Detailed analysis of these developments is provided in the other chapters of this book.

19 For a general discussion of the competitiveness issue in the banking sector cf. J. Parly and M. Poix (1987).

20 Cf. E. Davis (1988), J. Métais (1989).

21 The author wishes especially to acknowledge the very helpful contribution to this paragraph of Jean-Luc Menda of the Banque de France, who updated and made available to him the results of his former empirical research work: 'L'internationalisation du système bancaire français', a paper for the working party of the Commissariat Général du Plan, headed by the Deputy Governor, Philippe Lagayette, Perspectives du financement de l'économie française. The report of this working party was published under the same title by Documentation Française, Paris, 1987.

22 It should nevertheless be stressed here that Japan remains one of the foreign countries where French banks still hold a strong position: by total assets, at the end of March 1987, BNP, Société Générale, Crédit Lyonnais, and Indosuez respectively ranked second, third, fourth, and fifth among the foreign banking community in Japan. Paribas was eighth.

23 The United States alone accounts for thirty-six branches and agencies, as defined by the US regulations.

24 The study of J.-L. Menda (op. cit.), relying on two host countries (Germany and The Netherlands) in September 1985, shows that whereas domestic activity amounts to 70 per cent of the assets of French banks in Germany, this proportion is only 32 per cent in The Netherlands.

25 This argument is clearly stated by Paribas, which in addition to its subsidiary Paribas Capital Markets acquired in London the stockbroking firm of Quilter Goodison, which has a strong distribution network, able to complement the already well established placing power of that bank in the Benelux countries and Switzerland. Moreover, Quilter Goodison is more especially oriented towards European securities. Similar

arguments are developed by Indosuez about its stockbroking arm, W.I. Carr, which has a long established capability and expertise in Asia, where the bank has traditionally been active.

26 This is especially true of the markets for Treasury bills and bonds after the introduction of licensed primary dealers in Treasury securities along the lines of the systems already existing in London or New York. This market shows by far the largest turnover activity in the Paris securities markets. Another example is provided by the market for certificates of deposit. The primary market received strong impetus in 1987 after the liquidity of the secondary markets had been enhanced.

27 Although their position deteriorated slightly in 1988 – despite the premier position of Paribas – their overall market share still stood at 33 per cent.

28 Such market power in the medium run seems to be a typical feature of international capital markets today. For example, in the overall Euro-bond market the already noted dominance of CSFB was long before being successfully challenged by Nomura, which is now ahead of the book runners, with a market share of 13 per cent and 10 per cent in 1987 and 1988 respectively. This is very interesting from the standpoint of the degree of contestability of these markets and of the accuracy of the industrial economics arguments as applied to the financial markets. Cf. E. Davis, op. cit.

29 According to *International Financing Review*, 21 January 1989. In France, Crédit Lyonnais is also interested in this field and played a leading role in the biggest deals of 1988.

30 In its 1987 annual report Crédit Commercial de France claims that it actually follows such a niche strategy in the French franc and ECU Euro-bond sectors. The same seems even more true of Paribas in the ECU bond sector.

31 For a detailed analysis, cf. chapter 5, by Philippe Szymczak.

32 At the end of 1987 BNP had 40 billion frs. in loans outstanding to problem countries, Crédit Lyonnais thirty-two, and Société Générale twenty-eight (*Euromoney*, January 1989).

33 According to the results of two polls among bankers conducted by the magazine *European Banker*.

34 Association Française des Banques (1987).

35 Cf. P. Koenig (1989).

36 Cf. G. Humphreys (1987).

37 Cf. chapter 5, by Philippe Szymczak.

References

Aliber, R. (1984) 'International banking: a survey', *Journal of Money, Credit and Banking*, November.
Association Française des Banques (1987) *Rapport annuel.*
Banking Commission (Commission Bancaire): *Annual Reports.*
Baumol, W., Panzar, J., and Willig, R. (1982) *Contestable Markets and the Theory of Industry Structure*, San Diego: Harcourt Brace Jovanovich.
Bond, I. and Briault, C. (1983) 'The commercial banks' contribution to current debt difficulties', discussion paper, Bank of England, London.
Davis, E. (1988) 'Industrial structure and dynamics of financial markets: the primary Euro-bond market', discussion paper, Bank of England, London.
Gurley, J. and Shaw, E. (1960) *Money in a Theory of Finance*, Washington DC: Brookings Institution.
Humphreys, G. (1987) 'Rejuvenating *les trois vieilles*', *Euromoney*, April.
Koenig, P. (1989) 'The no idea man at Crédit Lyonnais', *Euromoney*, January.
Masson, P. (1982) 'Bilan du développement international des banques françaises', *Banque*, Mai.
Menda, J.L. (1987) 'L'internationalisation du système bancaire français', discussion paper, Banque de France, Paris.
Métais, J. (1989) 'Towards a restructuring of the international financial industry: some preliminary empirical and theoretical insights', in E.P.M. Gardener (ed.) *The Future of Financial Institutions*, London: Macmillan.
Michalet, C.A. and Sauviat, C. (1981) 'L'internationalisation bancaire: le cas français', in C.A. Michalet (ed.) *Internationalisation des banques et des groupes financiers*, Paris: Editions du CNRS.
Parly, J.M. and Poix, M. (1987) 'La compétitivité bancaire: une revue critique de la littérature', unpublished study for the Commissariat Général du Plan, mimeo, Paris, June.
Penati, A. and Protopapadakis, A. (1986) 'Implicit deposit insurance and banks' portfolio choices: a positive theory of international over-exposure', paper given at colloquium on Recent Developments in International Finance, HEC ISA, Jouy-en-Josas, France.
Saade, N.A. (1981) 'How banks can live with low spreads', *Euromoney*, November.
Szymczak, P. (1987) 'Elements de comparaison internationale des coûts et marges bancaires', *Revue d'Economie Financière* 1, June.
Vickers, J. (1985) 'Strategic competition between the few: some recent developments in the economics of industry', *Oxford Review of Economic Policy* 3.
Yarrow, G. (1985) 'Strategic issues in industrial policy', *Oxford Review of Economic Policy* 3.

Index

Index

Panzar, J. 133, 154, 187
Parly, J. 185, 187
Pastré, O. 135
payment systems 114
payment technologies 6, 89–91
Penati, A. 185, 187
Poix, M. 185, 187
policy innovations 24
postal financial services 8–9, 29, 43, 52, 53, 93
privatization of banks 22–3, 99, 129–30, 171
profitability of French banks 78, 102–33, 149
Protopapadakis, A. 185, 187
provisions 115–17, 126–7, 174–6
prudential rules 13–14, 68–78

ratio of permanent resources 71–2
regulatory dialectic 10–14
Renard, F. 134
repurchase agreements 29, 36, 47
reserve requirements 28, 44–5
retail banking 178–9
Revell, J. 135
risk asset ratio 69–70
risk distribution ratio 70

Saade, N. 185, 187
Sautter, E. 109, 135
Sauviat, C. 138, 140, 184
savings rates 15–16
Scrivener, C. 97

securitization 17, 38, 40, 50, 122, 151, 178
Shaw, E. 1, 25, 143
Silber, E. 5, 25
Sinclair, P. 133
Slater, M. 133
Smirlock, M. 114, 135
specialization of banks 22, 84, 89
Sterdyniak, H. 112, 135
sterilization policy 46
stockbrokers 13, 98–100
Strauss-Kahn, M.O. 134
subsidized credits 10–12
syndicated loans 172
system innovations 24
Szymczak, P. 106, 107, 109, 112, 135, 180, 186, 187

UCITS (undertakings for collective investment in transferable securities) 3, 10, 16, 30, 31, 35, 36, 41, 43, 73
unlisted securities market 99

velocity of money 4
Vickets, J. 133, 157, 187

White, L. 106, 135
Wholesale banking 178–9
Williamson, O. 114, 135
Willig, R. 114, 133, 157, 187

Yarrow, G. 157, 187

190